NEWCOMER'S HANDBOOK®

for

LOS ANGELES

3rd Edition

FIRST BOOKS

6750 SW Franklin
Portland, OR 97223
503-968-6777
www.firstbooks.com

Third edition

Newcomer's Handbook® is a registered trademark of First Books, Inc.

Authors: Joan Wai, Stacey Ravel Abarbanel
Series Editor: Bernadette Duperron
Publisher: Jeremy Solomon
Design and Production: Erin Johnson
Maps: Scott Lockheed

MTA transit map courtesy of the Los Angeles County Metropolitan Transportation Authority.

ISBN 0-912301-43-0
ISSN 1086-8879

Manufactured in the United States of America.

Published by First Books, Inc., 6750 SW Franklin, Portland, OR 97223.

CONTENTS

CONTENTS *(continued)*

WELCOME TO EL PUEBLO DE NUESTRA SEÑORA LA REINA DE Los Angeles (in English, the town of our lady the queen of the angels). That's the name the Spanish gave to this city in 1781 when 44 village settlers made their home in what is now downtown Los Angeles. Today, LA is a multi-ethnic, multi-cultural society as diverse as any city in the world. The city is so large you could fit St. Louis, Milwaukee, Cleveland, Minneapolis, San Francisco, Boston, Pittsburgh and Manhattan all within the municipal boundaries! People from more than 140 countries live in Los Angeles County, including the largest population of Mexican, Armenian, Korean, Filipino, Salvadoran and Guatemalan communities outside their respective home nations. In general, it's safe to say that with 9.6 million people living in the County of Los Angeles, there is indeed something for everyone.

For decades, people around the world have been attracted to Los Angeles for its promises of fame and fortune, and excellent year-round weather. While only a sliver of the population is famous and wealthy, the good weather here is no myth. Average temperatures range from 58 degrees Fahrenheit in December to 76 degrees in September, yet it's not uncommon to have an 80 degree day at the beach in February, while much of the rest of the country shivers under a layer of snow.

Los Angeles' traffic and other negatives like crime and racial tensions are perhaps as famous now as are her plusses. But as someone once said of LA, "If this is Hell, why is it so popular?"

Perhaps it's because in recent decades, Los Angeles has been the first city to confront the future on all fronts: culturally, artistically, politically and socially. That confrontation can be both exciting and frightening, challenging and rewarding. It is certainly that electric feel, that sense of change, that attracts people from other cities and countries. And for those who choose to call Los Angeles "home," she welcomes you with a wealth of opportunities.

WHAT TO BRING

A car; while LA has a large bus transit system and a new underground subway that's slowly growing, LA is simply too big to get around effectively without a car. And, public transportation by bus often means an even longer ride than if you drove yourself. Small, compact model cars are the most economical and ideal for maneuvering LA's tight parking spots. Be prepared to shell out the bucks for insurance coverage; auto insurance in LA is higher than most cities.

A map; it'll take newcomers a while to create a mental map of where one community is in relation to another, and to figure out how much time is necessary to get from one place to another. Traffic patterns create situations where the shortest route is not always the fastest. While many city streets are laid out in a grid, there are plenty of exceptions with streets that cross over, change names, and create not four, but five junctions at an intersection. A *Thomas Guide* street map (loose-leaf books of detailed LA neighborhood road maps) is perfect for finding alternate routes around gridlocked freeways. The *LA-County/Ventura* and *LA-County/Orange Thomas Guides*, veritable LA bibles, can be purchased at firstbooks.com or at most local bookstores.

A cell phone; most everyone has one for all those times they get stuck in traffic and to work on that movie deal. Besides, this is the kind of town where two lines on the rolodex for a home and work phone number doesn't cut it anymore. Many a professional will list a business phone number, cell phone number, fax number, and e-mail address on their business card.

An open mind and positive attitude; if this is your first time in Los Angeles, be prepared to interact with many different cultures and ethnicities. LA's primary airport (LAX) is one of the busiest international airports in the nation and the Port of Los Angeles ranks first in the nation in volume. Californians in general are famous for their laid-back attitude and many Angelenos are no different, however, the pace of life here *is* faster and more energetic than in smaller cities—but that's what makes it so fun! While this *Newcomer's Handbook® for Los Angeles* will introduce you to the area, nothing compares to discovering the area's many beautiful facets yourself. Welcome and enjoy.

A T FIRST GLANCE, LOS ANGELES APPEARS TO BE A SPRAWLING metropolis, with no clear demarcations from one municipality to the next, let alone distinct neighborhoods. It takes time and patience to understand the subtle qualities that make Santa Monica different from Venice, or Silverlake from the Fairfax district, but after a while, you will find neighborhoods in Los Angeles have quite different characteristics. Exploring LA's communities is easy and fun, and for newcomers especially, it's encouraged.

While cruising through the city you will no doubt encounter the "strip center" phenomenon—that is the appearance of two- to three-story mini-malls on every other block. While you will hear many complain that these modern strip centers are eyesores, take a closer look. They may be architecturally uninspiring, but some of these strip centers have become little neighborhood commerce centers in areas that previously had none.

Los Angeles' problems of crime and violence may be notorious, but in reality they reflect the nation's urban woes, and are certainly no better or worse here than in other major US cities. In fact, a recent *Money* magazine survey of FBI crime statistics ranked the fifteen most dangerous cities in the country, and Los Angeles didn't make the list. As in any city, a good dose of street smarts and common sense will help steer you away from trouble, and as safety experts are fond of reminding us, always be aware of your surroundings. Certain high-crime neighborhoods like South-Central and Watts are not recommended for outsiders or newcomers, but there are plenty of safe and affordable areas in which to live, work and play.

In general, you can expect the climate and air quality to be hotter and smoggier the further east you go, with the warmest temperatures and worst air pollution occurring in the summer months. For detailed information on the air quality in the areas you are considering calling home, contact the South Coast Air Quality Management District at 909-396-2000.

Due to the vastness of greater LA, this guide does not attempt to cover every neighborhood, but it does cover many. Some areas are separate incorporated cities, others are distinct communities within Los Angeles proper. What follows are comprehensive, yet concise descriptions of neighborhoods and cities that newcomers should check out. We start on the Westside with the beach communities, move more or less east, through downtown, then north, covering the Valley.

With so many neighborhoods and cities independent of the city of LA but within LA County, newcomers may wonder how it all comes together. Los Angeles County consists of 88 cities (such as Glendale, West Hollywood, Beverly Hills, etc.). These cities have independent city councils and their own municipal services like police and school districts. Residents proudly identify with their municipality and its reputation— taking offense when referred to as a "Los Angelenos." The remaining neighborhoods (Fairfax, Westwood, etc.) can be thought of as communities that are within the city of LA (roughly 470 square miles or 12% of the county). Incidentally, the city of LA is the second most populated city in the US with an estimated population of over 3.7 million in 1998. The city's patch-quilt like composition resulted from battles over a surprisingly simple commodity during its formation: water. Municipalities that were reluctantly annexed to the city in order to share in its water supply, often retained their community name.

Other useful information such as area codes: 213—downtown; 323—areas surrounding downtown, including Hollywood; 310 and 424—Westside and South Bay; 562—Long Beach; 818—the Valley, Glendale and Burbank; 661—Santa Clarita; and 626—Pasadena, zip codes, nearby post offices, district police stations, neighborhood hospitals, public libraries, community resources and public school information follows each neighborhood description. In some cases, the neighborhood boundaries are approximations, since areas that are not distinct cities tend to blend into one another.

Unless otherwise noted, housing statistics included in the neighborhood profiles are derived from Acxiom/DataQuick, www.dataquick.com, the same resource used by the *Los Angeles Times*, and real estate companies. In 1999, the median resale price for homes in Los Angeles County was nearly $200,000, this up from $175,500 in 1998. In itself, this number doesn't tell the full story since homes vary widely in price here, but the rising percentage prices, approximately 11%, are a good indicator of where the general LA market is headed.

The following neighborhoods are profiled:

West
Malibu
Topanga Canyon
Santa Monica
Venice
Marina del Rey
Playa del Rey
El Segundo
Manhattan Beach
Inglewood
Mar Vista, Palms, Cheviot Hills
Culver City
West Los Angeles
Brentwood
Westwood
Beverly Hills

East
West Hollywood
Fairfax District
Hancock Park
Hollywood
Los Feliz/Silverlake/Echo Park
Leimert Park
Downtown

South
Downey
La Mirada/Norwalk
Long Beach

North
San Fernando Valley
Encino
North Hollywood
Burbank/Glendale
Pasadena
Santa Clarita

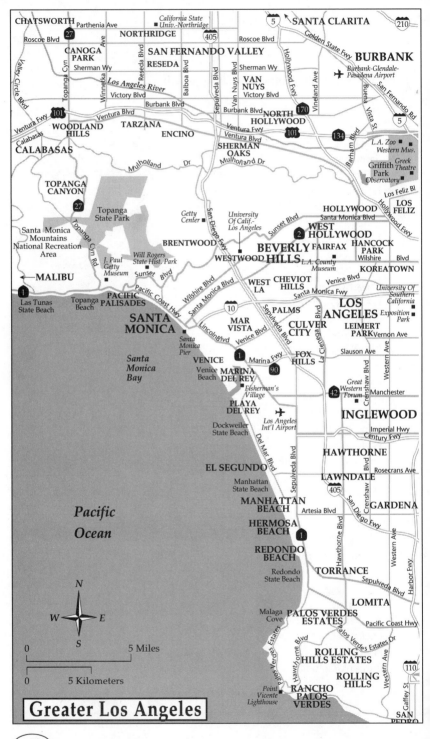

Greater Los Angeles

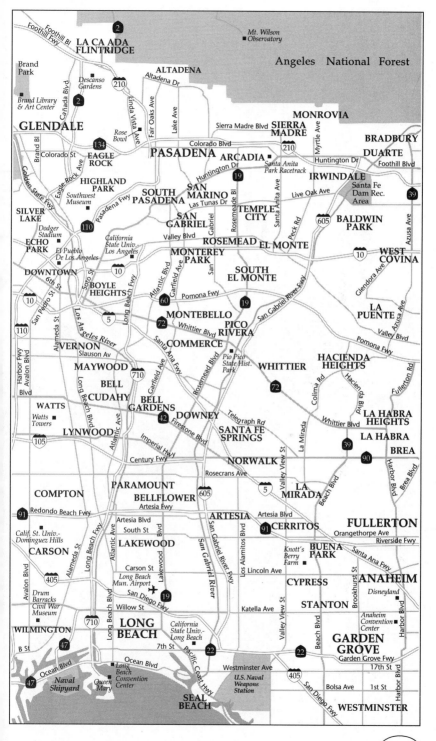

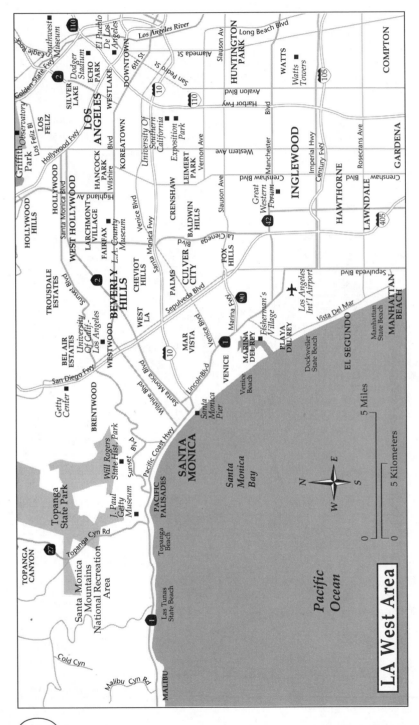

LA West Area

Pacific Ocean

MALIBU
Malibu Cyn Rd
Cold Cyn
Las Tunas State Beach
TOPANGA CANYON
Topanga Cyn Rd
Santa Monica Mountains National Recreation Area
Topanga State Park
Will Rogers State Hist. Park
J. Paul Getty Museum
Topanga Beach
PACIFIC PALISADES
Sunset Blvd
Pacific Coast Hwy
SANTA MONICA
Santa Monica Pier
Santa Monica Bay
Getty Center
BRENTWOOD
San Diego Fwy
BEL AIR ESTATES
University Of Calif.- Los Angeles
WESTWOOD
Wilshire Blvd
Santa Monica Blvd
Sunset Blvd
TROUSDALE ESTATES
BEVERLY HILLS
WEST LA
Sepulveda Blvd
PALMS
CHEVIOT HILLS
CULVER CITY
FOX HILLS
La Cienega Blvd
Santa Monica Fwy
MAR VISTA
Venice Blvd
Lincoln Blvd
VENICE
Venice Beach
MARINA DEL REY
PLAYA DEL REY
Fisherman's Village
Vista Del Mar
Dockweiler State Beach
EL SEGUNDO
Los Angeles Int'l Airport
Sepulveda Blvd
MANHATTAN BEACH
Manhattan State Beach
HAWTHORNE
LAWNDALE
Crenshaw Blvd
Century Fwy
Imperial Hwy
INGLEWOOD
Great Western Forum
Manchester
Western Ave
GARDENA
Rosecrans Ave
405
105
COMPTON
Slauson Av
Avalon Blvd
Harbor Fwy
San Pedro St
HUNTINGTON PARK
Long Beach Blvd
Alameda St
WATTS
Watts Towers
Slauson Ave
CRENSHAW
BALDWIN HILLS
LEIMERT PARK
Vernon Ave
Exposition Park
University Of Southern California
KOREATOWN
HANCOCK PARK
LARCHMONT VILLAGE
FAIRFAX
L.A. County Museum
Highland Av
Santa Monica Blvd
WEST HOLLYWOOD
HOLLYWOOD
HOLLYWOOD HILLS
Hollywood Fwy
Hollywood Blvd
LOS FELIZ
Los Feliz Bl
Griffith Observatory
Griffith Park
SILVER LAKE
ECHO PARK
Dodger Stadium
El Pueblo De Los Angeles
Los Angeles River
Eagle Rock
Golden State Fwy
Southwest Museum
LOS ANGELES
DOWNTOWN
WESTLAKE
6th St
Wilshire Blvd
Venice Blvd
110
2
10
110
10
1
90
42
27
2
2

5 Miles
5 Kilometers
0
0

N
E
S
W

NEIGHBORHOODS — WEST

MALIBU

Boundaries: North: Mulholland Highway; **East:** Tuna Canyon Road, Saddle Creek Road; **South:** Santa Monica Bay; **West:** Mulholland Highway

"Malibu—it's a state of mind." This message seen on license plate holders across Los Angeles may leave you scratching your head and wondering what it all means... until you get to the City of Malibu. Once you've traveled the twenty miles northwest of Santa Monica on the Pacific Coast Highway (PCH) you'll find Malibu is not so much a place as a peaceful vibe, something often absent in other parts of the region.

In fact, upon arrival Malibu is not so impressive. You'll find the usual fast-food stands, small shopping centers, and surf shops, sprinkled with a few fancy restaurants like Wolfgang Puck's star hangout, Granita. The pretty Malibu Pier offers fishing and food. Most non-residents come to Malibu for the beaches, which are some of the loveliest and cleanest (both sand and water) in the Los Angeles area. Zuma Beach is the most popular; nearby Point Dume is a bit less crowded, and Leo Carillo, a 1,600-acre beach situated further northwest, features three campgrounds. Surfrider Beach is still popular with surfers, as it was in the 1950s and '60s when Annette Funicello and Frankie Avalon frolicked here in their *Beach Blanket Bingo* movies. Even Pepperdine University has an ocean view in Malibu.

As for residents, Malibu is the home, or second home (or third, or fourth), to the rich and famous who enjoy its scenery and privacy. The most well-known spot for celebrities to live is the Malibu Beach Colony, a gated community right on the sand. Note that while the streets and homes in the Colony are not accessible to outsiders, the ocean is. The tidelands in California, defined as the area below the mean high tide, are considered public land. Hence, you can park along the road before or after the Colony property (or, for that matter, almost any other private beach area in the state), and walk along the wet, packed sand for a look at these beach-side villas. A few private beach communities have guards that will chase you off the dry, sandy part of the beach, but stick to the hard, wet sand along the tide and you should be okay.

Aside from the famous folks, Malibu has a fair share of successful

professionals, surfer dudes and dudettes, and just plain beach lovers living in its midst. Most are drawn to the area because living here offers
proximity to Los Angeles, without all the city-life hustle-bustle. As you
might imagine, rents and house prices in Malibu are most expensive at
the coast (beach front property sells for an average of $2.7 million), and
then decrease as you move inland, into the canyons (inland homes average $860,000). While the area is mostly owner-occupied, a diligent
hunter can locate a sprinkling of apartments, condominiums, and guest
and townhomes for rent. Renters should expect to write monthly checks
of $700 or more for a one-bedroom.

Because much of Malibu is hilly, dry canyon country, brush fires are
a problem here almost every summer. Then in the winter, since some of
the vegetation has been burned away, winter rains can cause land slides,
which then cause flooding. During heavy rains, rock slides are responsible for the occasional closures of the PCH, the main artery in and out of
Malibu. Through it all, most residents say the privacy and beauty of
Malibu make residing here worthwhile.

Web Site: www.ci.malibu.ca.us

Area Codes: 310, 424

Zip Codes: 90264, 90265

Post Office: Main Post Office, 23838 Pacific Coast Highway; La
Costa Station, 21229 Pacific Coast Highway; Point Dume Station,
29160 Heathercliff Road; 800-275-8777

Police District: Malibu is served by the Los Angeles County
Sheriff's Department, 27050 Agoura Road, Agoura, 818-878-1808.

Emergency Hospitals: Saint John's Health Center-Malibu, 23656
Pacific Coast Highway, 310-456-7551; Santa Monica UCLA Medical
Center, 1250 16th Street, 310-319-4000

Library: Malibu Library, 23519 West Civic Center Way, 310-456-
6438; Palisades Library, 861 Alma Real Drive, 310-459-2754

Community Resources: Pepperdine University, 24255 Pacific
Coast Highway, 310-356-4000, www.pepperdine.edu; Malibu
Bluffs Park, 24250 Pacific Coast Highway, 310-317-1364; Malibu
Equestrian Center, 6225 Merritt Drive, 310-317-1364; Charmlee
Nature Preserve, 2577 South Encinal Canyon Road, 310-457-7247

Public School Education: Santa Monica-Malibu Unified School

District: 1651 Sixteenth Street, Santa Monica, CA 90405, 310-450-8338, www.smmusd.org

Public Transportation: Call 800-COMMUTE for specific bus route schedule and information.

TOPANGA CANYON

Boundaries: North: Mulholland Drive; **East:** Topanga State Park; **South:** Santa Monica Bay; **West:** Los Flores Canyon

Curvy mountain roads, tangled trees and vines, an occasional hippie-type hitchhiking alongside the canyon passage way—are we in LA? Nestled in the Santa Monica Mountains between Santa Monica and Malibu, Topanga Canyon hardly seems like a part of a major metropolis. Its roots are firmly planted in the hippie, artist, and other alternative communities that have populated this unincoporated part of Los Angeles County for decades.

It's easy to see why people choose to live in Topanga Canyon. For starters, there is the beautiful, natural setting, complete with vistas (in some spots) of the Pacific Ocean. Another bonus is the *relatively* low cost of housing. Residences run the gamut from mountain cabins to newer, high-end houses, and rents and home prices (averaging $500,000) are much cheaper than in nearby, chic Malibu. Most area housing was built after 1950, and is filled by the recently arrived, many of whom were residents of the City of LA. Yes, the word is out, Topanga is more than just a good state park to take a day hike, hence today your next-door neighbor here is as likely to be a downtown lawyer as a stained-glass artist.

However, people used to the convenience of home-delivered Chinese food or 2 a.m. grocery shopping should think twice about living in Topanga Canyon. Although only a few miles down Pacific Coast Highway from Pacific Palisades, Topanga feels remote. At the crest of Old Topanga Canyon Road, a commercial strip caters to the basics like food and gas, but for the most part, once you've driven up the hill towards home, you've probably left the day's errands behind. And that's just the way Topanga Canyonites like it.

Hikers frequent Topanga Canyon, especially along the beautiful, hilly trails at Topanga State Park. Within Topanga Canyon is Topanga Creek, the third largest watershed draining into Santa Monica Bay. (Look out for the three turtle crossing signs in the neighborhood.) Another fun spot in the Canyon is the Will Geer Theatricum Botanicum, a rustic out-door theater now headed by actor Will Geer's daughter Ellen. A place where, on a warm summer evening, you can have a romantic, candle-lit picnic, then sit under the stars on comfy throw pillows and see Shakespeare and other plays and musical productions.

Finally, it's worth noting that if heavy rains hit during the winter, certain sections of Old Topanga Canyon Road and Topanga Canyon Boulevard, the primary arteries serving this community, are prone to clo-sure due to mud slides, especially along the creek beds. City crews are quick to bring in bulldozers, so the residents consider this a minor nui-sance in exchange for mountain living.

Web Site: www.topangaonline.com

Zip Code: 90290

Area Codes: 310, 424

Post Office: 101 South Topanga Canyon Boulevard, 800-275-8777

Police District: Topanga Canyon is served by the Los Angeles County Sheriff's Department, 27050 Agoura Road, 818 878-1808

Emergency Hospitals: Saint John's Hospital and Health Center, 1328 22nd Street, 310-829-5511; Santa Monica UCLA Medical Center, 1250 16th Street, 310-319-4000

Libraries: Malibu Library, 23519 West Civic Center Way, 310-456-6438; Palisades Library, 861 Alma Real Drive, 310-459-2754

Public School Education: LA Unified School District, 634 Cesar E. Chavez, Los Angeles, CA 90012; 800-933-8133, www.lausd.k12.ca.us

Community Resources: Topanga State Park in the Santa Monica Mountains National Recreation Area; Topanga Community House, 1440 Topanga Canyon Boulevard, 310-455-1980; Will Geer Theatricum Botanicum, 1419 North Topanga Canyon Boulevard, 310-455-3723

Public Transportation: Call 1-800-COMMUTE for specific **MTA** bus route and schedule information.

SANTA MONICA

Boundaries: North: San Vicente Boulevard; **East:** Centinela Avenue; **South:** Dewey Street; **West:** Santa Monica Bay, Pacific Ocean

Nicknamed "Santa Moscow" for its liberal city politics, Santa Monica, which is its own municipality, was once a highly coveted neighborhood for its rent-controlled, seaside apartments. However, rent control has ended and in its place is "vacancy decontrol" (started in 1999—see **Finding a Place to Live**) that allows landlords to set rent at whatever price they deem appropriate, once a formerly rent-controlled apartment has been vacated. With landlords eager to catch up on lost revenue, rental prices have now soared. Over time, this should level out, but for now, be prepared to pay a lot if you want to live here.

To soften the blow for renters, the City of Santa Monica maintains some level of control over the amount rent may be increased. Each year, at the beginning of September, the City's Rent Control Board determines the maximum percentage by which landlords may raise rent. So, while newcomers moving into an apartment will find their rent dramatically increased compared to what they would have paid previously due to the vacancy decontrol initiative, annual rental increases are a small fraction. For the 1999/2000 year, the general adjustment agreed upon by the board was set at one percent or four dollars, whichever was greater, up to nine dollars. In Santa Monica, Rent Control Board determinations only apply to multiple unit dwellings built before April 10, 1979. The majority of the rental units qualify. With so much potential for confusion, the City's rent control office provides special coordinators (310-458-8751) to help would-be renters determine what their legal rent should be.

Potential home buyers with low to moderate incomes can seek assistance from the Santa Monica Housing and Redevelopment Division (310-458-8702), an organization designed to provide affordable housing options, including low-cost housing for seniors and the disabled.

Committed to social and environmental sensitivity, Santa Monica has become one the first US cities to make it a matter of city policy to rely on sustainable, or renewable, resources. This is overseen by the Environmental Programs Division of the Environmental and Public Works Management Department. Electricity (generated by sustainable sources) and natural gas are the primary sources of energy within the city. There is also a strong recycling program in place for homeowners and renters, and aggressive campaigns to encourage residents to use water and energy efficient devices.

These environment-friendly policies must be having an effect. Area residents like to brag that the air is cleaner and the weather cooler here than anywhere else in LA, and it's true. While summer temperatures in Los Angeles can hover in the eighties and nineties, it's not uncommon for Santa Monica to sport temperatures that are fifteen degrees cooler than downtown or the Valley. Many apartments do not have air conditioners.

Approximately 20% of the housing stock in Santa Monica is composed of single family homes, the rest consist of multi-unit apartments and condos. Residential streets are lined with either rows of mature Magnolia trees or towering Palms. Like much of Los Angeles, the neighborhoods in Santa Monica tend to get more lavish as you move north. The area north of upscale shopping street Montana Avenue features some of LA's most beautiful (and priciest) homes, most built in the early 1960s. For those less financially endowed, the area south of Santa Monica Avenue offers mostly apartments and condominiums, while still boasting easy access to the area's cafes, coffeehouses, and shops. Be aware, street parking is extremely difficult to procure, especially in apartment neighborhoods.

Main Street is probably the hippest and beachiest area in this small city. The art galleries, restaurants and bars with patio seating, shops, and coffee houses overflow with cool looking singles (the average age here is 37) or young families with strollers in tow. To the west of Main Street are several walking lanes lined with some nice and some run-down beach cottages, but regardless, prices are high due to the proximity to the ocean. The hilly neighborhood just east of Main Street consists of apartments and condominiums, with a few funky houses mixed in.

The focus in downtown Santa Monica is the lively outdoor mall, Third Street Promenade, with shops, restaurants, and a multitude of theaters attracting huge crowds (and enterprising street performers) on weekends. The Promenade is also a mecca for book lovers, with the largest concentration of corporate superstores, fine used book stores, and independent book shops anywhere in the Los Angeles area. The Santa Monica Place Mall is on the southern end of the promenade and the Santa Monica Civic Center, Santa Monica College, and Santa Monica Municipal Airport are also located nearby. Well-tended community parks, active neighborhood watch programs, and strongly-supported social services for the elderly and disabled round out this sea-side neighborhood's offerings, making Santa Monica a favorite for families and singles alike.

Web Site: www.ci.santa-monica.ca.us

Area Codes: 310, 424

Zip Codes: 90401, 90402, 90403, 90404, 90405, 90406

Post Offices: Main Post Office, 1248 5th Street, Ocean Park Station, 2720 Neilson Way, Will Rogers Station, 1217 Wilshire Boulevard; 800-275-8777

Libraries: Main Library, 1343 Sixth Street, 310-458-8600; Fairview branch, 2101 Ocean Park Boulevard, 310-450-0443; Montana Avenue branch, 1704 Montana Avenue, 310-829-7081; Ocean Park branch, 2601 Main Street, 310-392-3804

Police District: Santa Monica is served by its own municipal police force, headquarters: 1685 Main Street, 310-458-8451, www.santamonicapd.org.

Emergency Hospitals: Saint John's Hospital and Health Center, 1328 22nd. Street, 310-829-5511; Santa Monica UCLA Medical Center, 1250 16th Street, 310-319-4000

Public School Education: Santa Monica-Malibu Unified School District, 1651 16th Street, Santa Monica, CA 90404, 310-450-8338; www.smmusd.org

Community Resources: City Information Desk, 310-393-9975; parking permits, 310-458-8291; Santa Monica College, 1900 Pico Boulevard, 310-450-5150; Lincoln Park, 1150 Lincoln Boulevard; Memorial Park, 1401 Olympic Boulevard

Public Transportation: The affectionately named, striking **Big Blue Bus** serves Santa Monica residents. Call 310-451-544 for specific Santa Monica Municipal Bus Line route and schedule information, or check www.BigBlueBus.com/bus.

VENICE

Boundaries: North: Dewey Street; **East:** Walgrove Avenue; **South:** Washington Street; **West:** Santa Monica Bay, Pacific Ocean

The funkiest of Los Angeles' beach communities, Venice is an eclectic mix of artists, surfers, bodybuilders and sightseers. It was founded in 1900 by Abbot Kinney, whose dream was to foster a cultural renaissance in America by recreating an Italian "Venice" here. Some of the area's original Venetian-style architecture still stands near the boardwalk, as do a few of the canals. Despite these Venetian touches, it is doubtful that Abbot Kinney had any idea just what kind of culture Venice would become known for.

Yes, men and women in skimpy bathing suits *do* rollerblade down the streets here. And yes, burly muscle men and women *do* perform their workouts and flex for tourists at Muscle Beach. But Venice is also home to a strong and thriving artists' community, composed of first-rate studios, galleries and artists' residences. The heart of the area is Ocean Front Walk (known as the boardwalk), a beach front collection of shops, outdoor cafes, street performers, jewelry and sunglasses stands, and the liveliest place in town to get your palm read, hair braided, or back massaged. Housing runs the gamut from beach cottages to reasonably priced apartments to ocean-front villas that in total support a residential population of over 40,000. Prices and quality vary greatly, but generally the closer you are to the ocean, the more you pay.

East of the boardwalk is Abbot Kinney Boulevard. While this street hasn't caught on like its Santa Monica neighbor Main Street (and some think that's just fine), it features an interesting mix of art galleries, antique stores, restaurants and shops. The surrounding homes and apartments are somewhat run down as the mode of lifestyle here suggests comfort over polish. A few old gems and some contemporary buildings get mixed in amongst the rest. Renters will have a slightly easier time than those seeking home-ownership, but when you do find a house, it will average $350,000.

Each Spring, artists open their studios and homes for the Venice Artwalk, an area fund-raiser. The canal neighborhood, located between Venice and Washington Boulevards east of Pacific Avenue, offers a unique and charming living situation. The houses along the canals vary from ramshackle cottages to newly built mini-mansions. Many residents have their own row boats for tooling through the area, and visiting romantics can even rent a gondola for a little taste of Italy, LA style.

While Venice's proximity to the beach and boardwalk and general outdoor lifestyle are definite pluses, beware that crime here is higher than average, and east of Sixth Avenue is a rough neighborhood called Oakwood. As Venice is one of the most popular tourist attractions in California, the city of Los Angeles is rectifying the crime situation with increased patrol efforts, especially on weekends.

Web Sites: www.venice.net; see also www.powershot.com for a "webumentary" of Venice.

Area Codes: 310, 424

Zip Code: 90291

Library: Venice branch, 610 California Avenue, 310-821-1769

Post Office: Main Post Office, 1601 Main Street, 800-275-8777

Police District: Pacific Division, 12312 Culver Boulevard, 310-202-4501

Emergency Hospital: Daniel Freeman Marina Hospital, 4650 Lincoln Boulevard, 310-823-8911

Public School Education: LA Unified School District, 634 Cesar E. Chavez, Los Angeles, CA 90012, 800-933-8133, www.lausd.k12.ca.us

Community Resources: Venice Recreation Center, Market Street and Ocean Front Walk; Westminster Park, 1234 Pacific Avenue

Public Transportation: Call 800-COMMUTE for specific **MTA** bus route and schedule information.

MARINA DEL REY

Boundaries: North: Washington Street; **East:** Centinela Boulevard; **South:** Ballona Creek; **West:** Santa Monica Bay, Pacific Ocean

Situated around the world's largest man-made small-boat harbor, Marina del Rey has a reputation as a singles area. Residents enjoy the Marina's waterfront locale and proximity to boating, sailing, wind surfing, water-skiing, tennis, and jogging and bicycling paths.

Marina del Rey boasts the highest density of restaurant seating in a one-square-mile area, outside of New York City. The area known as the Marina Peninsula is a strip of land between the ocean and the boat harbor, and is composed of streets and walkways that run perpendicular to the beach. Locals use the alphabetical, nautical street names, "Anchorage" down to "Yawl," to refer to not only to the streets themselves but to the beaches they abut. The Marina Peninsula offers both large (50-unit plus) and small condominiums and apartments, as well as upscale mini-mansions. In fact, real estate is at such a premium here that almost 90% of the residential buildings in Marina del Rey are multi-unit housing. Less than three percent are single detached homes, and these are primarily beach cottages. All are priced over a million dollars.

There is an abundance of modern apartments, many built since the 1980s, throughout the rest of Marina del Rey. Gyms, swimming pools and tennis courts are common features. At the western end of the 90 Freeway, you'll find new million dollar condos offering sweeping views of the city and ocean, complete with the finest amenities within their slender towers. Overall, housing prices in Marina del Rey lean toward the high end, so many young professionals fresh out of college team up here as housemates.

Web Site: www.marinadelrey.com

Area Codes: 310, 424

Zip Code: 90292

Post Office: Marina del Rey branch, 4748 Admiralty Way; 800-275-8777

Library: Marina del Rey branch, 4533 Admiralty Way, 310-821-3415

Police District: Pacific Division, 12312 Culver Boulevard, 310-202-4501

Emergency Hospital: Daniel Freeman Marina Hospital, 4650 Lincoln Boulevard, 310-823-8911

Public School Education: LA Unified School District, 634 Cesar E. Chavez, Los Angeles, CA 90012, 800-933-8133, www.lausd.k12.ca.us

Community Resources: Fisherman's Village, 13723 Fiji Way, 310-823-5411; UCLA Marina Aquatic Center, 14001 Fiji Way, 310-823-0048; LA County's Visitor Information for Recreation Boating, Facilities and Services, 4701 Admiralty Way, 310-305-9545

Public Transportation: Call 800-COMMUTE for **MTA** bus route and schedule information.

PLAYA DEL REY

Boundaries: North: Bollona Creek; **East:** Lincoln Bouelvard; **South:** Manchester Avenue; **West:** Pacific Ocean

Tucked in between Marina del Rey and LAX, residents say Playa del Rey (Spanish for "King's Beach") is their little private hideaway. Isolated from the rest of Los Angeles by wetlands and featuring a shack-style downtown strip of mom and pop restaurants and shops, Playa del Rey has the feel of a small California beach town. Since there are no public parking lots and street parking is limited, the beaches here are relatively uncrowded, even during the hot summer months. For years, there has been talk of developing the wetlands, once owned by Howard Hughes, with an office/residential park or movie production facilities. The most likely candidate, Dreamworks Studios, scrapped their planned move to Playa Vista. Once again, the wetlands remain a vacant, but effective barrier from the rest of the city.

Housing in Playa del Rey is approximately 45% owner-occupied and 55% renter-occupied. Lower Playa del Rey consists of the few streets right along the beach, and features mostly modern townhomes, condominiums and apartments. Heading east on Manchester Avenue is Upper Playa del Rey, and with the exception of some housing that offers magnificent views, this residential area is considered a bit less desirable than the spots right down by the water. On the other hand, if you're looking to rent or buy a house, you'll have the most luck in this upper area. Another plus, homes here tend to be newer than those found in other communities, many were built in the 1980s.

Playa del Rey is located just north of LAX, a fact which can be a plus or minus, depending on your needs. Frequent travelers will appreciate the light commute to the airport, but the noise, especially in Upper Playa del Rey, can be a nuisance. On the eastern border of this community is the Catholic Loyola Marymount University. Founded in 1865, it is the first college built in Los Angeles, and offers entertainment and educational opportunities to the public. Golf fans will notice the Westchester Golf Course is also adjacent.

Prospective residents might also like to know that Playa del Rey is the site of the Hyperion Treatment Plant, a sewage treatment facility at 12000 Vista del Mar. The Department of Public Works assures that state of the art technology is used to both monitor the environmental impact of the plant and to maintain safe standards. If you would like more information on the environmental monitoring of the plant, contact Heal the Bay, 310-581-4188, www.healthebay.org, a volunteer organization that monitors the health of the Santa Monica Bay (of which the Plant dumps into).

Web Sites: www.ci.la.ca.us, www.co.la.ca.us

Area Codes: 310, 424

Zip Code: 90293

Post Office: Playa del Rey branch, 215 Culver Boulevard; 800-275-8777

Library: Marina del Rey branch, 4533 Admiralty Way, 310-821-3415

Police District: Pacific Division, 12312 Culver Boulevard, 310-202-4501

Emergency Hospital: Daniel Freeman Marina Hospital, 4650 Lincoln Boulevard, 310-823-8911

Community Resources: Loyola Marymount University, Loyola Boulevard at West 80th Street, 310-338-2700; Del Rey Lagoon Park, 6660 Esplanade; Westchester Recreation Center, 8740 Lincoln Boulevard, 310-649-3317; Westchester Golf Course, 6900 West Manchester Avenue, 310-670-5110

Public School Education: LA Unified School District, 634 Cesar E. Chavez, Los Angeles, CA 90012, 800-933-8133, www.lausd.k12.ca.us

Public Transportation: Call 800-COMMUTE for specific **MTA** bus route and schedule information.

EL SEGUNDO

Boundaries: North: Imperial Highway; **East:** Aviation Boulevard; **South:** Rosecrans Boulevard; **West:** Vista del Mar Boulevard

Located directly south of Los Angeles International Airport and fourteen miles southwest of downtown LA, the city of El Segundo, Spanish for "the second," is so named because in 1911, Standard Oil Company selected it as the site of its second oil refinery. In fact, a 1920s newspaper advertisement described the town as "the Standard Oil payroll city." The 1,000-acre refinery, now run by Chevron USA, is still a major part of El Segundo, encompassing the southwestern quadrant of the city. The rest of the city is 80% zoned for commercial/industrial use and 20% is composed of the tranquil residential enclave west of Sepulveda Boulevard.

In addition to the oil refinery, El Segundo, a 1980s hot spot for aviation and defense industry companies, is now home to Mattel Toys,

Merisel, Raytheon, Northrop Grumman, Xerox, and Computer Sciences Corporation. Many people commute to this community to work. In fact, its daytime population exceeds approximately 70,000 compared to its resident population of about 15,000.

You can expect most of the housing here to be modern—generally built between 1950 and 1980, but rather nondescript. The average price for a home in El Segundo is $330,000. Apartments are rare, but average $650 for a one-bedroom. El Segundo residents love the small-town atmosphere and the fact that it has its own school district. However, due to its close proximity to LAX, overhead noise can be distracting. Also, intermittent fumes from the Hyperion sewage treatment plant (see section on **Playa del Rey**) have given the area the nickname "El Stinko." On the upside, big business has provided the community with the means for recreational amenities including The Lakes at El Segundo Golf Course and a recreational park located at East Pine Avenue and Eucalyptus Drive. Serviced by the 405 San Diego and 105 Century/Glen Anderson freeways and the Metro Green Line, access to the southwestern part of LA and its beaches is second to none.

Web Site: www.elsegundo.org

Area Codes: 310, 424

Zip Code: 90245

Post Office: El Segundo branch, 200 Main Street; 800-275-8777

Library: El Segundo Public Library, 111 West Mariposa Avenue, 310-322-4121

Police District: El Segundo is served by its own municipal police force, headquarters: 348 Main Street, 310-322-9114.

Emergency Hospitals: Centinela Hospital Medical Center, 555 East Hardy Street, 310-673-4660; Daniel Freeman Memorial Hospital, 333 North Prairie Avenue, 310-674-7050

Public School Education: El Segundo Unified School District, 641 Sheldon Street, El Segundo, 90245; 310-615-2650

Community Resources: The Lakes at El Segundo Golf Course, 3355 South Sepulveda Boulevard; Recreation Park, East Pine Avenue and Eucalyptus Drive

Public Transportation: Call 800-COMMUTE for specific **Metro Green Line** and **MTA** bus route and schedule information.

MANHATTAN BEACH

Boundaries: North: Rosecrans Avenue; **East:** Aviation Boulevard; **South:** Artesia Boulevard; **West:** Pacific Ocean

Ever wondered what happened to Susie Sorority and Frank Fraternity after graduation? They moved to Manhattan Beach. It may be a bit more of a commute to work, but the youthful residents, generally in their thirties, think the beautiful beaches and lively shops, restaurants, and bars are worth the drive.

Upscale beach life here centers around The Strand, a cement promenade popular with skaters, joggers, and walkers, and the South Bay Bicycle Trail that also runs along the beach. The sandy beach draws droves of sunbathers and volleyball players, who can choose their game site from among over one hundred courts located just steps away from beachfront homes.

A short walk from the city's white, sandy beach is the vibrant and charming shopping district centered around Manhattan Avenue and Manhattan Beach Boulevard. The area is densely packed with cafes, bars, bookstores and clothing shops. Weekend nights can take on the feel of a college town as scores of young hipsters walk the streets to take in the local bar and restaurant scene.

Housing options near the ocean include quaint beach cottages with porches or balconies that open right onto the sandy strip and multi-unit apartment buildings, most of which were built during the 1950s. Since Manhattan Beach is on a slight hill, many units boast ocean views and while rents for these units are understandably higher, they are comparable to LA's other beach communities. The area east of Ardmore Avenue is more family-oriented, with mostly single family houses.

As with many beach communities, residential streets are narrow and parking is impossible, especially on weekends when beach goers flock to the area. It is important to note that although Manhattan Beach is located only about 20 miles southwest of downtown Los Angeles, the weekday commute to downtown can be as long as 45 minutes to over an hour, each way. If your job requires a lot of flying, though, Manhattan Beach is conveniently located near LAX.

Web Site: www.ci.manhattan-beach.ca.us

Area Codes: 310, 424

Zip Code: 90266

Post Offices: Main Post Office, 1007 North Sepulveda Boulevard; Substation, 425 15th Street; 800-275-8777

Library: Main Library, 1320 Highland Avenue, 310-545-8595

Police District: Manhattan Beach is served by its own municipal police force, headquarters: Manhattan Beach Police Department, 420 15th Street, 310-545-5621.

Emergency Hospital: South Bay Medical Center, 514 North Prospect Avenue, 310-376-9474

Community Resources: Marine Avenue Park, Marina Avenue and Redondo Avenue; Live Oak Park, North Valley Drive and 21st Street; Polliwog Park, Manhattan Beach Boulevard and North Peck Avenue; Manhattan Village Mall, 3300 North Sepulveda Boulevard, 310-546-5555

Public School Education: Manhattan Beach Unified School District, 1230 Rosecrans Avenue, Manhattan Beach 90266, 310-725-9050, www.manhattan.k12.ca.us

Public Transportation: Call 800-COMMUTE for specific **MTA** bus route and schedule information.

INGLEWOOD

Boundaries: North: 64th Street; **East:** Van Ness Avenue; **South:** Imperial Highway; **West:** 405 Freeway

Sports fans remember Inglewood as the home of The Great Western Forum, the original site of the Los Angeles Lakers, Kings and Clippers before their move to the Staples Center downtown. It is also the site of the Hollywood Park horse race track where bettors play the ponies. Planes departing and approaching nearby LAX are quite apparent and security bars and gates are a must in this urban neighborhood, though the eastern side is generally thought of as more secure with its gated streets.

Housing in Inglewood consists of two- and three-bedroom homes, the majority built between 1940 and 1960. Some streets seem to be waging an on-going fight with graffiti and litter, others are neater and tidier. A handful of multi-unit apartment buildings are also located here. It's highly recommended that potential renters locate vacancies that include secured parking. Downtown Inglewood is centered around the shopping district of Market Street and Manchester Avenue, offering day-to-day amenities such as grocery stores, pharmacies and hair salons. The largest patch of green in the community is the Inglewood Park Cemetery, located to the north of the racetrack. The 405 San Diego Freeway borders the western edge, and the relatively new 105 Transit Highway, which is elevated above Inglewood, creates an unwelcome forest of concrete pillars along Inglewood's southern border.

Web Sites: www.ci.la.ca.us, www.co.la.ca.us

Area Codes: 310, 424

Zip Codes: 90301-5

Post Offices: Main Post Office, 300 East Hillcrest Boulevard; Crenshaw Imperial Station, 2672 West Imperial Highway; Lennox Branch, 4443 Lennox Boulevard; Morningside Park Station, 3212 West 85th Street; North Station, 811 North La Brea Avenue; 800-275-8777

Libraries: Main Library, 101 West Manchester Boulevard, 310-412-5380; Crenshaw-Imperial Branch, 11141 Crenshaw Boulevard, 310-412-5403; Morningside Park Branch, 3202 West 85th Street, 310-412-5400

Police District: Inglewood is served by its own municipal police force, headquarters: 1 Manchester Boulevard, 310 412-5210.

Emergency Hospitals: Daniel Freeman Memorial Hospital, 333 North Prairie Avenue, 310-674-7050; Centinela Hospital Medical Center, 555 East Hardy Street, 310-673-4660

Public School Education: Inglewood Unified School District, 401 South Inglewood Avenue, Inglewood, 90301, 310-419-2500

Community Resources: Hollywood Park, West Century Boulevard and Prairie Avenue; Centinela Park, 700 Warren Lane; Rogers Park, North Oak Street and North Eucalyptus Avenue

Public Transportation: Call 800-COMMUTE for specific **Metro Green Line** and **MTA** bus route and schedule information.

MAR VISTA, PALMS, CHEVIOT HILLS

Boundaries: North: 10 Santa Monica Freeway; **East:** Motor Avenue; **South:** Venice Boulevard; **West:** 405 Freeway

Mar Vista, and **Palms**, located within LA proper, just northwest of Culver City, attract those looking for reasonably priced housing, both for rent and purchase. This easy to access Westside location not only offers plenty to choose from housing wise, but its small commercial center—easy to access neighborhood restaurants and stores along Motor Avenue—is popular with the locals as well.

Of the two neighborhoods, Mar Vista is more geared toward family living. It has more single family homes and fewer apartment buildings than Palms, and the affordable home prices are attractive to young families. A few streets running atop the hill in Mar Vista boast ocean and city views. As evidence of the population in this area, the lovely Mar Vista Park at McLaughlin and Palms is usually filled with families (or kids with nannies) using the facilities. The park's recreation department caters to children, offering summer camps, gym classes, and toddler programs.

The Santa Monica Airport, which sits on the northern border of Mar Vista, can be a noise nuisance. Those viewing Mar Vista should know that many people often get this neighborhood confused with the housing project located west of Culver City called Mar Vista Gardens.

Venice Boulevard, the southernmost boundary for both Palms and Mar Vista, is a commercial strip seemingly overflowing with businesses where you can find everything from ethnic food to discount futons to auto parts. A short drive or walk north on Motor Avenue just under the 10 Freeway leads to lovely **Cheviot Hills**, a hilly residential neighborhood of mostly vintage Southern California homes. Continuing north on Motor Avenue will lead to the popular Cheviot Hills Park, offering 14 lit tennis courts, archery, swimming, basketball courts, baseball diamonds, and to Rancho Park, reputed to be one of the busiest public golf courses in the country. Motor Avenue continues north into the Twentieth Century Fox studio lot, and although it's closed to the public, you may spot the old movie set street from "Hello, Dolly" as you drive by.

Web sites: www.ci.la.ca.us, www.co.la.ca.us

Area Codes: 310, 424

Zip Code: 90034

Post Offices: Mar Vista Station, 3865 Grand View Boulevard; Palms Station, 3751 Motor Avenue; 800-275-8777

Libraries: Mar Vista branch, 12006 Venice Boulevard, 213-390-3954; Palms-Rancho Park Library, 2920 Overland Avenue, 310-838-2157

Police District: Pacific Division, 12312 Culver Boulevard, 310-202-4501

Emergency Hospital: Brotman Medical Center, 3828 Delmas Terrace, 310-836-7000

Community Resources: Mar Vista Recreation Center, 11430 Woodbine Street, 310-398-5982; Cheviot Hills Park and Recreation Center, 2551 Motor Avenue, 310-837-5186; Rancho Park Golf Course, 10460 West Pico Boulevard, 310-838-7373; Hillcrest Country Club, 10000 West Pico Boulevard, 310-553-8911

Public School Education: LA Unified School District, 634 Cesar E. Chavez, Los Angeles, CA 90012; 800-933-8133; www.lausd.k12.ca.us

Public Transportation: Call 800-COMMUTE for specific **MTA** bus route and schedule information. Santa Monica's Municipal **Big Blue Bus** has lines in the area, call 310-451-5444 for route and schedule information. For the **Culver City Municipal Bus Line**, call 310-202-5731.

CULVER CITY

Boundaries: North: Venice Boulevard; **East:** Jefferson Boulevard; **South:** Slauson Avenue; **West:** 405 Freeway

Culver City is the original and current home to several major movie studios, including the landmark site of Metro Goldwyn Mayer, now the location of Sony Studios. Such movie classics as "Citizen Kane," "King Kong," "ET," and the scene of Atlanta burning in "Gone with the Wind" were all filmed on the lots of Culver City movie studios. Today Columbia, Tri-Star and several other major film and televisions producers are located here.

Though only five square miles and bordered on all sides by parts of LA, Culver City is its own municipal entity. It is bisected by Ballona Creek which empties into the Pacific Ocean. The majority of Culver City is zoned for commercial, industrial and light industrial business, however, those looking to reside here can find pockets of single-family homes. Prospective homeowners are enticed to relocate here based on city offered housing incentives (see their web site). The majority of homes are simple, two- or three-bedroom homes, generally built between 1950 and 1980. Because Culver City did not begin developing until the 1940s, the homes in this community are newer than many other Los Angeles neighborhoods. Apartment rentals are pricey due to its Westside location—for a one-bedroom apartment, you can expect to pay about $900. Home seekers can expect to pay somewhere in the mid to low $300,000s for a Culver City zip code.

The lively commercial district of Culver City has over three million square feet of retail space. Retailers include the 140-store Fox Hills Mall and a handful of auto dealerships. As a workplace hub, the old industrial area known as the Hayden Tract, located between National Boulevard and Higuera Street and north of Ballona Creek, now consists of a collection of recently built art and design studios, high-tech marketing firms and architecture offices. Two unique buildings designed by award-winning architect Eric Owen Moss, one on National Boulevard and another on Hayden Avenue, have also focused attention on this area for their eye-catching appearance.

On weekends, residents take to the sidewalk cafes and retail stores along Washington Boulevard. During the weekday, the wide thoroughfares of Venice, Washington, and Culver boulevards provide alternatives to the 10 Santa Monica Freeway into Marina Del Rey and Santa Monica. After rush hour, when Culver City's daytime workforce population has left, area residents are able to enjoy a less hurried pace.

Web Site: www.ci.culver-city.ca.us

Area Codes: 310, 424

Zip Code: 90230, 90232

Post Office: Main Post Office, 11111 Jefferson Boulevard; Gateway Station, 9942 Culver Boulevard; 800-275-8777

Library: Culver City Library, 4975 Overland Avenue, 310-559-1676

Police District: Culver City is served by its own municipal police force, headquarters: 4040 Duoquesne Avenue, 310-837-1221.

Emergency Hospital: Brotman Medical Center, 3828 Delmas Terrace, 310-836-7000; Washington Medical Center, 12101 West Washington Boulevard, 310-391-0601

Public School Education: Culver City Unified School District, 4034 Irving Place, Culver City, 90232-2848; www.ccusd.k12.ca.us

Community Resources: Culver City Park, Duoquesne Avenue and Jefferson Boulevard; Veterans Memorial Park, 4417 Overland Avenue

Public Transportation: For the **Culver City Municipal Bus Line**, call 310-202-5731. Call 800-COMMUTE for specific **MTA** bus route and schedule information. Santa Monica's **Big Blue Bus** has lines in the area, call 310-451-5444 for route and schedule information.

WEST LOS ANGELES

Boundaries: North: Santa Monica Boulevard; **East:** Beverly Glen Boulevard; **South:** Pico Boulevard; **West:** Centinela Avenue

While still centrally located on the Westside, the area known as West LA tends to be less expensive than nearby Westwood and Brentwood. Here, the streets are more urban, dotted with convenience shops, gas stations, and strip malls, many of which could use a new coat of paint.

Housing stock mainly consists of bunched together, non-descript, three-story apartments dating from the 1960s and '70s. Many do not have air conditioners, though the air is cooler here, with the ocean just a stone's throw away in the beach community of Santa Monica. Street parking generally is available, and some buildings provide back-alley parking spaces, though many are not gated. The positives for this Westside location include convenient access to major freeways, including the 10 Santa Monica and 405 San Diego, and mid- to low-end rental rates. The area certainly makes up for in affordability what it lacks in architectural charm, creating a good choice for people on a budget who want to live on the Westside.

Aficionados of Japanese food and culture should check out Sawtelle Boulevard north of Olympic Boulevard, where a number of Japanese restaurants and Japanese-owned nurseries can be found. Also worth a visit is the funky Art Deco movie house called the Nuart (on Santa Monica Boulevard just west of the 405 Freeway), which features foreign and alternative films, plus a weekly Saturday midnight showing of "The Rocky Horror Picture Show."

If you like to shop, you should know that West LA is also the locale of two major malls. The indoor Westside Pavillion mall offers basic shopping amenities. The upscale outdoor Century City Shopping Mall is conducive to window shopping and caters to a fashion-conscious crowd; it even offers valet parking. The Century City Mall's movie theater complex is especially popular with Westsiders and is frequently sold out on weekends. The weekday lunch crowd—business suited men and women from the nearby work district (heavy in the entertainment and law fields) fills the mall's food court.

Web Sites: www.ci.la.ca.us, www.co.la.ca.us

Area Codes: 310, 424

Zip Code: 90025

Post Office: West Los Angeles branch, 11420 Santa Monica Boulevard; 800-275-8777

Library: West Los Angeles Library, 11360 Santa Monica Boulevard, 310-575-8323

Police District: West Los Angeles Division, 1663 Butler Avenue, 310-575-8402

Emergency Hospital: UCLA Medical Center, 10833 LeConte Avenue, 310-825-9111

Public School Education: LA Unified School District, 634 Cesar E. Chavez, Los Angeles, CA 90012; 800-933-8133; www.lausd.k12.ca.us

Community Resources: Westwood Park, 1350 South Sepulveda Boulevard; Westside Pavillion Shopping Mall, Overland Avenue and Ayres Avenue; Century City Shopping Mall, 10250 Santa Monica Boulevard

Public Transportation: Call 800-COMMUTE for specific **MTA** bus route and schedule information. Santa Monica's **Big Blue Bus** has lines in the area, call 310-451-5444 for route and schedule information.

BRENTWOOD

Boundaries: North: Sunset Boulevard; **East:** 405 Freeway; **South:** Wilshire Boulevard; **West:** Centinela Avenue

The lushly planted, upscale Brentwood exudes prestige for those with the means to live here. Brentwood's central position on the Westside and numerous apartment buildings makes it a natural choice for new and established professionals. What this community may lack in character, it makes up for with a vanilla safe environment. Running through Brentwood's center, the busy San Vicente Boulevard offers brand-name clothiers, upscale restaurants, bookstores, coffee shops, and gourmet groceries. The Boulevard also acts as a divider for area residences, with houses located to the north of it, and stylish contemporary apartments and condominiums to the south. The northwestern-most part of Brentwood is an affluent residential area of palatial homes on shady streets. Multiple bedrooms, i.e., more than three, are typical in these custom homes tucked on quiet streets that curve through hills. These hillside residences translate into big price tags ($1 million is the average here). Higher-end rent also applies to Brentwood's apartments.

The area around Brentwood Village, the quaint shopping area where Barrington Avenue meets Sunset Boulevard, includes cafes, bakeries, hair salons, a post office, and park. Many joggers and dog walkers especially love the wide, grassy meridian that makes up San Vicente Boulevard, which, for the truly motivated, will take exercisers all the way west to the coastline in Santa Monica.

Brentwood is also home to the Getty Center, a billion dollar "campus" of buildings housing, among other art related programs and institutions, the late J. Paul Getty's collection of European antiquities and art. Designed by noted architect Richard Meier, the mountain top museum has been a hit with locals and visitors alike who must wait in line to ride the meandering electric tram up the mountain. Be aware, the museum's popularity has increased traffic in the area, especially on weekends, much to the dismay of area residents. However, the snarls are minor compared to the frequently sardine-packed 405 San Diego Freeway which serves as the main north/south artery in and out of Brentwood for commuters.

Web Site: www.ci.brentwood.ca.us

Area Code: 310

Zip Code: 90049

Post Office: Barrington Station, 200 South Barrington Avenue, 800-275-8777

Library: Brentwood branch-Donald Bruce Kauffman Library, 11820 San Vincente Boulevard, 310-575-8273

Police District: West Los Angeles Division, 1663 Butler Avenue, 310-575-8402

Emergency Hospital: UCLA Medical Center, 10833 LeConte Avenue, 310-825-9111

Public School Education: LA Unified School District, 634 Cesar E. Chavez, Los Angeles, CA 90012; 800-933-8133; www.lausd.k12.ca.us

Community Resources: The Getty Center, 1200 Getty Center Drive, 310-440-7300; Barrington Recreation Center, 333 South Barrington Avenue, 310-476-3807; Brentwood Country Club, 590 Burlingame Avenue, 310-451-8011

Public Transportation: Call 800-COMMUTE for specific **MTA** bus route and schedule information. Santa Monica's **Big Blue Bus** has lines in the area, call 310-451-5444 for route and schedule information.

WESTWOOD

Boundaries: North: Sunset Boulevard; **East:** Beverly Glen Boulevard; **South:** Santa Monica Boulevard; **West:** 405 Freeway

South of the tony hills of Bel Air lies Westwood, most famous for being the home of the University of California Los Angeles (UCLA). The area around the campus is filled with fraternities, sororities, and student-inhabited apartment buildings, but non-students also enjoy the proximity to Westwood Village's many shops, restaurants, and movie theaters, as well as the sporting and cultural events held on campus.

During the 1980s and early 1990s, Westwood Village was *the* weekend hangout for young people. At night, the crowd often got so big that police were forced to close most of the Village streets to automobiles, allowing only foot traffic. Sadly, during the early 1990s, the congestion and high concentration of youths in the area got out of hand, and on a few occasions, screenings of violent and/or race-related movies touched off riots and looting. Additionally, Westwood Village became the too-frequent site of muggings and other crimes. Today many of the folks who used to stroll shoulder to shoulder in Westwood Village, now do so in Santa Monica's Third Street Promenade.

While the Village doesn't quite hum with the same amount of enthusiasm today, the area is secure and restaurants and shops continue to offer a variety of entertainment options. In fact, the popular Mann Theaters owns several large movie houses in Westwood.

Apartment rentals in Westwood are expensive due to the UCLA student population's voracious need for housing. When there is an apartment vacancy, especially during the school year, it is not unusual for students to double up in a one bedroom, or bunk four to a two-bedroom.

For those newcomers to Westwood with a car and no garage, a word of warning: hunting down street parking in Westwood requires a lot of patience. And beware the meter maids—Westwood has some of the quickest ticket writers in the county.

In the northern portion of Westwood, you'll find pretty, custom-built homes along winding, eucalyptus lined streets, many on cul-de-sacs. With the exception of the city's meticulously groomed National Cemetery located between Veteran Avenue and the 405 Sepulveda Freeway, Westwood is surrounded by affluence. The Bel Air Country Club lies just to the north, the Los Angeles Country Club to the east, and the posh outdoor shopping mall, Century City Center, to the south. The price of comfort and convenience doesn't come cheaply, with homes here easily going for a half million on up.

Prices ease up a bit as you move farther away from campus, especially going south toward the 10 Santa Monica Freeway. There's a little less green (both the kind you grow and the kind you earn) found south of Wilshire Boulevard, the trade-offs here being cheaper housing and easier parking. As you head closer to Los Angeles, apartments and houses are still modern and clean, but mingle with commercial zones, making for heavier traffic. Many professionals and singles reside and work in the area. The Federal Office Building, where many of the city's federal offices are housed, is at Wilshire and Sepulveda Boulevards, and the high profile Getty Museum is a stone's throw across the 405 Sepulveda Freeway in neighboring Brentwood.

Web Sites: www.ci.la.ca.us, www.co.la.ca.us

Area Code: 310

Zip Code: 90024

Post Office: Veterans Administration Building branch, 11000 Wilshire Boulevard, 800-275-8777

Library: West Los Angeles Branch, 11360 Santa Monica Boulevard, 310-575-8323

Police District: West Los Angeles Division, 1663 Butler Avenue, 310-575-8402

Emergency Hospital: UCLA Medical Center, 10833 LeConte Avenue, 310-825-9111

Public School Education: LA Unified School District, 634 Cesar E. Chavez, Los Angeles, CA 90012; 800-933-8133; www.lausd.k12.ca.us

Community Resources: Westwood Park, 1350 South Sepulveda Boulevard; Holmby Park, 601 Club View Drive; Los Angeles Country Club, 10101 Wilshire Boulevard; UCLA-Armand Hammer Museum, 10889 Wilshire Boulevard, 310-443-7000

Public Transportation: Call 800-COMMUTE for specific **MTA** bus route and schedule information. Santa Monica's **Big Blue Bus** has lines in the area, call 310-451-5444 for route and schedule information. The **LADOT** also operates here, call 310-808-2273 for commuter route and schedule information.

BEVERLY HILLS

TROUSDALE ESTATES
BEL AIR ESTATES

Boundaries: North: hills above Sunset Boulevard; **East:** Doheny Drive; **South:** Whitworth Drive; **West:** Whittier Drive

The above boundaries are rough outlines of Beverly Hills—residents are very particular about what constitutes a Beverly Hills address. There's even something called "Beverly Hills P.O." which refers to areas that may not look as meticulously groomed as Beverly Hills, but fall within the coveted Beverly Hills postal code, therefore entitling such residents to the city's civic amenities. One reason that locals are so concerned about who's in and who's out is that, as its own city, and a well-funded one at that, Beverly Hills' municipal services (police, fire, public education, etc.) are considered top notch in Los Angeles county. Even the well stocked Beverly Hills public library requires its patrons have library cards (that are gold-colored, by the way) separate from the Los Angeles library system's.

With a worldwide reputation as the home of the rich and famous, many multi-bedroomed residences in the Beverly Hills housing market begin at the million dollar mark and go upward. The tree-rich **Trousdale Estates** is another exclusive community of custom built homes tucked in the winding hills north of Beverly Hills, and **Bel Air Estates** sports mansions nestled in canyon country to the west.

Apartments, though similar in look and style to much of West Los Angeles (i.e., Spanish stucco), are harder to find and understandably pricier too. Tenacious bargain hunters may find more affordable pricing in the area known as "below the tracks." Though long since removed, train tracks once ran through Beverly Hills along Santa Monica Boulevard, and the site serves to mark the high rent from the not-so-high rent district of the city.

Downtown Beverly Hills (including the famous Rodeo Drive) starts south of Santa Monica Boulevard and continues south to Wilshire Boulevard. Along Wilshire Boulevard are high-rise office buildings, large upscale department stores (Neiman Marcus, Saks Fifth Avenue) and the stately Regent Beverly Wilshire Hotel. South of Wilshire Boulevard is the area where more affordable apartments and flats are located. The majority of these buildings were constructed before the 1940s and many offer hardwood floors and molded ceilings. Harder to find, but worth hunting for are the gatehouses and apartments over garages that are part of many of the Beverly Hills homes in "the flats," the palm tree-lined residential streets between Sunset and Santa Monica Boulevards, and to a lesser extent in the hills above Sunset Boulevard.

Beverly Hills streets are kept clean and have strict parking rules that nearly fill the length of the lamp posts on which they're posted. No freeways are immediately accessible from Beverly Hills, which means surface streets such as Wilshire Boulevard and Santa Monica Boulevard serve as surrogate freeways in and out of this city—preserving the exclusivity of the neighborhood, just the way residents like it.

For housing leads in Beverly Hills try the classifieds in the local *Beverly Hills Courier*.

Web Site: www.ci.beverly-hills.ca.us

Area Codes: 310, 424

Zip Codes: 90210, 90211, 90212

Post Office: Main Post Office, 325 North Maple Drive; Crescent Station, 469 North Crescent Drive, 800-275-8777

Library: Beverly Hills Library, 444 North Rexford Drive, 310-288-2222

Police District: Beverly Hills is served by its own municipal police force; headquarters: 464 North Rexford Drive, 310-550-4800.

Emergency Hospital: Cedars-Sinai Medical Center, 8700 Beverly

Boulevard, 310-855-5000

Community Resources: Parking Permits, 310-285-2551; La Cienega Park Community Center, 8400 Gregory Way, 310-550-4625; Roxbury Park Community Center, 471 South Roxbury Drive, 310-550-4761; Beverly Gardens Park, Santa Monica Boulevard and Bevely Drive, 310-285-2537

Public School Education: Beverly Hills Unified School District, 255 South Lasky Drive, 310-277-5900

Public Transportation: Call 800-COMMUTE for specific **MTA** bus route and schedule information.

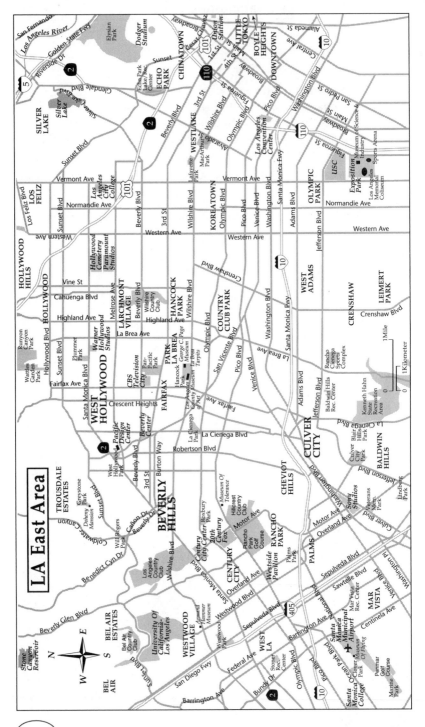

LA East Area

San Fernando
Los Angeles River
Golden State Fwy
Riverside Dr
Glendale Blvd
Elysian Park
Dodger Stadium
Cesar Chavez
Broadway
Sunset
Union Station
LITTLE TOKYO
Alameda St
BOYLE HEIGHTS
5
2
Echo Park Lake Rec. Area
ECHO PARK
Sunset Blvd
CHINATOWN
Main St
1st St
110
101
4th St
Broadway
Figueroa St
DOWNTOWN
Central Ave
San Pedro St
Washington Blvd
10
SILVER LAKE
Silver Lake
Sunset Blvd
2
Beverly Blvd
WESTLAKE
3rd St
MacArthur Park
Wilshire Blvd
Alvarado St
Lafayette Park
Olympic Blvd
Los Angeles Convention Center
Pico Blvd
Main St
Broadway
110
Figueroa St
Museum of Science & Industry
USC
Sports Arena
LOS FELIZ
Los Feliz Blvd
Vermont Ave
Los Angeles City College
101
Normandie Ave
Beverly Blvd
3rd St
Wilshire Blvd
KOREATOWN
Vermont Ave
Olympic Blvd
Venice Blvd
Washington Blvd
Adams Blvd
Santa Monica Fwy
OLYMPIC PARK
Normandie Ave
Exposition Park
Los Angeles Memorial Coliseum
HOLLYWOOD HILLS
Western Ave
Sunset Blvd
Western Ave
Western Ave
Western Ave
HOLLYWOOD
HOLLYWOOD
Hollywood Cemetery
Paramount Studios
Vine St
Cahuenga Blvd
Melrose Ave
Highland Ave
LARCHMONT VILLAGE
Wilshire Country Club
HANCOCK PARK
Crenshaw Blvd
COUNTRY CLUB PARK
WEST ADAMS
CRENSHAW
LEIMERT PARK
Runyon Canyon Park
Wattles Garden Park
Hollywood Blvd
Sunset Blvd
Plummer Park
Warner Hollywood Studios
La Brea Ave
Wilshire Blvd
Highland Ave
PARK LA BREA
George C. Page Museum
La Brea Tarpits
Olympic Blvd
San Vicente Blvd
Pico Blvd
Venice Blvd
Washington Blvd
Santa Monica Fwy
Adams Blvd
10
Crenshaw Blvd
1 Mile
1 Kilometer
0
Rancho Cienega Sports Complex
Santa Monica Blvd
Fairfax Ave
CBS Television City
Pan-Pacific Park
Hancock Park
Los Angeles County Museum of Art
WEST HOLLYWOOD
Crescent Heights
FAIRFAX
Pacific Design Center
Beverly Center
La Cienega Park
La Cienega Blvd
La Cienega Blvd
Robertson Blvd
Kenneth Hahn State Recreation Area
Baldwin Hills Rec. Center
Jefferson Blvd
BALDWIN HILLS
Blair Hills Park
2
West Hollywood Park
Beverly Blvd
3rd St
Burton Way
Beverly Dr
Robertson Blvd
Museum Of Tolerance
Roxbury Park
Hillcrest Country Club
CHEVIOT HILLS
CULVER CITY
La Cienega Blvd
Culver City Park
Culver Blvd
Sony Studios
Veterans Mem. Park
Lindberg Park
Jefferson Blvd
TROUSDALE ESTATES
Greystone Park
Doheny Mansion
Sunset Blvd
Canon Dr
Beverly Dr
Coldwater Canyon
Will Rogers Park
BEVERLY HILLS
Century City Center
20th Century Fox
CENTURY CITY
Rancho Park Golf Course
RANCHO PARK
Motor Ave
Motor Ave
PALMS
Culver Blvd
Motor Ave
Overland Ave
Washington Blvd
Culver Blvd
Sepulveda Blvd
MAR VISTA
Washington Pl
Venice Blvd
Benedict Cyn Dr
Los Angeles Country Club
Wilshire Blvd
Santa Monica Blvd
Westside Pavilion
Palms Park
Overland Ave
Sepulveda Blvd
405
Barrington Ave
Sawtelle Blvd
Mar Vista Rec. Center
Centinela Ave
Stone Canyon Reservoir
Beverly Glen Blvd
BEL AIR ESTATES
Bel Air Country Club
University Of California Los Angeles
Armand Hammer Museum
WESTWOOD VILLAGE
Westwood Park
Westwood Blvd
WEST LA
Federal Ave
Sepulveda Blvd
Sawtelle Blvd
Bundy Dr
Olympic Blvd
Pico Blvd
Santa Monica Municipal Airport
Museum Of Flying
Clover Park
Santa Monica College
Penmar Golf Course
Marine Park
N
W   E
S
BEL AIR
Sepulveda Blvd
San Diego Fwy
Barrington Ave
2
Olympic Blvd
10
Stoner Rec. Center
Santa Monica Blvd

NEIGHBORHOODS — EAST

WEST HOLLYWOOD

Boundaries: North: Sunset Boulevard (to the west), Fountain Avenue (to the east); **East:** La Brea Avenue; **South:** Beverly Boulevard (to the west), Willoughby Avenue (to the east); **West:** Doheny Drive

West Hollywood made headlines in 1984 when the city elected America's first openly gay mayor, Valerie Terrigno. Though only 1.9 square-miles in size with 37,000 residents, this community, identified by a lush grass and rainbow flag lined meridian down Santa Monica Boulevard, is high profile for its gay and lesbian community.

The area is also home to a large Jewish and Russian immigrant population that clusters on the southern and eastern borders, while the western side is made up of gay men and women from all ethnicities. Jewish immigrants were the first group to come to the area, spilling west from the Fairfax District where they had settled post-World War II. The gay community was next to discover West Hollywood. Some were attracted to the growing design community here and others by the relative security of living in this then-unincorporated area in LA County, which was under the jurisdiction of the county sheriff and not the Los Angeles Police Department (said to frequently raid gay clubs).

On a stroll through Plummer Park on Santa Monica Boulevard, you can see the mosaic of neighbors who seem to have found a peace, albeit at times uneasy, amongst each other. As an example of how the local government is responsive to its citizenry, West Hollywood was the first US city to declare Yom Kippur (the Jewish New Year) a legal holiday. The social and politically minded residents of this community were also responsible for paving the way to outlaw discrimination against people with AIDS. One weekend every June the city plays host to one of the largest gay pride festivals in the country.

Residents enjoy the city's numerous amenities, including chic shopping and dining, and the beautiful Spanish-style architecture that graces many West Hollywood streets. Santa Monica Boulevard runs the length of the city and has a business base as diverse as the community itself. On the western end of the street there are many retail stores, cafes, and nightclubs catering to the gay and lesbian community, which is estimated to be anywhere from 25-40% of the city's population. (Check out *Gay USA* by Lori

Hobkirk for a concise, useful chapter on LA for the gay arrival.) A burgeoning group of gyms and related fitness and beauty businesses have transformed the area near City Hall into Health Row. And further east, the boulevard is home to the entrepreneurial efforts of the thriving Russian-Jewish immigrant community. Head south to Melrose and you'll find many more posh eateries including Elixir, 8612 Melrose Avenue, which features a lab-coated Asian herbalist concocting restorative tonics, and O2, at 8788 Sunset Boulevard, actor Woody Harrelson's oxygen bar and restaurant.

West Hollywood is also the site of the Pacific Design Center, a huge collection (1.2 million square feet) of interior design showrooms which anchors the myriad interior decorating businesses along Melrose, Beverly, and Robertson boulevards. The Center itself is affectionately known as "The Blue Whale," due to the scale and bright blue hue of the original building. Added later was an equally large, bright green building, Center Green, with even more showrooms. Further south on La Cienega Boulevard is the chic Beverly Center, a multi-level indoor mall, and its humbler sister the Beverly Connection, a smaller outdoor mall.

The northern most part of West Hollywood features some of the trendiest sites on Sunset Boulevard, including nightclubs like House of Blues, The Viper Room and The Laugh Factory. The club *du-jour*, Standard, is at 8300 Sunset Boulevard in the Sunset Strip Hotel; lit up like a gray-blue mirage it exudes plenty of too-cool-for-you attitude. On weekend nights you'll find this section of the Boulevard choked with traffic and exhausted car valets as club-goers cruise the scene, hoping for a peep through the windows of Larry Flynt's Hustler Hollywood. Farther west is Sunset Plaza, a tony strip of sidewalk cafes and designer label retailers, where celebrity sightings are not unusual.

Clean and well tended apartments and condominiums make up the majority of residences lining the leafy streets radiating out from this section of Santa Monica Boulevard. The buildings are a mix of older Spanish-style homes, and the modern but boxy three- to four-story stuccos. A handful of retirement/assisted living apartments are also located in the area.

While the recently instituted "vacancy decontrol," brought on by the Costa-Hawkins bill (which allows landlords to raise rent in a previously rent-controlled apartment to market value, after a tenant vacates the apartment) is in effect for all of California, including West Hollywood, prospective renters will be interested to know that West Hollywood has a strict and intricate rent control that regulates the maximum percentage (typically around 1.25% or less) a landlord may raise rent. This adjustment is based on the consumer price index and is released every July. Rent control does not apply to single family dwellings, some condominiums and any apartments that received a certificate of residency after 1979. Apartment vacancies are not difficult to find and the stock of available condominiums is especially healthy. Only seven percent of the housing in West Hollywood consists of detached homes, which generally go for $300,000—if you can find one for sale. The city's Department of Rent Stabilization publishes a list of residential units available for rent. Call their 24-hour Residential Referral List Hotline 323-848-6419 for more information. Limited street parking dictates the use of permits. Weekend parking is made scarcer by Angelenos of all persuasions looking for a night on the town in West Hollywood.

Web Site: www.ci.west-hollywood.ca.us

Area Code: 310

Zip Code: 90069

Post Office: West Branch, 820 North San Vicente Boulevard, 800-275-8777

Police District: West Hollywood is contracted with the County of Los Angeles Sheriff's Department, 720 North San Vicente boulevard, 310-855-5000.

Emergency Hospital: Cedars-Sinai Medical Center, 8700 Beverly Boulevard, 310-855-5000

Library: 715 North San Vicente Boulevard, 310-652-5340

Community Resources: West Hollywood Permit Parking Divison, 323-848-6400; Department of Rent Stabilization, 323-848-6450; Convention & Visitor Bureau, 800-368-6020

Public School Education: LA Unified School District, 634 Cesar E. Chavez, Los Angeles, CA 90012; 800-933-8133; www.lausd.k12.ca.us

Public Transportation: The **West Hollywood City Line** offers shuttle services within the city of West Hollywood, call 800-447-2189 for specific route and schedule information. Santa Monica's **Big Blue Bus** services West Los Angeles and Santa Monica, call 310-451-5444 for route and schedule information. For all other areas, call 800-COMMUTE for specific **MTA** bus route and schedule information.

FAIRFAX DISTRICT (MID-WILSHIRE)

Boundaries: North: Willoughby Avenue; **East:** La Brea Avenue; **South:** Pico Boulevard; **West:** La Cienega Boulevard

Long the center of Los Angeles' Orthodox Jewish community, the Fairfax District includes a blend of cultures and lifestyles, including Indian, Ethiopian, African-American, and urban hip mixed in with the daytime office folk. Indeed, Fairfax Avenue itself is a cultural mish-mash where one can find family-run kosher butchers, Ethiopian restaurants, African artifacts, and Indian spice shops. Even Canter's Delicatessen reflects the diversity of the neighborhood, serving up matzo ball soup to elderly Jewish residents by day while featuring jazz and blues in the adjoining "Kibitz (Yiddish for "chat") Room" at night.

The Farmers' Market at Fairfax Avenue and Third Street is a favorite for tour bus stops and Fairfax District locals who come for fresh, picture-perfect fruits and vegetables and cafes. It's also a busy lunch spot for business people, especially the nearby television and movie industry executives (CBS's Television City is right next door and the Writer's Guild of America is across the street).

A retail district along Third Street between La Cienega Boulevard and Crescent Heights is dotted with new and used clothing and furniture stores, and La Brea Avenue to the east boasts several trendy furniture stores and eateries, as well as some of the area's most well kept Spanish-style apartment buildings along Sycamore Avenue, just east of La Brea. Finally, there is the famous, incense infused Melrose Avenue, popularized by the television series, "Melrose Place." Melrose, on the Hollywood border, is LA's funkiest shopping street and definitely *the* place to go to find the latest chic fashion and food items. The street's denizens are some of LA's most urban and cutting-edge, with pierces and tattoos practically *de rigueur*.

Besides the wonderful mix of local residents in the Fairfax District, the architecture of much of the housing here is another plus. You can find reasonably priced rentals in everything from multi-unit apartment buildings to small houses. If it's within your budget and you're lucky enough to locate a vacancy, the real gems are the 1920s and '30s duplexes. Usually two-story stuccos, with one unit on the top and another below, many of these duplexes feature such touches as hardwood floors, built-in cabinetry, leaded or stained glass windows, ceramic tiled bathrooms and kitchens, and spacious rooms. It's typical for the landlord to live in one unit and rent out the other, and often the backyard is available for shared access.

Web Sites: www.fairfaxla.com

Area Codes: 310, 213

Zip Codes: 90035, 90211, 90048, 90036, 90019

Post Office: Bicentennial Station, 7610 Beverly Boulevard, 800-275-8777

Libraries: Fairfax Branch, 161 South Gardner Street, 323-936-6191; Wilshire Branch, 149 North Saint Andrews Place, 323-957-4550

Police District: (north of Beverly Boulevard) Hollywood Division, 1358 North Wilcox Avenue, 213-485-4302; (south of Beverly Boulevard) Wilshire Division, 4861 Venice Boulevard, 213-485-4022

Emergency Hospital: Cedars - Sinai Medical Center, 8700 Beverly Boulevard, 310-855-5000

Public School Education: LA Unified School District, 634 Cesar E. Chavez, Los Angeles, CA 90012, 800-933-8133, www.lausd.k12.ca.us

Community Resources: Parking Permits, 310-485-8291; Wiltern Theatre, 3790 Wilshire Boulevard, 213-380-5005

Public Transportation: Call 800-COMMUTE for specific **MTA** bus route and schedule information.

HANCOCK PARK

LARCHMONT VILLAGE

Boundaries: North: Melrose Avenue; **East:** Western Avenue; **South:** Wilshire Boulevard; **West:** La Brea Avenue

Hancock Park is noted for its rolling, well-groomed front lawns and stately pre-World War II homes, previous residences of Los Angeles' powerful elite. Some of the area's oldest and grandest homes may be viewed here. The Getty House, built in 1921, is the Mayor's official residence, located on Irving Boulevard. Hardwood floors and built-in cabinetry are typical features of homes in this area. The posh Wilshire Country Club begins just north of Third Street, and residents enjoy the proximity to the business district along Wilshire Boulevard. Miracle Mile, as the boulevard is called, was developed during the 1930s when art deco was in its heyday, and many buildings display this architectural influence. Here, the LA County Museum of Art and the Wiltern Theater, preserved in all its art deco glory, offer cultural entertainment year round. Tony Beverly Hills is located to the west, much to the delight of "shopaholics." And for all you bread lovers, the La Brea Bakery, 624 South La Brea Avenue, is known for its artisan breads, including a fresh baked chocolate cherry creation, and scrumptious rectangular toasting bread. Banks, gas stations and bus stops are conveniently dotted throughout the area. Hancock Park is popular with Jewish families, and a number of orthodox and conservative synagogues are located within walking distance.

Bordered by Koreatown to the east and Mid-City to the south, Hancock Park offers potential home owners slightly cheaper prices than on the Westside. Pricey, modern apartments are clustered in Park La Brea, a gated and grassy community just East of Hancock Park. Parking within Hancock Park can be hell for visitors, but heaven for residents as many streets are restricted and require permits after business hours.

More affordable apartments and flats—and slightly more relaxed parking regulations—may be found near quaint **Larchmont Village** and along upper Rossmore. Within Larchmont Village, you'll find a string of mom and pop retail businesses and restaurants located along Larchmont Avenue. The small older buildings along the street and general lack of pretension of the stores and cafes are in stark contrast to many of Los Angeles' more trendy neighborhoods, though it still has an upscale feel. Business owners can be seen sweeping their sidewalks and addressing their customers by name. No tourist attractions here, just tidy residences with well-kept lawns and small florists, dry cleaners, bookstores, eateries and the like.

Web Sites: www.ci.la.ca.us, www.co.la.ca.us

Area Codes: 323, 213

Zip Codes: 90004-5 90019-20, 90010, 90036

Post Office: Oakwood Station, 265 South Western Avenue, 800-275-8777

Libraries: Memorial Branch, 4625 West Olympic Boulevard, 323-938-2732/2733; Wilshire Branch, 149 North Saint Andrews Place; 323-957-4550; Fairfax Branch, 161 South Gardner Street, 323-936-6191

Police District: (north of Beverly Boulevard) Hollywood Division, 1358 North Wilcox Avenue, 323-485-4302; (south of Beverly Boulevard) Wilshire Division, 4861 Venice Boulevard, 323-485-4022

Emergency Hospitals: Westside Hospital, 910 South Fairfax Avenue, 323-938-3431; Queens of Angels Hollywood Presbyterian Medical Center, 1300 North Vermont Avenue, 213-413-3000

Public School Education: LA Unified School District, 634 Cesar E. Chavez, Los Angeles, CA 90012; 800-933-8133; www.lausd.k12.ca.us

Community Resources: Parking Permits, 310-485-8291; Pan Pacific Recreation Center, 141 South Gardner Street, 323-939-8874; Los Angeles County Museum of Art (LACMA), 5905 Wilshire Boulevard, 323-857-6000

Public Transportation: Call 800-COMMUTE for specific **MTA** bus route and schedule information.

HOLLYWOOD

HOLLYWOOD HILLS

Boundaries: North: Mulholland Drive (in the west), Griffith Park (in the east); **East:** Vermont Avenue; **South:** Melrose Avenue; **West:** Crescent Heights

With images from Hollywood's golden era often in newcomer's minds, many come to Hollywood expecting to rub elbows with the stars and find work in the studios. The reality is that only a handful of studios, Paramount among them, remain in Hollywood, and most working actors try to avoid the tourists. In fact, much of Hollywood has become a budget-rent apartment district and tired tourist destination, dotted with souvenir shops and strip clubs, and is further tarnished by the urban realities of homelessness and crime. The closest most get to a star is at the Walk of Fame where the celebrities' names are engraved in stars lining the sidewalk. The good news however, the presence of transients and prostitutes have been reduced, thanks to a revitalization effort.

The famous Sunset Boulevard ("the Strip") runs through the heart of Hollywood, providing access to neighboring West Hollywood, a place known for a bustling nighttime social scene. Along Hollywood Boulevard, the recently renovated Mann's Chinese, twenties-era theaters, the Egyptian and the El Capitan, are *the* place to go for opening night movies. Many die-hard movie fans will happily stand in line two or more hours for seats and costume themselves according to the movie's theme.

To be content to call Hollywood home, you must love the energy and edginess of the area. Most apartment complexes in central Hollywood were built in the 1950s and '60s, and despite the area's lack of garages and tight street parking, these apartments are filled with many budget-minded singles pursuing their American dream. Amenities much appreciated by the locals include plentiful Laundromats®, car washes, and cheap eats.

In sharp contrast, the exclusive **Hollywood Hills** is but a few minutes north of Sunset Boulevard. The Hills feature some of Los Angeles' most sought-after residential areas, and many in the entertainment business call the neighborhood home. Here you'll find million dollar custom-built homes located on windy, twisting hillsides, complete with the prerequisite BMW Z3 or Mercedes Benz, or both.

Nestled at the base of the Hills is the Hollywood Bowl, summer home of the Los Angeles Philharmonic and a popular attraction among Angelenos of all ages. The summer series includes orchestral, jazz, and popular tunes, and some nights the music is accompanied by glorious fireworks. And if these entertainment amenities aren't enough, the Hollywood Hills location also offers quick access to neighboring Beverly Hills and the Westside via Sunset Boulevard.

Outside the Hills and south of the apartments, but just north of hip Melrose Avenue, a pocket of charming, Santa Fe style homes run along tree-lined sidewalks. Rental and housing prices tend to be high, due to the proximity to Melrose Avenue's trendy shopping boutiques and restaurants.

Overall, Hollywood lays out like a geographic hierarchy of the entertainment business, with those who have "made it" living in the Hills north of Franklin Avenue and those still trying, living south. In-between the hills and the flats, you'll find a few gentrified bohemian enclaves, but overall, Hollywood's population is a mix of working class people, professionals, artists and aspiring actors.

Web Sites: www.chamber.hollywood.com; www.ci.la.ca.us

Area Codes: 213, 323

Post Office: Hollywood Station, 1615 North Wilcox Avenue, 800-275-8777

Zip Codes: 90028, 90068, 90078

Police District: Hollywood Division, 1358 North Wilcox Avenue, 213-485-4302

Emergency Hospitals: Kaiser Permanente Hospital, 4867 Sunset

Boulevard, 323-783-4011/2000, Queen of Angeles Hollywood Presbyterian Medical Center, 1300 North Vermont Avenue, 213-413-3000; Hollywood Community Hospital, 6245 Delongpre Avenue, 323-462-2271

Libraries: Goldwyn Hollywood Library, 1623 North Ivan Avenue, 323-467-1821; John C. Fremont Branch, 6121 Melrose Avenue, 323-962-3521

Public School Education: LA Unified School District, 634 Cesar E. Chavez, Los Angeles, CA 90012, 800-933-8133

Community Resources: Lake Hollywood, northern end of Weidlake Drive; Barnsdall Park, 4800 Hollywood Boulevard; Plummer Park, 7377 Santa Monica Boulevard

Transportation: Call 800-Commute for specific **MTA** bus route and schedule information.

LOS FELIZ, SILVERLAKE PARK, ECHO PARK

Boundaries: North: Mulholland Drive (in the west), Griffith Park (in the east); **East:** Vermont Avenue; **South:** Melrose Avenue; **West:** Crescent Heights

More affordable than the Westside, these are the funky communities that hug the Santa Monica Mountains, between Hollywood and Dodger Stadium. Los Feliz, Silverlake, and Echo Park residents vary greatly, from entertainment industry workers to blue collar folk. The appearance of residential (a near 50-50 mix of houses and apartments) and commercial zones are likewise varied, ranging from mansion sized homes with well-tended lawns to modest residences with security bars.

Los Feliz defines the start of East Los Angeles and is the furthest north among these three communities. Residents here are a well-to-do and often colorful lot with outrageous hairdos, pierced tongues, and cutting edge urban fashion quite the norm.

Los Feliz is the closest of the three to Griffith Park, the largest publicly owned park in the United States. The park occupies 4,400 acres in the hills and features the Los Angeles Zoo, the Griffith Park Observatory Planetarium and Laserium, the Greek Theater, Travel Town Train Park, and the Gene Autry Western Heritage Museum. There are also picnic areas, a soccer field, and 50 miles of hiking and horseback riding trails. Los Feliz is the most prestigious community within this area with many of its streets winding into the hills at the mountain base of Griffith Park. Along Hillhurst Avenue near Franklin Avenue is Los Feliz Village, the site of trendy eateries and clothing boutiques to the stars. Speaking of trendy, many wing-tipped dancers frequent The Derby, 4500 Los Feliz Boulevard, a bar and restaurant that offers free swing lessons in the evenings.

Located along Franklin Avenue, the two-story, multi-bedroom homes, built in the old-style of Hollywood mansions, attract many a budding starlet. Madonna resides behind wrought iron gates with the letter "M" sculpted on it. Area architecture varies greatly from stucco to medieval, but the majority of the residences feature 1930s opulence. The houses are of mansion proportions with price tags to match. Those hunting for a home here should know that street access to residences is occasionally congested by concert goers heading in and out of the Greek Theater in Griffith Park.

Silverlake, located further south, offers more shopping districts with the usual cafes, antique stores and bookstores, along Vermont and Hyperion Avenues. A number of private residences designed by 1930s architect Richard Neutra line the 2200 block of East Silverlake Boulevard. Lucky residents even get a view of the tree-lined Silverlake Reservoir. The well-kept Spanish style homes are on the modest side when compared with their neighbors to the north. Silverlake's gay enclave is more low key than that of West Hollywood, but gay and lesbian residents enjoy their own cluster of bars and clubs in the area, and transsexuals, cross-dressers and other alternative lifestylists seem to prefer Silverlake. The 5 Golden State Freeway borders the northeast section of Silverlake.

Further southeast is **Echo Park**. Established in the 1920s, this largely blue-collar, Latino community hugs the base of the hills, facing a man-made lake which offers paddle-boating on sunny weekends. Well preserved Victorian and Craftsman-style homes, built when the area was in its heyday, are clustered along Carroll Avenue. Spanish architecture makes up the rest of the selection in the neighborhood's housing stock. There are a variety of mom-and-pop shops and restaurants in Echo Park offering the latest in Latino pop music and the best in Mexican and Spanish food and wares.

Also located in Echo Park is Dodger Stadium (near Elysian Park Avenue and West Sunset Boulevard), which can make navigation into these communities difficult during sporting events, and Elysian Park, second in size only to Griffith. Proximity to downtown LA (just a hop onto the nearby 110 Pasadena Freeway) is a plus for local commuters. Heat and smog become especially noticeable during the summer, but nothing air conditioners can't handle. Prospective homebuyers should know that prices here are reasonable, and architecturally interesting older homes abound. Security, however, may be an issue, and many home-owners elect to subscribe to private patrols to supplement the city's.

Web Sites: www.losfeliz.com, www.ci.la.ca.us, www.co.la.ca.us

Area Code: 323

Zip Code: 90026

Post Office: Silverlake branch, 1525 North Alvarado Street; 800-275-8777

Library: Los Feliz Branch, 1801 Hillhurst Avenue, 323-913-4714; Echo Park Branch, 515 North Laveta Terrace, 213-250-7808

Police District: Northeast Division, 3353 San Fernando Drive, 213-485-2563

Emergency Hospitals: Children's Hospital of Los Angeles, 4650 Sunset Boulevard, 213-660-2450; Queen of Angels Hollywood Presbyterian Medical Center, 1300 North Vermont Avenue, 213-413-3000

Public School Education: LA Unified School District, 634 Cesar E. Chavez, Los Angeles, CA 90012, 800-933-8133, www.lausd.k12.ca.us

Community Resources: Barnsdall Park, 4800 Hollywood Boulevard; Echo Park Lake and Recreation Center, Bellevue Avenue and Glendale Boulevard, 213-250-7808; Elysian Park, 1880 Academy Drive, 323-226-1402; Dodger Stadium, 1000 Elysian Park Avenue, 323-224-1500

Transportation: Call 800-COMMUTE for specific **MTA** bus route and schedule information.

LEIMERT PARK

BALDWIN HILLS
CRENSHAW

Boundaries: North: Martin Luther King Jr. Boulevard; **East:** Leimert Boulevard; **South:** Vernon Avenue; **West:** Crenshaw Boulevard

Located seven miles southeast of downtown LA and nestled in the Crenshaw District, Leimert Park is one of the first planned communities in Los Angeles. Development here began in the early 1930s and grew around the park itself (located at the triangular intersection of Leimert and Crenshaw), created by Olmsted & Olmsted, a later incarnation of the same firm that designed New York's Central Park. The surrounding area of shops, 1940s-style duplexes, and houses on wide, tree-lined streets is known as Leimert Park Village.

Leimert Park is characterized by its lovely homes and tight African-American community. Most residences in Leimert Park consist of homes and duplexes which boast 1930s and 1940s architecture not found in many other parts of the city. Housing costs are moderate, with a typical home averaging $200,000.

Stroll down Degnan Boulevard and you will find galleries, art centers, jazz clubs, and bookstores, all highlighting African-American themes. In August, an annual jazz festival here draws music lovers from all over the city. The large Baldwin Hills Crenshaw Plaza mall offers convenient shopping.

In comparison, the nearby **Crenshaw** neighborhood, distinguishable by its gridded city streets, has a more urban feel, with wrought iron security bars on houses and businesses a common sight.

The LAX airport, located a few miles to the southwest, is a convenience to those who fly frequently, and a noise nuisance to others.

Neighboring to the west is the community of **Baldwin Hills**, an unincorporated patch of oil-rich, but hilly land dotted with more oil pumps than homes.

Web Sites: www.ci.la.ca.us, www.co.la.ca.us

Area Code: 213

Post Office: Crenshaw Station, 3894 Crenshaw Boulevard, 800-275-8777

Zip Code: 90008

Libraries: Angeles Mesa Branch, 2700 West 52nd Street, 213-292-4328; View Park Branch, 3854 West 54th Street, 213-293-5371

Police District: Southwest Division, 1546 West Martin Luther King Jr. Boulevard, 213-485-2582

Emergency Hospitals: LA County - USC Medical Center, 1200 North State Street, 213-226-2622; Daniel Freeman Memorial Hospital, 333 North Prairie Avenue, 310-674-7050

Public School Education: LA Unified School District, 634 Cesar E.

Chavez, Los Angeles, CA 90012, 800-933-8133, www.lausd.k12.ca.us

Community Resources: Leimert Park, 4395 Leimert Boulevard; Baldwin Hills Crenshaw Plaza Mall, Crenshaw Boulevard and Martin Luther King Junior Boulevard; Rancho Cienega Sports Center Park, 5001 Rodeo Road, 323-294-6788

Transportation: Call 800-COMMUTE for specific **MTA** bus route and schedule information.

DOWNTOWN

WESTLAKE
BOYLE HEIGHTS
CHINATOWN
LITTLE TOKYO

Boundaries: North: Montana Street (in the west), Washington Boulevard (in the east); **East:** west of Michilinda Avenue; **South:** Columbia Street (in the west), California Boulevard (in the east); **West:** Hills West of Linda Vista Avenue

Generally, Downtown is considered a business district, not a residential neighborhood. During the day, a large number of white-collar workers employed in law, finance and advertising occupy the tightly packed high-rise office buildings. At night, after most day-timers have gone home and retailers have pulled down their iron gates over storefronts, the streets take on a ghost-town feel. The district's homeless, estimated at 12,000, seek refuge from the cold in the city's cluster of homeless shelters and soup kitchens at Fourth and Los Angeles Streets. With this in mind, LA's downtown core may not be where you want to take up residence, however, many of the city's finest cultural institutions are situated here. The Arata Isozaki-designed Museum of Contemporary Art (MOCA), the Music Center, the Dorothy Chandler Pavilion, and LA's newly restored Central Library, the Downtown Convention Center, the largest on the West Coast, and the newly built Staples Center sports arena are all located Downtown. And, the Disney Concert Hall is scheduled for completion in 2002. Also calling this environ home is the University of Southern California, a compact, but beautiful private college campus. The 110 Harbor Freeway, 10 Santa Monica Freeway, and 101 Hollywood Freeway all border Downtown, making entry to and exit from this area easy, albeit slow during rush hour.

Downtown is where you'll find the city's flower, jewelry, textile, garment, toy and produce districts. While primarily a wholesale district, many businesses do retail to the public. This makes for *beaucoup* savings for savvy bargain hunters unmindful of the no-frills display of wares. The ethnic hamlets Chinatown, Little Tokyo and the Mexican village-style Olvera Street are also situated in Downtown.

In 1993, Los Angeles opened the first phase of the long-awaited subway, the Metro Red Line. Starting at the beautiful, historic Union Station on North Alameda Street, residents can ride through most of Downtown in seven minutes. The Red Line now extends to Hollywood and ends at Universal City. The Blue Line light rail transports passengers from Downtown to Long Beach. While not as well received initially as transit officials would have liked, the Metro is now catching on. Ridership is up on this clean and well patrolled, though not yet comprehensive, system. To get just about anywhere in LA, hop on a bus. LA bus drivers are famous for muscling their way through traffic in their zealousness to keep to their schedules.

For those looking to set up residence in Downtown, and some do, a smattering of artists-in-residence and loft-type housing dot central LA, including the large Santa Fe Art Colony at 2401 South Santa Fe and The Brewery at 1920 North Main Street. Finding a vacancy requires good luck and timing as most Downtown residences are limited to low-rent single-occupancy hotels and apartments.

Those wanting a central locale might also check just outside the business district in the ethnically diverse neighborhoods of **Westlake** (west of Alvarado Street), **Boyle Heights** (east of the Los Angeles River), **Chinatown** (slightly north of Cesar E. Chavez Avenue), or **Little Tokyo** (east of San Pedro Street) to locate housing. Blue- and white-collar families and recent immigrants (mostly Hispanic, Chinese, and Japanese) are the majority of residents in these neighborhoods. The quality of housing is uneven, varying from aging buildings in need of improvement to the well preserved or newly built. Most, if not all, of the stores and restaurants here are bilingual and cater to the tastes of area residents.

Web Sites: www.ci.la.ca.us; www.co.la.ca.us; www.cityofla.org

Area Code: 213

Post Office: Terminal Annex, 900 North Alameda, 800-275-8777

Zip Codes: 90012-15, 90017, 90057

Libraries: Central Library, 630 West 5th Street, 213 228-7000; Little Tokyo Branch, 244 South Alameda Street, 213 612-0525; Chinatown Branch, 536 West College Street, 213-620-0925

Police District: Hollywood Division, 1358 North Wilcox Avenue, 213-485-4302

Emergency Hospitals: Good Samaritan Hospital, 1225 Wilshire Boulevard, 213-977-2121; White Memorial Medical Center, 1720 East Cesar Chavez Avenue, 213-268-5000; LA County - USC Medical Center, 1200 North State Street; 213-226-2622

Public School Education: LA Unified School District, 634 Cesar E. Chavez, Los Angeles, CA 90012, 800-933-8133, www.lausd.k12.ca.us

Community Resources: Los Angeles Conservancy provides downtown walking tours, 213-623-CITY; Exposition Park at Figueroa Street and Exposition Boulevard; University of Southern California at Figueroa Street and Jefferson Boulevard, 213-740-2311; Los Angeles Memorial Coliseum, 3911 South Figueroa Street; Dodger Stadium, 1000 Elysian Park Avenue; Staples Center, 1111 South Figueroa Street

Transportation: Call 800-COMMUTE or 800-371-LINK for specific **MTA** bus or **Metro Rail** (respectively) route and schedule information. The **DASH** is a $.25 fare mini-bus that runs exclusively in Downtown between the area's major tourist stops and office buildings, call 213-808-2273 for route and schedule information.

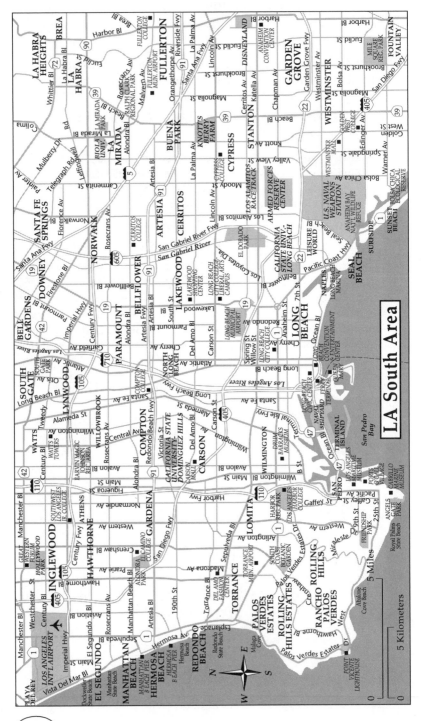

LA South Area

5 Miles

5 Kilometers

NEIGHBORHOODS — SOUTH

DOWNEY

BELLFLOWER
LAKEWOOD

Boundaries: North: Telegraph Road; **East:** San Gabriel River; **South:** Forest Road (in the east), Gardendale Street (in the west); **West:** the Rio Hondo River

A southern suburb of Los Angeles, the City of Downey is a self-contained community with its own downtown, civic theater, school district, and fire and police departments. Most of the housing is owner-occupied, two- to three-bedrooms, and built between 1950 and 1980.

Despite its tract housing origins, many homes here have since been customized. Remodeling styles vary and the presence of security bars and doors appear to be the exception rather than the rule. While there's a small percentage of apartments, the family owned home is big here, making this a pleasant, south of central LA community for first-time homebuyers.

The area's biggest industry is aerospace. The industrial complex known as the Rockwell International Space Division, near Lakewood Boulevard off the 105 Century Freeway, manufactures parts for NASA. Bordered by the 710 Long Beach Freeway to the west and the 5 Santa Monica Freeway to the east, Downey offers quick access to the southern border of Los Angeles County, explaining why more than three-quarters of its residents work outside of Downey in other parts of LA County. The busy international Port of Long Beach/Los Angeles is approximately twelve miles away, equally close is the northern border of Orange County.

The Civic Theater in downtown Downey presents Broadway shows and musicals and is home to the Downey Symphony Orchestra and the Downey Civic Light Opera. Typical of other downtowns, there are a number of restaurants, hotels and office buildings to be found here. For strolling, the intersection of Florence Avenue and Paramount Boulevard is a busy commercial hub dotted with bookstores, restaurants, gift shops, grocery stores and offices. The Stonewood Center at 251 Stonewood Street, is a large shopping mall with over 100 stores. The prominent presence of parks, playgrounds and movie theaters typifies this family centered community.

Further south, heading toward Long Beach, is the cozy, 6.4 square mile, City of **Bellflower**. In terms of housing, it is similar in composition to Downey, however, the presence of overhead power and telephone lines are noticeable here, especially down the wide thoroughfares that define Bellflower's city blocks. (Most LA cities route their power lines underground.) These imposing steel posts fade away, however, once you turn off onto the side streets. Lots of green yards and trees compliment the tidy, single-story homes in this working class community.

A story similar to Bellflower can be told of the City of **Lakewood**, located to the south. Defined by the San Gabriel River to the east and Long Beach to the south, Lakewood is slightly larger occupying nearly 10 square miles. The city sponsored Lakewood's Home Beautiful Awards, recognizing well-groomed homes, only hints at the area's civic pride. The neighborhood around Lakewood High School is especially picturesque, and a number of parks dot the primarily residential neighborhood. There's also the Lakewood Center Mall for shopping. About one-third of Lakewood households have school-aged youngsters, and incredibly, three school districts lay claim to this area. Residents are trying to form their own school district, which has yet to reach fruition. Just to the east, past the river, runs the 605 San Gabriel River Freeway for easy access into Orange County.

Web Sites: www.downeyca.com; www.bellflower.org; www.lakewoodcity.org

Area Code: 562

Zip Codes: 90241-2, 90706, 90712-3

Post Offices: Downey branches: 10345 Lakewood Boulevard; 13003 Dahlia Street, 8051 Imperial Highway, 8111 Firestone Boulevard; Bellflower branch, 9835 Flower Street; Lakewood branch, 5200 Clark Avenue; 800-275-8777

Libraries: Downey, 11121 Brookshire Avenue, 562-923-3256; Norwalk: Alondra Library, 11949 East Alondra Boulevard, 562-868-7771; Bellflower: Clifton M. Brakensiek, 9945 East Flower Street, 562-925-5543; Lakewood: Angelo M. Iacoboni Library, 4990 Clark Avenue, 562-866-1777; George Nye Jr. Library, 6600 Del Amo Boulevard, 562-421-8497

Police District: Downey is patrolled by its own police force,

Downey City Police, 10911 Brookshire Avenue, 562-861-0771. The Cities of Bellflower and Lakewood contract with the Los Angeles County Sheriff's Department for law enforcement services. Lakewood Sheriff's Station, 5130 North Clark Avenue, 562-866-9061.

Emergency Hospitals: Downey Community/Rio Hondo Hospital, 11500 Brookshire Avenue, 562-904-5000; Rio Hondo Memorial Hospital, 8300 East Telegraph Road, 562-806-1821; Bellflower Medical Center, 9542 East Artesia Boulevard, 562-925-8355; Kaiser Foundation Hospital - Bellflower, 9400 East Rosecrans Avenue, 562-461-3000; Lakewood Regional Medical Center, 3700 East South Street, 562-531-2550

Public School Education: Downey Unified School District, 11627 Brookshire Avenue, 562-904-3500; Bellflower Unified School District,16703 Clark Avenue, Bellflower, CA 90706, 562-866-9011. For Lakewood, consult the following districts: Bellflower Unified School District (see above); Long Beach Unified School District, 1515 Hughes Way, Long Beach, CA 90810, 562-997-8000; and LA Unified School District, 634 Cesar E. Chavez, Los Angeles, CA 90012, 800-933-8133, www.lausd.k12.ca.us.

Community Resources: Heritage Park, 12100 Mora Drive; Los Amigos Golf Course, 7295 Quill Drive, 562-869-0302; Dennis the Menace Park, 9125 Arrington Avenue; Furman Park, 10419 South Rives Avenue; Downey Art Museum, 10419 South Rives Avenue, 562-861-0419; Downey Civic Theatre, 8345 Firestone Boulevard, 562-861-8211; Lakewood City Information Line, 562-925-4357

Transportation: Call 800-COMMUTE for specific **MTA** bus route and schedule information. This area is also serviced by **Downey LINK**, 562-529-LINK; the Metro **Greenline** 800-320-9442; and the **Bellflower Bus**, 562-865-7433.

LA MIRADA, NORWALK

Boundaries: North: Leffingwell Road; **East:** Beach Boulevard; **South:** Alondra Boulevard; **West:** San Gabriel River

A modest southern suburb of Los Angeles, on the northern border of Orange County, is the City of **La Mirada**. This relatively new community (incorporated in 1960) occupies just 7.8 square miles and includes the large La Mirada Park and Golf Course and the private Biola University. Known for its civic beauty, landscaped streets and lush greenbelts abound, and pine, palm, and other trees can be found lining residential streets. While the city's cultural and sporting amenities have yet to fully blossom, the La Mirada Performing Arts Center and its ten parks are nice options for local entertainment.

Two recently built tract housing communities along Visions Drive, Treasures and Visions, feature three- and four-bedroom homes ranging in the low- to mid-$200,000's. The median range for existing three-bedroom, single-story homes in this area hover in the mid- to upper-$100,000's. La Mirada is one of the few California cities which levies no property tax. It has its own school district, but receives some city services (such as fire) from Los Angeles County. Typical of many new or yet to be developed communities with land to spare, residences are comfortably spaced apart. The 5 Santa Ana Freeway borders La Mirada's southern edge, making access easy to downtown LA for La Mirada's commuters.

Directly west of La Mirada is the City of **Norwalk**, a blue-collar community dating back to the nationwide housing boom of the 1940s. Correspondingly, the houses tend to be single-story, two- and three-bedroom homes, similar in composition to neighboring Downey. Area homes are neat and well-kept, but more tightly packed together compared to La Mirada. Some homes share driveways, but most everybody still gets a front or back yard. Architecturally speaking, most of these 1950s homes are unremarkable, but their affordability (average, mid- to low-$100,000's) appeals to many first-time, budget-minded homeowners. Security doors and windows are visible. Typically, the breadwinners of Norwalk commute to neighboring commercial districts such as Downey's Rockwell International Space Division for work. Norwalk civic amenities include the Cerritos Community College, located on the southwest corner of Norwalk, the Norwalk Sports Complex, and Paddison Square Mall.

Web Sites: www.cerritos.edu/lamirada, www.lmchamber.org, www.ci.norwalk.ca.us

Area Code: 562

Zip Codes: 90638, 90650

Post Offices: La Mirada, 14901 Adelfa Drive; Norwalk: 12415 Norwalk Boulevard; 14011 Clarkdale Avenue; 800-275-8777

Libraries: La Mirada Library, 13800 La Mirada Boulevard, 562-943-0277; Norwalk Library, 12350 Imperial Highway, 562-868-0775;

Alondra Library, 11949 East Alondra Boulevard, 562-868-7771

Police District: La Mirada and Norwalk contract with the Los Angeles County Sheriff's Department for law enforcement services. Norwalk-La Mirada Sheriff's station, 12335 Civic Center Drive, 562-863-8711

Emergency Hospital: Los Angeles Community Hospital of Norwalk, 13222 Bloomfield Avenue, 562-863-7011

Public School Education: Downey Unified School District, 11627 Brookshire Avenue, 562-904-3500; Norwalk-La Mirada Unified School District, 12820 Pioneer Boulevard, Norwalk, 562-868-0431, ext. 2122

Community Resources: La Mirada Park, 13701 South Adelfa Road; Biola University, 13800 Biola Avenue; La Mirada Theatre for Performing Arts, 14900 La Mirada Boulevard; Cerritos College, 11110 East Alondra Boulevard; Norwalk Sports Complex, 13000 Clarkdale Avenue

Transportation: Call 800-COMMUTE for specific **MTA** bus route and schedule information. This area is also serviced by **Downey LINK**, 562-529-LINK and the Metro **Greenline** 800-320-9442.

CITY OF LONG BEACH

Boundaries: North: Carson Street; **East:** 605 San Gabriel River Freeway; **South:** Pacific Ocean; **West:** 710 Long Beach Freeway

With 35 miles of beach, in a city of 50 square miles, it's easy to see why the founding residents named their home "Long Beach" (incorporated in 1888). From a population of 1,500 and an area of just three square miles in those early years, the city has grown to an estimated 440,000, making it the second most populous city in LA County. As the home of the busiest port on the west coast, the Port of Los Angeles/Long Beach and the Long Beach Marina (the largest city-run marina in the country with nearly 4,000 slips), many area residents are employed in the shipping industry. And, with the recent completion of the Aquarium of the Pacific, an anchor to the dry-docked luxury cruise ship of yesteryear, the Queen Mary, this city is simply blossoming.

The newly built Aquarium was part of a $650 million renovation of the Long Beach waterfront. Adjacent is downtown Long Beach, a pleasant outdoor shopping village of New England style buildings, known as

Shoreline Village, and the Long Beach Convention & Entertainment Center, which was expanded to triple its original size in the early 1990s. Along the coast, favorable sailing waters with offshore breakwaters and a natural bay hosts the Congressional Cup, Transpac and Olympic trial races. Further inland are three major golf courses and a country club. Hugging the 405 San Diego Freeway is the Long Beach Municipal Airport (see **Transportation**). The city is a popular and convenient weekend getaway for Angelenos who can enjoy a sparkling waterfront and all the amenities of a full-fledged city without the urban grit.

Considering the city's proximity to the coast, homes are surprisingly affordable (averaging $250,000 for a typical three-bedroom house, or $650 per month for a two-bedroom apartment), which may explain why there are so few vacancies. Residents are almost equally divided between renters and owners with renters slightly outnumbering owners. Over 40% of the single-family dwellings were constructed between 1940 and 1960. The quality of housing differs from other beachfront communities in that older, lower-income neighborhoods surround the water and downtown, and homes get newer and costlier as you move inland toward Cal State University Long Beach. Just down the street from the university is the newly built Los Altos Market Center (at North Bellflower Boulevard and Stearns Street), which offers local shopping options including a major grocer and bookstore. The residential streets and main thoroughfares of Long Beach are well tended and tree lined.

Getting in and out of Long Beach can be a bit of a hassle because the 710 Long Beach Freeway, which runs north-south, is narrow and often clogged with trucks taking shipments in and out of the port; running east-west is the perpetually busy 405 San Diego Freeway. In an effort to ease the commute, the nation's first public bike station was constructed at First Street and The Promenade (for more info, call 562-436-2453 or visit www.bikestation.org). Billed as a bike-transit facility, it loans brand new cruiser-type bicycles to downtown employees or residents for free. The commute to downtown LA may be an inconvenience, but often is viewed as a relatively minor trade-off by those seeking affordable housing in a bustling seaside community.

Web Site: www.ci.long-beach.ca.us

Area Code: 562

Zip Codes: 90802-46

Post Offices: Main Post Office, 2300 Redondo Avenue; 2234

North Bellflower Boulevard; 300 North Long Beach Boulevard; 101 East Market Street; 800-275-8777

Police District: Long Beach Police Department, 400 West Broadway, Long Beach, 562-570-7301

Emergency Hospitals: Long Beach Community Hospital and Medical Center, 1720 Termino Avenue, 562-498-1000; Long Beach Memorial Medical Center, 2801 Atlantic Avenue, 562-595-2000; Pacific Hospital of Long Beach, 2776 Pacific Avenue, 562-595-1911

Libraries: Long Beach Public Library, 101 Pacific Avenue, 562-570-7500, www.lbpl.org; Alamitos branch, 1836 East Third Street, 562-436-6448; Bay Shore Branch Library, 195 Bay Shore Avenue, 562-570-1039

Public School Education: Long Beach Unified School District, 1515 Hughes Way, Long Beach, 90810, 562-997-8000, www.lbusd.k12.ca.us

Community Resources: Shoreline Park, East Shoreline Drive and Pine Avenue; Bixby Park, Cherry Avenue and East Ocean Boulevard; Skylinks Golf Course, 4800 Wardlow Road, 562-429-0030; Virginia Country Club, 4602 Virginia Road, 562-424-5211

Public Transportation: Call 800-COMMUTE for specific **MTA** bus route and schedule information. The **Metro Blue Line** runs between Long Beach and downtown LA, call 213-626-4455 for Metro schedule information. **Long Beach Transit**, call 562-591-2301 for route and schedule info. **Long Beach Passport Bus Shuttle**, is a free downtown bus shuttle, 562-591-2301. For free bike loans, contact the **Long Beach Bikestation**, 562-436-BIKE.

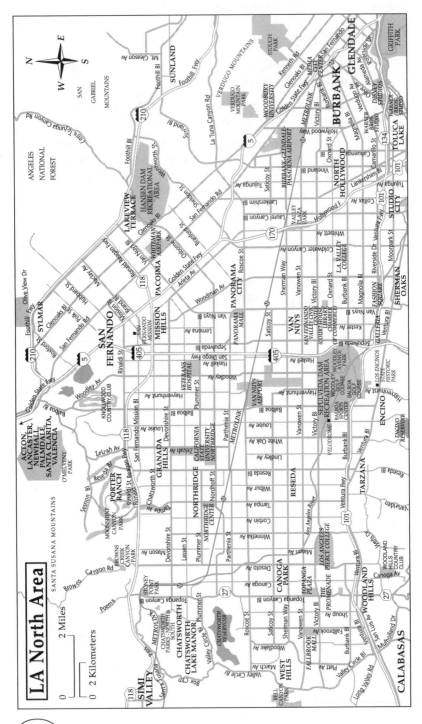

LA North Area

SANTA SUSANA MOUNTAINS

N
W E
S

2 Miles
0
2 Kilometers
0

SANTA SUSANA MOUNTAINS

SAN GABRIEL MOUNTAINS

ANGELES NATIONAL FOREST

GRIFFITH PARK

SUNLAND

GLENDALE

BURBANK

VERDUGO MOUNTAINS

VERDUGO MOUNTAIN PARK

STOUGH PARK

WOODBURY UNIVERSITY

MEDIA CENTER

DISNEY STUDIOS

WARNER BROS. STUDIO

LAKEVIEW TERRACE

HANSEN DAM RECREATIONAL AREA

BURBANK-GLENDALE-PASADENA AIRPORT

NORTH HOLLYWOOD

TOLUCA LAKE

STUDIO CITY

WHITEMAN AIRPARK

PACOIMA

SYLMAR

SAN FERNANDO

MISSION HILLS

VALLEY PLAZA PARK

PANORAMA CITY

PANORAMA MALL

VAN NUYS

L.A. VALLEY COLLEGE

FASHION SQUARE

SHERMAN OAKS

SAN FERNANDO VALLEY CIVIC CENTER (COURT HOUSE, LIBRARY, CHAMBER OF COMMERCE)

VETERANS HOSPITAL

VAN NUYS AIRPORT

SEPULVEDA DAM RECREATION AREA

WOODLEY AVENUE PARK

LOS ENCINOS STATE HISTORIC PARK

ENCINO

KNOLLWOOD COUNTRY CLUB

ACTON, LANCASTER, PALMDALE, SANTA CLARITA, VALENCIA

O'MELVENY PARK

PORTER RANCH

GRANADA HILLS

CALIFORNIA STATE UNIVERSITY NORTHRIDGE

NORTHRIDGE

NORTHRIDGE CENTER

BALBOA SPORTS CENTER

VELODROME

BALBOA GOLF COURSE

ENCINO RESERVOIR

TARZANA

MOONSHINE CANYON PARK

BROWNS CREEK CANYON PARK

STONEY POINT PARK

CHATSWORTH

RESEDA

LOS ANGELES PIERCE COLLEGE

WOODLAND HILLS COUNTRY CLUB

CHATSWORTH LAKE MANOR

CHATSWORTH RESERVOIR

CANOGA PARK

TOPANGA PLAZA

WEST HILLS

THE PROMENADE

WOODLAND HILLS

FALLBROOK MALL

CALABASAS

SIMI VALLEY

NEIGHBORHOODS — NORTH

SAN FERNANDO VALLEY

Just north of the Hollywood Hills, via either the 405 San Diego Freeway or 101 Hollywood Freeway, is a large, flat basin called the San Fernando Valley. The Valley, as it's known, is the land of the famed Valley Girl ("Like oh-my-God!").

The Valley has traditionally been a suburban neighborhood for the middle and upper-middle class. Even its earliest settlers, the Gabrielino Indians, and later the missionaries who founded the San Fernando Rey de Espana Mission in 1797, recognized the Valley's great qualities. Its fertile land was groomed into prosperous farming and ranching communities which became world-famous for oranges, lemons, walnuts and persimmons. Following World War II, housing tracts sprouted across the Valley and the area became a working model for the American dream. By the 1950s, the Valley was a bastion of white suburbia, offering Los Angelenos affordable homes complete with two-car garages and a patch of lawn to call their own.

Today, nearly four million people live in the Valley, which is considered a "neighborhood" of the City of Los Angeles. However, Valley residents started a secession measure in 1999 to make the Valley its own municipality. LA and Valley leaders are still wrangling over the details of the parting, which, if it happens, will require that the Valley be responsible for maintaining its own city services, such as fire and police departments. Visit www.valleyvote.org to keep abreast of secession issues.

Generally the Valley offers cheaper, more laid-back living options, and a close proximity to many businesses, including the entertainment studios and related businesses in the eastern communities of Burbank, Glendale and Universal City. Also, home buyers find that they can get more house for their money in the Valley, and while the temperatures are hotter (by 10 to 20 degrees) and the smog worse, the 'burbs lifestyle is what many seek. In addition, this formerly white enlcave has taken on a more racially and ethnically mixed flavor in recent years due to an influx of African-American, Asian, and Latino residents.

Ventura Boulevard runs east-west through the southern portion of the Valley, and is a thriving business and restaurant strip. All forms of housing are represented; single family homes tend to be located in the side streets that run east and west while apartments and condos line the main streets going north and south. Ventura Boulevard (running parallel to the 101 Hollywood Freeway) begins in Studio City, and heads west through Sherman Oaks, Van Nuys, the City of Encino, Woodland Hills and the City of Calabasas (the latter three are known as the West Valley). Continuing northeast from the western border of the Valley are the communities of West Hills, Reseda, and Northridge (the East Valley).

The West Valley, with its well established planned communities have been so well tended they still feel new and suburby. There are occasional pockets of redevelopment where new homes have been built over old, but they're rare. People looking for newly built homes now search westward in the neighborhoods of Ventura County, which offer the planned and gated communities of Thousand Oaks and Westlake Village. Others looking to buy the latest search northward in the City of Santa Clarita, where the communities of Valencia and Newhall occupy the northernmost border of LA County. The commute from these northern areas can be an hour plus for those who work in Los Angeles proper, but for many, the suburban lifestyle offered by these environs makes the hours spent behind the wheel worthwhile.

The eastern communities of LA County (that is, east of the 5 Golden State Freeway) defy easy categorization as they're not part of the San Fernando Valley nor are they technically part of the City of LA. These communities start with the City of Burbank, City of Glendale, and include the City of Pasadena, City of South Pasadena, and unincorporated Altadena. The freeways that service these areas are confusing. The 134 Ventura Freeway runs east west and eventually becomes the 210 Foothill Freeway in Pasadena. The northern tip of the 110 Harbor Freeway begins in Pasadena, but this wide strip of pavement isn't really a freeway and is also known as South Arroyo Parkway, which is also a leg of the Historic Route 66. Whatever its name, the major road, a busy commercial strip, transforms in South Pasadena to a bonafide freeway (the 110) which takes commuters downtown. To add more confusion, the 210 Foothill Freeway also runs north (at the junction that the 134 Ventura Freeway becomes the 210) and yet still has the same name as its twin, the other 210 Foothill Freeway, which runs east. (Just be sure you buy a *Thomas Guide!*)

But enough about freeways, let's look at the communities...

ENCINO

**WOODLAND HILLS
SHERMAN OAKS
VAN NUYS**

Boundaries: East: 405 San Diego Freeway; **South:** Santa Monica Mountains; **North:** 101 Ventura Freeway; **West:** Reseda Boulevard

Pretty Encino is located on the north side of the Santa Monica Mountains, facing the San Fernando Valley. Adjacent to the west is another well tended community, Woodland Hills. To the northeast is Van Nuys, a busy, but more middle-class community in comparison. Homey Sherman Oaks is Encino's eastern neighbor and not as modest as Van Nuys, but not as polished as Encino or Woodland Hills either. The bordering 405 San Diego and 101 Ventura freeways provide easy access for commuters.

Encino and **Woodland Hills** are similar in that they're both upper-middle-class, homogenous communities. Streets are clean and homes well maintained. A number of celebrities reside in these family-oriented neighborhoods which feature modern or Spanish-style architecture. Most of the single-family homes are 3- or 4-bedrooms with single level floor plans. In 1999 the average selling price for Encino was $430,000, in Woodland Hills it was $350,000. The reason for the difference, Woodland Hills is not as fully developed as Encino, but that gap is expected to close as growth continues. Their business districts, the bulk of which line Ventura Boulevard and Warner Center, boast the greatest number of banks and savings and loans of any Valley community. Retail districts are being developed or expanded, especially in Woodland Hills. Three large malls, Topanga Canyon Plaza, Fall Brook Mall, and The Promenade Mall are within a few blocks of each other. Residents enjoy any one of six golf courses and there are several parks in the area. The Sepulveda Dam Recreation Area offers two thousand acres of open space and is popular for hiking, picnicking, biking and paddle-boating. The Los Encinos State Historical Park offers five acres dedicated to the preservation of the area's history, including a building that is over 150 years old.

Van Nuys is host to the Van Nuys Airport, which does not take commercial flights, but serves as home base for private and corporate jets and helicopters. A huge collection of car dealerships are clustered along Van Nuys Boulevard, just north of Riverside Drive. Discount retailers located further north on the same street blare Mexican pop music and reflect the preferences of area residents. The majority of residences here are in the form of apartments, with only about 30% being single family houses. Affordable housing ($175,000 is the average selling price; rent for a one bedroom can go as low as $425) has made this community attractive to recent immigrants and young singles. Upkeep of residences varies greatly, some streets show a lot of care, while others sport security bars and could use sprucing up.

Sherman Oaks is a mix of flat and hilly land. Residential streets south of Ventura Boulevard wind into the hills, where homes feel more exclusive and are pricier than those north of the Boulevard. It is north of the Boulevard where you will find more middle class homes lining the side streets and a respectable choice of apartments along main thoroughfares. Residential architecture varies from ranch homes to boxy stuccos. Many have back and front yards that are tended by hired gardeners who mow and trim their way from one house to the next down the same street. Housing prices average $400,000 and one-bedroom rentals start at $525; vacancies are not difficult to find. When the Northridge earthquake of 1994 hit (Northridge is northwest of Sherman Oaks), scattered parts of Sherman Oaks were hard hit, especially along Hazeltine Avenue. But with the rebuilding of apartments and homes, the community looks better than ever. Typical of many neighborhoods in the Valley, the majority of area businesses line Ventura Boulevard, including a pleasant mall called the Sherman Oaks Fashion Square, chain grocery stores, banks, restaurants and a variety of other retailers serving the needs of the local community. Weekend evenings find the locals, their children, and the family dog out on the sidewalks of Ventura Boulevard just west of Van Nuys Boulevard for dinner, ice cream, and window shopping.

Web Sites: www.sfvalley.org/encino; www.valleyquest.com

Area Code: 818

Zip Codes: Encino: 91316, 91436; Woodland Hills: 91364-7; Van Nuys: 91401-35; Sherman Oaks: 91401

Post Offices: Encino branch, 5805 White Oak Avenue; Woodland Hills branch, 22121 Clarendon Street; Van Nuys Main Post Office: 15701 Sherman Way; Sherman Oaks branch, 14900 Magnolia Boulevard; 800 275-8777

Police District: Encino and Woodland Hills are patrolled by the LAPD's West Valley Division: 19020 Vanowen Street, 818-756-8542; Van Nuys and Sherman Oaks are patrolled by the LAPD's Van Nuys

Division: 6240 Sylmar Avenue, 818-756-8343.

Emergency Hospitals: Encino Tarzana Regional Medical Center - Encino Campus, 16237 Ventura Boulevard, 818-995-5000; Kaiser Foundation Hospital - Woodland Hills, 5601 De Soto Avenue, 818-719-2000; Van Nuys Hospital, 15220 Vanowen Street, 818-787-0123; Valley Presbyterian Hospital, 15107 Vanowen Street, 818-782-6600; Sherman Oaks Hospital & Health Center, 4929 Van Nuys Boulevard, 818 981-7111

Libraries: Encino-Tarzana Library, 18231 Ventura Boulevard, 818-343-1983; Woodland Hills Library, 22200 Ventura Boulevard, 818-887-0160; Platt Branch Library, 23600 Victory Boulevard, 818-340-9386; Van Nuys Library, 6250 Sylmar Avenue, 818-989-8453; Sherman Oaks Library, 14245 Moorpark Street, 818-981-7850

Public School Education: LA Unified School District, 634 Cesar E. Chavez, Los Angeles, CA 90012; 800-933-8133, www.lausd.k12.ca.us

Community Resources: Sepulveda Basin Recreation Area, 405 Freeway and Victory Boulevard, 818-784-5180; Los Encinos State Historic Park, 16756 Moorpark Street, 818-784-4849; Encino Community Center, Balboa and Ventura Boulevards, 818-995-1690; Van Nuys-Sherman Oaks Park, Huston Street near Hazeltine Avenue

Transportation: Call 800-COMMUTE for specific **MTA** bus route and schedule information.

NORTH HOLLYWOOD

TOLUCA LAKE
STUDIO CITY

Boundaries: East: Cahuenga Boulevard; **South:** Ventura Boulevard; **North:** Saticoy Street; **West:** Van Nuys Boulevard

North Hollywood, located within the Valley, is great for cheap apartments and easy access to almost any place in LA without actually being in Los Angeles proper—as long as you have a car. Serviced by the 101 Hollywood Freeway (driver beware, this schizophrenic freeway goes both north-south and east-west), the largely Hispanic North Hollywood neighborhood is a working class enclave. You'll find rents are more affordable as you go north, though proximity to industrial and commercial zones make for noisier and grittier living. If you stick close to main thorough-fares like Riverside Drive or Moorpark Street (the southern end of North Hollywood) you will find residences that combine North Hollywood's affordability with the neighboring security of the Toluca Lake (to the east) and Studio City (to the west) communities.

Available street parking runs the gamut and depends on whether the street you live on is crowded with apartments or homes. The good news is permits are not required, street parking is usually unrestricted, and most apartments provide gated parking spaces.

Vacant apartments and homes are not hard to find. Among other things, rents here depend on proximity to the more prestigious Toluca Lake and Studio City zip codes. Affordable housing and easy access to the studios make North Hollywood a good bet for transplants interested in the entertainment business.

Judging by the large selection of individual serving sized portions of food in neighborhood grocery stores, this town is home to a significant singles population. Grocery shopping abounds with every major super-market chain represented in the area. For those on the move, dry clean-ers and gas stations can be found on virtually every street corner. Used book stores (Dutton's Books at 5146 Lauren Canyon Boulevard is con-sidered the best in LA) and thrift shops dot the area, convincing many a bargain hunter they've died and gone to heaven.

A plethora of restaurants exist to satisfy every stomach and wallet size from the cellphone-armed executive with a fat expense account to the would-be-starlet. Actors, writers and producers, with their irregular work schedules, keep stores and restaurants hopping throughout the week and weekend. For a fun and tasty evening, book a reservation at Tokyo Delve, 5239 Lankershim Boulevard, a rock and roll sushi bar where the chefs not only prepare such morsels as the Godzilla Roll, they boogie with their customers in a thumping dance-club atmosphere.

The recent renovation of NoHo, North Hollywood's ambitious attempt to create a Melrose-type arts district, has yielded a collection of small actor's theaters, coffee shops, used bookstores and bargain furni-ture stores along Lankershim Boulevard. Occasional weekend crafts fairs add to the pickings. The Academy of Television Arts and Sciences also calls this area home.

A pleasant place for a stroll is City Walk at nearby Universal Studios. It's a self-contained outdoor "entertainment complex" (read: theme restaurants, stores and movie theaters) drawing tourists and locals alike, especially on weekends. Natives who like to cozy up to their VCR or DVD will appreciate the selection at Odyssey Video or Eddie Brant's Saturday Matinee, on Vineland Avenue.

The neighboring communities of **Toluca Lake** and **Studio City** are higher income neighborhoods with plush apartments, recently built condos, and single level family homes. The fact that Toluca Lake and Studio City are just minutes from the media districts of Burbank and Universal City means that a lot of entertainment industry people live in the area. Comedian Jay Leno, an avid car collector, can sometimes be seen hanging with fellow grease monkeys at the oldest remaining Big Boy Restaurant, Bob's Big Boy, 4211 Riverside Drive, which hosts antique car shows and car hop service on weekends.

Within Studio City, you'll find a mix of owners and renters. Single family residences that cluster behind Magnolia trees, south of Ventura Boulevard (the main thoroughfare), are slightly more expensive than the homes lining streets that run east-west, just north of Ventura Boulevard. Apartments are grouped to the north of Ventura along north-south running streets. Ventura Boulevard is a long, bustling street with a wide variety of restaurants and retail merchants; a great place to meander and browse or just people watch.

Web Site: www.noho.org

Area Code: 818

Zip Codes: 91601-91606

Post Offices: North Hollywood Station, 7035 Laurel Canyon Boulevard; Chandler Station, 11304 Chandler Boulevard; Toluca Lake Station, 10063 Riverside Drive; Studio City Station, 3950 Lauren Canyon Boulevard; 800-275-8777

Libraries: North Hollywood Regional Branch, 5211 Tujunga Avenue, 818-766-7185; Valley Plaza Branch, 12311 Vanowen Street, 818-765-0805; Studio City Branch, 4400 Babcock Avenue, 818-769-5212

Police District: North Hollywood Division: 11640 Burbank Boulevard, 818-623-4016

Emergency Hospitals: Hospitals serving this area are located within neighboring communities: Providence Saint Joseph Medical Center, 501 South Buena Vista Avenue, Burbank, 818-843-5111; Sherman Oaks Hospital & Health Center, 4929 Van Nuys Boulevard, Sherman Oaks, 818-981-7111

Public School Education: LA Unified School District, 634 Cesar E. Chavez, Los Angeles, CA 90012; 800-933-8133; www.lausd.k12.ca.us

Community Resources: North Hollywood Recreation Center, Chandler Boulevard and Tujunga Avenue, 818-763-7651; Studio City Recreation Center, Rye Street and Beeman Avenue, 818-769-4415

Public Transportation: Call 800-COMMUTE for specific **MTA** bus routes and schedule information.

BURBANK, GLENDALE

Boundaries: East: 5 Golden State Freeway; **South:** 134 Ventura Freeway; **North:** Verdugo Mountains; **West:** Clybourn Avenue

One of the oldest Los Angeles suburbs, the City of Burbank began life as a humble sheep pasture. Named after Dr. David Burbank, a sheep ranching dentist, it wasn't until 1928 with the development of a small airplane manufacturing site owned by Alan Loughead (who changed the spelling to Lockheed), that modern Burbank began to form. Around the same time, a motion picture studio laid roots here and was eventually acquired by Warner Brothers. Today, Burbank's big industry is entertainment, home to NBC's west coast headquarters, Disney Studios, Nickelodeon Animation Studios, and a host of other entertainment related businesses. City leaders are aggressively establishing Burbank as the "Media Capital of the World" and have even nicknamed the town Media City.

With an older town, you might expect worn architecture and fully filled out lands. By those standards, Burbank hardly reveals its true age. Most of the existing homes today were built in the 1960s and have been well cared for. While this community may not be as leafy as others, many of the stucco homes, built to maximize the land allotted to them, sport lush lawns. The residences here are well tended and often display the unique characteristics of their owners. The housing stock is nicely balanced between renters and homeowners, about 45% are single family homes and the remaining 55% are townhomes, condos and apartments. Existing homes average $250,000.

Many condos were recently built; apartments, however, range from the recently built to the well preserved. Rents vary; you'll find bargain rates for a one-bedroom in an older building but will pay one quarter to one third more to live in the same in a new building. Prospective home buyers might want to check nearby Verdugo Hills (dubbed the Burbank Hills) for newly built 3- to 8- bedroom Spanish architecture homes, complete with panoramic views.

The cost of living in Burbank is slightly lower than in most Los Angeles County communities; business taxes and licenses are lower, as are water and electricity. The Burbank-Glendale-Pasadena Airport offers travelers the choice of some major airlines (see **Transportation**), without the congestion and confusion often experienced at LAX. The airport's increasing popularity (4.7 million travelers in 1998 according to airport authorities) and plans for expansion are being met with opposition by area residents who fear additional noise pollution.

Starting in the mid 1990s, community leaders revamped the city's 22 parks (including three senior centers), built a brand new police and fire headquarters, and opened a three-story, indoor mall, the Media City Shopping Center at 201 East Magnolia Boulevard. Nearby Brand Avenue in downtown Burbank is a popular evening hangout for residents who patronize the mall's large theater complex. The huge Swedish discount furniture store, IKEA, is located here, providing put-it-together-yourself furniture at reasonable prices. Horse lovers should note that the lovely Los Angeles Equestrian Center is in Burbank. Neighborhood restaurants lean toward comfort food rather than gourmet type fare. The decades old Barrons Family Restaurant, 4130 West Burbank Boulevard, serves one of the best breakfasts in the nation, this according to *Gourmet Magazine* and huge morning crowds.

With a small town feel, clean streets and one of the most responsive police departments around, Burbank also feels contemporary and metropolitan. It is this city's charm, affordability and total lack of attitude common to other LA towns that makes Burbank a stand-out for young families and senior citizens.

Adjacent to Burbank, just east of the 5 Golden State Freeway, is the City of **Glendale**. It too has undergone a great deal of change in the past two decades, becoming an ethnically diverse population of nearly 200,000 people in its 30 square miles. Glendale, the third largest city in Los Angeles County, has a more urban feel and pace in comparison to Burbank.

Single and multi-family units were once the predominant housing type here, but today, multi-family units comprise 60% of the city's housing stock. In fact, Glendale has one of the highest percentages of multi-family dwelling units of any city in California, many of which were built in the 1980s. Most apartment buildings are clustered around downtown—a bright and cheery business district located just south of the 134 Ventura Freeway. Some of the newest two-story, stucco, red-tiled homes are poised above Chevy Chase Drive, east of Highway 2. Most existing homes were built between 1950 and 1980 and can be found north of Foothill

Boulevard. The average price for a typical home in Glendale is $300,000. Glendale's affordability makes it a popular choice for newcomers and has attracted a large Asian, Middle-Eastern, and Mediterranean population. In fact, Colorado Street, Glendale's main thoroughfare, is lined with the charming restaurants and sumptuous bakeries of many ethnic persuasions. Overall, streets are clean, business districts well tended and social amenities abundant, and include the large indoor mall, Glendale Galleria, and 32 city parks. Recently, the city's growth has slowed somewhat, and available land has been built-out, giving city leaders a chance to catch up with civic beautification, including the renovation of Colorado Street and tree plantings along its neighborhood streets.

Web Site: www.ci.burbank.ca.us; www.ci.glendale.ca.us

Area Code: 818

Zip Codes: 91501-91523, 91201-91213

Post Offices: Main Post Offices, 2140 North Hollywood Way; 313 East Broadway Street; 800 275-8777

Police District: Burbank Police Headquarters: 311 East Orange Grove, 818-238-3333; Glendale Police Department: 140 North Isabel, 818-548-3106

Emergency Hospitals: Providence Saint Joseph Medical Center, 501 South Buena Vista Avenue, Burbank, 818 843-5111; Glendale Memorial Hospital and Health Center, 1420 South Central Avenue, Glendale, 818-502-1900

Libraries: Main Burbank Library, 110 North Glenoaks Boulevard, 818-238-5600; Buena Vista Branch, 401 North Buena Vista, 818-953-9747; Northwest Branch, 3323 West Victory Boulevard, 818-953-9750; Main Glendale Library, 222 East Harvard Street, 818-548-2027; Brand Branch, 1601 West Mountain Street, 818-548-2051; Casa Verdugo Branch Library, 1151 North Brand Boulevard, 818-548-2047; Chevy Chase Branch, 3301 East Chevy Chase Drive, 818-548-2046

Public School Education: Burbank Unified School District, 330 North Buena Vista Street, Burbank, 91505, 818-558-4600; www.burbank.k12.ca.us; Glendale Unified School District, 223 North Jackson Street, Glendale, 91206-4380, 818-241-3111

Community Resources: Olive Recreation Center and George

Izzay Park, 1111 West Olive Avenue, 818-238-5385; Verdugo Recreation Center, 3201 West Verdugo Avenue, 818-238-5390; Burbank Tennis Center, 1515 North Glenoaks Boulevard, 818-843-4105; Johnny Carson Park, 400 South Bob Hope Drive; Starlight Amphitheatre, 1249 Lockheed View Drive, 818-238-5400/5300; De Bell Municipal Golf Course, 1500 East Walnut Avenue, 818-845-5052; Burbank Family YMCA, 321 East Magnolia Boulevard, 818-845-8551; Los Angeles Equestrian Center, 480 Riverside Drive, 818-840-9066; Glendale Central Park, East Colorado Street and South Louise Street

Transportation: Call 800-COMMUTE for specific **MTA** bus routes and schedule information. Downtown Glendale has a .25 cent shuttle known as the **"Beeline,"** call 818-548-3961 for route and schedule information

PASADENA

ALTADENA
SAN MARINO
SOUTH PASADENA

Boundaries: North: Montana Street (in the west), Washington Boulevard (in the east); **East:** West of Michilinda Avenue; **South:** Columbia Street (in the west), California Boulevard (in the east); **West:** Hills West of Linda Vista Mountain Way

Pasadena's claim to fame is the always-sunny New Year's Day Tournament of Roses Parade and Rose Bowl, but this city's roots, like much of the Valley, are in agriculture. Pioneers who came to this area in the late 1800s found success growing oranges and olives, and named their community Pasadena (derived from an Ojibwa word and translated into "Crown of the Valley").

By the turn of the 20th century, the town had become a winter retreat for wealthy Midwesterners such as David B. Gamble of Proctor & Gamble and chewing gum magnate William Wrigley Jr. Through the next several decades it was known as a quiet, pretty, and conservative place in which to raise a family.

Over the past few years, a revitalized "old town" has sparked new interest in the area. Colorado Boulevard is Pasadena's main artery, and the heart of Old Pasadena. The city's original business district, Old Pasadena is bounded by Pasadena Avenue, Walnut Street, Arroyo Parkway and Green Street, and the newly-renovated historic buildings offer a unique array of retailers, art galleries, movie theaters, antique shops, restaurants, and offices. On weekend nights, the sidewalks are brimming with people.

Those arriving in Pasadena via the 134 Ventura Freeway are greeted by a magnificent view of the intricate and recently restored Colorado Street Bridge (Colorado Boulevard at Arroyo Seco). Carefully preserved, turn of the century homes grace the streets, and Pasadena residents take pride in the city's small town atmosphere. At first glance, single family homes appear to make up the majority of the residential offerings, however, about half of the city's residents are renters. Most homes were built in the 1950s, with about 30% constructed before 1939. The average Pasadena home will set you back about $300,000, and a one-bedroom rental generally starts at $600 on up, depending on the age of the building and its location. The neighborhood is clean, palm tree-lined, with plenty of grassy front yards. Pah-*sad*-na, as some intentionally, but affectionately mispronounce the name is a lovely place to own a home. Twenty-three square miles in size, it has an average of nine residents per acre.

Would-be homebuyers who fall in love with Pasadena may elect to buy in the neighboring, yet to be incorporated **Altadena**, just north of Pasadena. Residents of this leafy suburb find they can still enjoy the benefits of Pasadena without the higher price tag attached (DataQuick reports that in 1999 homes averaged $260,000). Suburban to its core, Altadena has plenty of room yet for development. Some homeowners keep horses on their land and many backyards open right on to mountain trails. Paved sidewalks and apartment buildings are scarce. Newly built single family residences can be found along La Vina Lane, these 3- to 5- bedroom homes begin at $350,000.

If money is not a concern, try the **City of San Marino**, Pasadena's southern neighbor which also offers a cozy community with beautiful, rolling tree-lined streets. The posh Ritz-Carlton Huntington Hotel & Spa offers pampering to the ladies who lunch—they number more than a handful here. Picture-perfect, multiple bedroom homes average $820,000. This storybook neighborhood was featured in the Steve Martin film, "Father of the Bride." To the south of Pasadena is—surprise—the **City of South Pasadena**. It too features Craftsman and Mission revival architecture. Located between Pasadena and Los Angeles, it acts as a buffer between these two environs, and consequently some streets aren't as well tended in comparison to its northern sister. Despite its more urban feel, homes here consistently fetch prices that rival those in Pasadena.

In the commercial districts of these residential neighborhoods, boutique shops and gourmet grocery stores mingle with general retailers, providing plentiful shopping options. South Lake Avenue is where you'll find designer label boutiques. Preservation of area historic sites adds to the village-like feel of these communities. Pasadena's public library is housed in a Renaissance-style building. One of the country's oldest soda fountains, the Fair Oaks Pharmacy and Soda Fountain, 1526 Mission Street, South Pasadena, still dishes out malts and egg creams much like it did back in the 1920s.

The Jet Propulsion Laboratory, Cal Tech, Pasadena Center (the city's convention center), Pasadena Playhouse (built in 1917), lavish Huntington Gardens and Library, and the privately owned and recently renovated Norton Simon Museum, featuring Western European painting and Asian sculpture, round out the first rate cultural and educational offerings in the area.

Depending on where you work, Pasadena, serviced by the 210 Foothill and 134 Ventura Freeways, can be an easy half-hour or less commute to downtown Los Angeles or parts of the Valley—or a long haul if you need to head to the western and southern communities of Los Angeles. A car is definitely needed here, unless you plan to work in an area easily accessed by bus. The Metro has plans to run the Blue Line from downtown Los Angeles to Pasadena by the year 2002, but with so many delays troubling subway construction, nobody is holding their breath.

On the downside, Pasadena, nestled as it is in the foothills of the San Gabriel Mountains, can get hot and smoggy. Still, Pasadena and its neighboring cities remain a wonderful place to call home ... just be on the lookout for central air conditioning when house hunting here.

Web Sites: www.ci.pasadena.ca.us; www.pasadenavisitor.org; www.ci.south-pasadena.ca.us; www.aaaim.com/altadena

Area Code: 626

Zip Codes: Pasadena: 91101-91126; South Pasadena: 91030; San Marino: 91108; Altadena: 91001

Post Offices: Pasadena Main Post Office, 600 North Lincoln Avenue; South Pasadena Main Post Office, 1001 Fremont Avenue; Altadena branches: 2271 Lake Avenue and 3021 Lincoln Avenue; many more locations, call 800-275-8777.

Police District: Pasadena is served by its own municipal police force: Pasadena Police Headquarters, 207 North Garfield Avenue, 626-744-4501; ditto for South Pasadena: South Pasadena Police Headquarters, 1422 Mission Street, 626-799-1122, www.sppd.org; San Marino Police Department Headquarters, 2200 Huntington Drive, 626-300-0720.

Emergency Hospitals: Huntington Memorial Hospital, 100 Congress Street, 626-397-5000; Las Encinas Hospital, 2900 East Del Mar Boulevard, 626-795-9901; St. Luke's Medical Center, 2632 East Washington Boulevard, 626-797-1141

Libraries: Main Library, 285 East Walnut Street, 626-405-4052; County Sunnyslope Library, 346 South Rosemead Boulevard, 626-792-5733; South Pasadena Public Library, 1100 Oxley Street, 626-799-9108; San Marino Public Library, 1890 Huntington Drive, 626-282-8484; Altadena Bob Lucas Memorial Library and Literacy Center, 2659 North Lincoln, 626-798-8338

Community Resources: Norton Simon Museum, 411 West Colorado Boulevard, 626-449-6840; Huntington Library, Art Collections & Botanical Gardens, 1151 Oxford Road, 626-405-2100; Pacific Asia Museum, 46 North Los Robles Avenue; 626-449-2742; Tournament House & Wrigley Gardens, 391 South Orange Grove Boulevard, 626-449-7673; Rose Bowl, 991 Rosemont Boulevard, 626-577-3100; Brookside Park, 360 North Arroyo Boulevard; California Institute of Technology, 1201 East California Boulevard, 626-395-6811

Public School Education: Pasadena Unified School District, 351 South Hudson Avenue, Pasadena, 91109, 626-441-5700, www.pasadena.k-12.ca.us; South Pasadena Unified School District, 1020 El Centro Street, 626-441-5700, www.spusd.k-12.ca.us; San Marino Unified School District, 1665 West Drive, San Marino, 91108, 626-299-7000, www.san-marino.k-12.ca.us; Altadena is part of the La Canada Unified School District, 5039 Palm Drive, La Canada Flintridge, 91011, www.lcusd.k-12.ca.us

Public Transportation: Call 800-COMMUTE for **MTA** bus route and schedule information. **Foothill Transit** contributes regular and express bus service here, 800-743-3463. **LADOT** also operates commuter express lines here, 213-580-5444. Free Pasadena **ARTS Buses** shuttle the shopping and entertainment districts, call Transit Services at 626-744-4055 for routes and hours.

SANTA CLARITA

NEWHALL
VALENCIA
LANCASTER
PALMDALE
ACTON

Boundaries: East: Angeles National Forest; **South:** Junction of the 5 Golden State and 14 Antelope Valley Freeways; **North:** Angeles National Forest; **West:** 5 Golden State Freeway

Santa Clarita only became a city in 1987 and by 1999 was selected as one of 30 finalists in the All-American City Award competition. Sponsored by the National Civic League (www.ncl.org), the award recognized Santa Clarita for its Youth Plan for troubled kids which resulted in a significant drop in gang membership—from 1,300 to 500 by 1998. In 1999, the city was also named the fifth most kid-friendly suburban city in the nation by Zero Population Growth. The group cited the community's schools, low crime and low high school drop out rates as factors. Santa Clarita's Public Information Officer, 661-255-4314 can provide additional details.

The 42 square mile city, with a population of over 147,000 is located 26 miles north of Los Angeles, in between the 5 Golden State and the 14 Antelope Valley freeways, near the Six Flags Magic Mountain Theme Park (incidentally, the city's largest employer). The established community of Newhall and the new tract-housing community of Valencia are both within Santa Clarita.

Much of Santa Clarita's existing housing was built in the 1960s, however, during the late 1990s the city experienced another housing boom. Prices here are affordable, primarily due to Santa Clarita's far-flung location. While 26 miles may not sound far, with traffic, an hour-plus commute into central LA would not be unusual. (You could opt for the Metrolink, which takes residents to Burbank, Glendale, or downtown LA.) Despite the longer than average commute to LA, many newcomers are drawn Santa Clarita's affordable housing. And, according to FBI statistics Santa Clarita is one of the safest cities of its size in the nation.

According to the city's web site (see below), typical housing in Santa Clarita consists of recently built 4-bedroom, two story homes, averaging $297,000. A new condominium runs about $155,000. The average monthly rent is $940 with a 98% average occupancy rate on rentals. Young families make up a large segment of the population—the median age here is about 30. Santa Clarita sponsors Pride Week every April, an organized effort to keep the community clean. Call organizers at 661-255-4918 for more details. A word of warning to newcomers from cold climates, Santa Clarita is in desert country and gets quite hot during the summer.

"New" seems to be the best adjective to describe the communities of Santa Clarita. Three parks were recently constructed: 17-acre Canyon Country Park; 5-acre Begonias Lane Neighborhood Park (both in Canyon Country); and, most recently, the 8-acre Creekview Park in Newhall. The city's commitment to creating a family-friendly environment is obvious. For those who can't easily get to a park, they can ask the city to bring its "mobile park," a sort of playground on wheels, to their community (call 661-255-4910).

Revitalization efforts and civic dollars are also being invested in downtown **Newhall**. The typical chain restaurants, houseware stores, and grocery stores can be found in the myriad of recently built strip malls. School buildings here are also new. (Note that separate districts represent elementary schools and high schools here—in LA, both are usually lumped together into one district.) The California Institute of the Arts (Cal Arts), the Disney sponsored arts college where many top animators graduate, is located in Newhall, and there are plans to build a new theater complex and major recreation area and skateboard park in adjacent Canyon Country.

Over in **Valencia**, community amenities are similar to neighboring Newhall's but the buildings appear even newer. Valencia residents are especially keen on preserving the neighborhood's spacious environs. Oak trees and generous green belts are plentiful here, supported by residents who pay an annual assessment for public landscape upkeep. (Not so in other nearby communities where *au natural* tends to be the rule.) This tract-housing community is also noted for excellent traffic flow within its well planned streets.

Further north of Santa Clarita are the City of **Acton**, the City of **Lancaster** and the City of **Palmdale**. All three are located in Antelope Valley with Lancaster and Palmdale bordering Edwards Air Force Base. This is truly desert country, hot dry air, no smog and bargain-priced homes garnished with freshly planted trees. The commute to LA is even longer than what it would be from Santa Clarita; Acton is the most southern of the trio and it is nearly 50 miles from LA. According to the city's web site 40% of the two-story, two-bedroom homes in this area were built in the mid 1980s. The average home in these cities starts at $100,000. The older residences date from between 1950-1970. Rentals make up a modest 27% of the housing stock here. Three- to four-bedroom homes are sprouting up all over with commercial districts blossoming alongside. New homebuyers might be interested in the Legends Way development in Palmdale. The prices of these homes begin at $150,000. These towns make lovely selections for first-time homebuyers who enjoy desert suburban life.

Web Sites: www.ci.santa-clarita.ca.us; www.scvonline.com; www.city.lancaster.ca.us; www.city.palmdale.ca.us, http://city.acton.ca.us

Area Code: 661

Zip Codes: Santa Clarita: 91381-2, Acton: 93510, Lancaster: 93534, Palmdale: 93550

Post Offices: Santa Clarita branch, 24355 Creekside Road; Acton branch, 3632 Smith Avenue; Lancaster branches: 1008 West Avenue J2, 567 West Lancaster Boulevard; Palmdale branches: 2220 East Palmdale Boulevard, 38560 9th Street East; 800-275-8777

Libraries: Valencia Library, 23743 West Valencia Boulevard, 661-259-8942; Newhall Library, 22704 West Ninth Street, 661-259-0750; Santa Clarita Valley Bookmobile for Acton, 661-259-0750; Lancaster Library, 601 West Lancaster Boulevard, 805-948-5029; Palmdale City Library, 700 East Palmdale Boulevard, 661-267-5600

Police District: Santa Clarita is patrolled by the LA County Sheriffs, their headquarters: 4700 Ramona Boulevard, 661-255-1121.

Emergency Hospitals: In Valencia, Henry Mayo Newhall Memorial Hospital, 23845 West McBean Parkway, 661-253-8000; In Newhall, Newhall Community Hospital, 22607 6th Street, 661-259-4555; for Lancaster and Acton: Antelope Valley Hospital Medical Center, 1600 West Avenue J, 661-949-5000; LAC-High Desert Hospital, 44900 North 60th Street West, 661-948-8581; Lancaster Community Hospital, 43830 North 10th Street West, 661-948-4781; for Palmdale: Desert Palms Community Hospital, 1212 East Avenue South, 661-273-2211

Public School Education: Saugus Union School District, 24930 Avenue Stanford, Santa Clarita, 91355, www.saugus.k12.ca.us; William S. Hart Union High School District, 21515 Redview Drive, Santa Clarita, 91350-2948, www.hart.k12.ca.us; Newhall School District, 25375

Orchard Village Road, Valencia, 91355, www.newhall.k12.ca.us; Acton-Agua Dulce Unified School District, 32248 North Crown Valley Road, Acton, 93510, www.aadusd.k12.ca.us; Antelope Valley Union High School District, 44811 Sierra Highway, Lancaster, 93534, www.avdistrict.org; Lancaster School District, 44711 North Cedar Avenue, Lancaster, 93534, www.lancaster.k12.ca.us; Palmdale School District, 39139-49 10th Street East, Palmdale, 93550, www.psd.k12.ca.us

Community Resources: Santa Clarita Community Center, 24406 San Fernando Road, 661-286-4151; Newhall Park, 24923 Newhall Avenue, 661-286-4073; Valencia Meadows Park, 25671 Fedala Road, 661-286-4040; Santa Clarita Park, 27285 Seco Canyon Road, 661-286-4046; City recreation programs, 661-255-4910; Cal Arts, 24700 McBean Parkway, 661-225-1050; Acton County Park, Syracuse Avenue and Crown Valley Road, 661-269-0133

Transportation: Santa Clarita Transit/Bus route and schedule information: 661-294-1287; for **Metrolink** information, 800-371-LINK; for bus transfer information call 661-294-IBUS, or pick up a schedule on the bus.

OST MAJOR LOS ANGELES STREETS FOLLOW A STANDARD grid pattern, running east-west and north-south, but there are plenty that snake around, stop at one block, then continue down another with little rhyme or reason. We offer a general guide to LA's thoroughfares and city layout. Nearby cities may have their grids laid out differently. Ultimately, the best way to figure out where you are, or where you want to go is to pull out your trusty *Thomas Guide*. And, unless you're in a tough part of town, don't be shy about asking for directions. Every Angeleno has gotten lost at one time or another in this sprawling metropolis.

Roads that run east-west are usually boulevards (Pico Boulevard) and if they're numerical, they're streets (Third Street). Those that run north-south are avenues (but there are plenty of exceptions like Westwood Boulevard). The grid pattern extends to downtown, except the grid is tilted about 45 degrees to Hoover Street. Continue south and downtown returns to an upright grid at Martin Luther King Junior Boulevard. (The east-west street numbers continue through South Central.)

The approximate center of the grid is downtown at Main Street and First Street. All streets that run north-south below First Street increase in number as you travel south. For north-south streets above First Street, the numbers increase in number as you head north. For example, La Brea Avenue is one long north-south street. First Street, bisects La Brea Avenue into South La Brea Avenue (south of First) and North La Brea Avenue (north of First) in Hancock Park—but most Angelenos refer to a street without the "south" or "north." So an address like 1400 La Brea Avenue can be in Culver City or Hollywood. (Always ask for a cross street when getting the address of a new location.) The same goes for many of the streets that run east-west. If the east-west street runs west of Main

Street, "West" is attached to the street moniker and the numbers increase as you head further west, if the east-west street runs east of Main Street, "East" is the modifier and the street numbers increase as you head further east of Main Street.

Outside of downtown, some numbered streets make up the side streets, while main thoroughfares have names such as Wilshire Boulevard or Beverly Boulevard. Beyond that, there is little logic behind the names of city streets. Until you familiarize yourself with the city, keeping a map in the car is almost as important as your insurance card.

The lack of a formal system in street planning might be blamed on the fact that many of the communities came into being before incorporating with the City of Los Angeles. Fortunately, the city's main thoroughfares are easy to identify—they're heavy with traffic because they're used as alternatives to the freeways. Some of the main arteries include:

Santa Monica Boulevard: begins in Silverlake at Sunset Boulevard, and runs west and ends in Santa Monica, on Ocean Avenue. This is a heavily traveled street on the Westside.

Wilshire Boulevard: begins at Grand Avenue, downtown, and ends at Ocean Avenue on Santa Monica Boulevard. It is heavily traveled throughout its length.

Ventura Boulevard: this Valley based street begins in Universal City where Cahuenga Boulevard ends and runs west to Woodland Avenue in Woodland Hills.

Sepulveda Boulevard: begins at San Fernando Boulevard in Mission Hills (in the Valley) and runs south, paralleling the 405 Freeway into the 91 Artesia Freeway in Manhattan Beach. Often used by commuters looking for an alternative to the 405 Freeway, especially along the "Sepulveda Pass" the passage that joins the Valley with LA.

Laurel Canyon Boulevard: begins at Sunset Boulevard in Hollywood and runs north into the Valley to Webb Avenue. A popular (but winding) alternative to the 101 and 405 Freeways because it's centrally located, making it easy to go between the Valley and LA proper.

A S IN ALL MAJOR METROPOLITAN AREAS, YOU CAN FIND APARTMENTS, condos, single-family homes, mansions, and everything in between in Los Angeles. Your choice will depend on your needs and your financial resources.

Scan the classifieds for one-bedroom apartments, and you'll find them averaging $600 in Los Angeles. There's plenty of leeway in either direction depending on the neighborhood, area resources, and building amenities. Location can mean the difference between a cramped single with ancient appliances in Santa Monica or a cheery one-bedroom with central air and a fireplace in Van Nuys.

If you're looking to own, condominiums can be cheaper than a townhouse or detached house, but offer little in way of a front or back yard and neighbors that aren't separated by a fence. Condos and town-homes are popular choices here for would-be homeowners who feel they can get more house for the buck in comparison to a single detached home. There are also high-end condos that cost as much as mid-level homes yet feel like a mansion once you step inside.

New or old home? If you're looking for something within greater LA, you'll have better luck finding a recently built condo rather than a brand new house. Residential land in Los Angeles is fully built out and buyers have to look at the suburbs, even outside of LA County if they want a new home. Those looking to keep costs down may want to consider purchasing an existing home in need of remodeling. Because many LA residences were built decades ago, you should definitely hire an inspector to perform a thorough check of the property you are considering buying. Ask your realtor for a reference.

APARTMENT HUNTING

Finding an apartment in the Los Angeles area can be simple or difficult, depending on where you are looking and your budget. First, determine how much money you are willing to spend on your monthly rent, and how big an apartment you want. If you need a two-bedroom place but can only afford $600 per month, there is no need to look in Beverly Hills.

Once you have determined your rent budget and size needs, walk or drive through the neighborhoods in which you would like to live. Not only will this give you a feel for the areas, but often you can find "For Rent" posted at available apartments—often unlisted anywhere else.

Finally, ask around. Co-workers and friends may know of vacancies in their buildings, and landlords are often quite willing to take a referral from a trustworthy tenant.

Below are some other ways to find your new digs.

NEWSPAPER CLASSIFIED ADVERTISEMENTS

A key resource for would-be renters are the classified advertisements. The *Los Angeles Times* lists pages of rentals, with the largest selection in its Sunday edition; web-goers try: www.latimes.com/rentals. Tip: most grocery and convenience stores and newspaper stands get an early Sunday edition of the *Los Angeles Times*, including the classified ads, on Saturday. Pick up a copy Saturday morning and begin your hunt ahead of the pack. Smaller regional and weekly alternative newspapers like the *LA Weekly*, the *Santa Monica Outlook*, *Beverly Hills Courier*, *New Times*, and *The Tolucan Times* also have rental ads. For those looking at mid- to higher-end apartments, you can pick up free, monthly apartment listing directories from: Von's and Ralph's grocery stores, 7-Eleven stores, AM-PM Mini Markets, and other convenience stores, motels and hotels, real estate agents, banks, moving companies, and airports. Look for: the *Apartment Guide*, 818-893-1249, www.apartmentguide.com, *The Renter*, 818-908-1608 and the *Original Apartment Magazine*, www.aptmag.com.

RENTAL AGENTS

Using a real estate agency for apartment rentals is not the norm here, as area agents generally are used for those trying to locate townhouses, condos or houses for sale or lease. The apartment finding services that do exist in LA require a fee before you can view their listings. If convenience outweighs cost—say you are relocating from out of state with limited time, try one of the following:

- **Rent Times,** 323-653-RENT, www.rentimes.com
  For a $29 fee, you can view their on-line listings which include over 1,000 active vacancies and sublets, including houses and guest homes.

- **HomeHunters,** 323-848-3490, www.bestrents.com
  For a $69 fee, you can view their listings of 900 weekly vacancies
  and sublets, including houses and condos. The majority of their listings are located in the Westside.
- **PRM Relocation,** 800-522-6863, www.prmrelo.com
  For a $500 fee, you will receive a relocation package and a repre-
  sentative who will do all the legwork of locating an apartment for
  you based on your preferences and lifestyle.

SHARING

Sharing a two-bedroom with a roommate is often more economical than
getting a one-bedroom by yourself. The same classified ads sources men-
tioned above also have a "Rentals to Share" section. Another possibility
are roommate services that strive to match you with a compatible
roomie. Similar to rental agencies, a fee is charged to conduct a search.
Consider one of the following:

- **Roommate Matchers,** 323-653-ROOM, www.roommatematchers.com
  For a $29 membership fee, they will match you up with compatible
  roommates. You can also browse pictures of potential roomies and
  descriptions of their housing.
- **Roommate Express,** 213-250-1095, 310-330-3910, 818-842-5010,
  www.e-roommate.com
  For a $39 membership fee, they will match you to a roomie looking
  to rent or one who already has housing to share.
- **Roommate Access,** www.RoommateAccess.com
  Free matching service offered only via the internet and e-mail.

OTHER PLACES TO LOOK

Keep your eyes peeled. Many neighborhood coffee shops, grocery stores,
pet stores, and Laundromats® have bulletin boards or wall space devoted
to posting neighborhood announcements. Tucked between flyers for
yoga classes and dog walkers, you may find notices of apartment or
house rentals. More often, you'll find flyers for apartment shares. Some of
the best rental bargains are only advertised with a sign on the window or
front yard of an apartment building. The web sites of the city or neighborhood you're interested in will likely have leads as well. (See the
Neighborhoods chapter.)

CHECKING IT OUT

It's two months into your lease and suddenly, that cozy budget bachelor pad you found is feeling claustrophobic and the police choppers buzzing overhead are keeping you awake at night. To avoid this scenario we suggest you bring a checklist of your musts and must-nots. In addition, you should make a quick inspection to make sure the apartment's beauty is not just skin deep. A little time and a few questions asked now can save you a lot of time, money, and headache later on. Specifically, you may want to look for the following:

- Are the kitchen appliances clean and in working order? Do the stove's burners work? How about the oven? Is there enough counter and shelf space? Be aware, often apartments in Los Angeles do not come with refrigerators, and you may need to buy or rent your own. Some landlords offer rentals on refrigerators they have in the building.
- Do the windows open, close and lock? Do the bedroom windows open onto a noisy or potentially dangerous area? Is there an air-conditioning unit or central air?
- Are there enough closets and is there enough storage space?
- Are there enough electrical outlets for your needs? Do the outlets work?
- Are there any signs of insects?
- What about laundry facilities? Are they in the building or nearby?
- How did the building fare in the last earthquake? Superficial cracks along the walls or ceiling don't necessarily indicate a serious structural problem. The city's building inspector office (213-977-6941 or 888-LA4BUILD) can provide you with information if you are unsure.
- Outside, do you feel comfortable? Will you feel safe here at night? Is there secured parking? How many spaces? If two, are they tandem (so that one car blocks the other) or side by side? Is there an extra fee for parking? What about public transportation and shopping?
- Are you responsible for paying gas, water, and/or electricity? This policy varies from place to place and paying any combination or none at all are possible.

Ed Sacks' Savvy Renter's Kit contains a thorough renter's checklist for those interested in augmenting theirs.

If it all passes muster, be prepared to stake your claim without delay!

STAKING A CLAIM

While it is not necessary to wear your Sunday best, good grooming impresses landlords and apartment managers as much as it impresses the rest of us. Landlords are looking for responsible tenants who will pay their rent on time, and take good care of their unit. Try to look the part.

Come with checkbook in hand. Often the person who is willing to put down a deposit first will get the apartment. Have ready access to your references, both credit and personal.

LEASES, SECURITY DEPOSITS AND RENT CONTROL

In most cases, leases and security deposits fall under the jurisdiction of state law. If you have any questions regarding your lease, security deposit, or rent control, contact your rent stabilization board (see below).

The lease is a legally binding contract which outlines both your obligations to your landlord, and your landlord's obligations to you. Of course, you should read your lease carefully, and get a full written explanation for anything that does not make sense to you.

Here are some things to consider in your lease:

- Is this a month-to-month lease, one-year, or longer?
- Are pets allowed?
- Are water beds allowed?
- Are you allowed to barbecue on the property?
- Can you sublet your unit?

Under California law, in most instances the security deposit cannot exceed two months rent for an unfurnished unit or three months rent for a furnished unit. The deposit can be collected in addition to the first month's rent. In some cities, for instance in West Hollywood, landlords are required to pay interest on your security deposit. Again, check with your rent board.

In addition, your landlord cannot raise your rent during a lease period unless the lease specifically allows it—so read your lease carefully. If you have a month-to-month agreement, your landlord can increase rent after giving you 30-day's notice.

LANDLORD PROBLEMS

You should try to resolve any problems with your landlord first. However, if your efforts are fruitless there are a number of city and state housing advocates to call on.

- **California Fair Employment and Housing Department**, 800-233-3212, handles discrimination claims.
- **City of Los Angeles Tenant & Landlord Information Line**, 800-994-4444, handles landlord-tenant disputes. If you reside in another city, contact the housing department or general information line of your city for a referral.
- **Coalition for Economic Survival**, 323-656-4410, specializes in legal problems with regards to tenants' rights.
- **Fair Housing Council of San Fernando Valley**, 818-373-1185, investigates housing discrimination in the Valley.
- **Legal Aid Foundation of Los Angeles**, 213-640-3881, can refer a lawyer for handling disputes.
- **Lock-Out Hotline**, 213-252-3890, provides recorded information on eviction procedures.
- **San Fernando Valley Neighborhood Legal Services**, 800-433-6251, provides information and assistance to low-income renters regarding evictions and landlord problems.
- **US Department of Housing and Urban Development**, 800-669-9777, handles discrimination and other housing problems.

RENT STABILIZATION

In an effort to offer affordable rental housing, several cities in the Los Angeles area have enacted rent stabilization. Rent control laws and their effects vary according to city.

The most recent development in rent control, and one that is beneficial to the landlord more than the tenant, is the Costa-Hawkins Bill (also known as "vacancy decontrol") which went into effect in 1999. This bill allows landlords to raise the rents of vacated rent-controlled units to current market value. This law has resulted in a significant loss of bargain priced rentals. In 1999 close to ten percent of Santa Monica's total rental units converted to market value. It is worth noting that rental units affected by the Costa-Hawkins Bill are still covered by rent control in terms of how much rent may be raised from year to year during a tenancy. However, this type of rent control does nothing to prevent the rent of recently vacated apartments from being immediately raised to current market value. Cities with rent control have counselors who can help a renter sort it all out. Contact the following rent stabilization boards to learn how rent control works in your area.

- **Beverly Hills Rent Office,** 455 North Rexford Drive, 310-285-1031
- **Los Angeles Department of Housing,** 111 North Hope Street, 213-847-7368
- **Santa Monica Rent Control Board,** 1685 Main Street, Room 202, 310-458-8751
- **West Hollywood Dept. of Rent Stabilization,** 8611 Santa Monica Boulevard, 323-848-6450

RENTER'S/HOMEOWNER'S INSURANCE

Renter's insurance provides a relatively inexpensive policy against theft, water damage, fire, quakes and in many cases personal liability. It does not cover structural damage to the building, only personal belongings. Go for the replacement value over cash-value policy. As with all insurance, be sure you understand your policy completely and ask questions. While most larger insurance companies offer renter's insurance, call to be sure. (Check with your auto insurance agency to see if they offer renter's insurance—some agencies offer discounts for multiple policy holders.) **Allstate, Farmers, Metlife, Prudential** and **State Farm** are some of the larger insurance agencies in the area.

Ditto for homeowner's insurance. Expect this to be a necessary part of negotiating with the bank when buying a home. After the 1994 Northridge Earthquake, some companies stopped selling earthquake insurance altogether. Be sure to find an insurance company that offers earthquake coverage, and get it.

When you obtain insurance, you will have to provide a detailed inventory of your possessions. Photograph or videotape your furniture, jewelry, electronics, and anything else of value to supplement your documentation. Store this inventory separate from your home, in a safe-deposit box or with a family member or trusted friend.

BUYING

In Southern California's tight housing market, becoming a homeowner is a good financial investment. Over the long-term, the cost of renting can exceed that of owning, especially in high rent districts.

Whatever your reasons for buying, a newcomer to Los Angeles

would be well advised to rent or sublet for at least one year before buying, time to learn about the various neighborhoods. The general rule of thumb is to buy if you expect to spend at least seven years in one place, however, people here seem to buy and sell much more frequently.

The search for a condo, townhome, or house is similar to renting. You'll want to start by browsing the "Housing" section of the Sunday *Los Angeles Times*. Free real estate brokerage guides: *Homes & Land*, 800-277-7800, www.homes.com, *The New Home Buyers Guide*, 800-273-HOUSE, www.hbg.com, and *Coldwell Banker Homes*, 800-733-1380 or 800-589-9866, www.coldwellbanker.com, can be found on racks at grocery stores, pharmacies, and newspaper stands. City web sites (see **Neighborhoods**) will often offer links to real estate options.

REAL ESTATE BROKERS

Most home buyers in Los Angeles prefer to supplement their search with a real estate broker/agent to do the foot work for them. Agents will take a percentage of the sale to cover their services. This percentage is usually negotiable, but rarely runs higher than six percent.

RECOMMENDATIONS FOR FINDING A REAL ESTATE BROKER

Seek the referrals of friends, family, and co-workers. Browse the classifieds and/or Internet for a broker who handles listings that appeal to you. Investigate the vicinity you're interested in and look for smaller firms that operate only in the area—that broker will likely have intimate knowledge of the neighborhood. Call a realty agency or check out their web site for a field office in the community you're interested in.

The following **major realtors** have offices throughout Los Angeles and can direct you to a specific branch that handles the community you are interested in:

- **Coldwell Banker-Jon Douglas Company,** 800-733-1380, www.coldwellbanker.com
- **Century 21,** 800-346-9118, www.c21allproperties.com
- **Fred Sands Realtors,** 310-820-6880
- **Prudential California Realty,** 818-889-1431, www.prucalhomes.com
- **Ramsey-Shilling Associates,** 818-763-5162, www.ramseyshillingassoc.com
- **Re/Max,** 800-603-7828

Following is a sample list of brokers grouped by community. Since LA is such a sprawling city, many brokers do not limit their expertise to the neighborhood where their office is based. A West Los Angeles broker, for example, may also be able to find you a home in Century City, Los Angeles, or Santa Monica. Some brokers stationed in Santa Clarita can also assist in your search for homes in Glendale or Burbank. Always inquire directly with the broker to determine how well he or she knows the community you're interested in.

BEVERLY HILLS & THE WESTSIDE

- **Ashner Dann & Associates**, 301 North Canon Drive, Beverly Hills, 90210, 310-777-6287, www.ashnerdann.com
- **Auburn Companies**, 11630 Barrington Court, Brentwood, 90049-2929, 310-440-3700, www.auburn-companies.com
- **Beverly Hills Real Estate Co.**, 433 North Camden Drive, 4th Fl, Beverly Hills, 90210, 310-550-5550
- **Century 21 Beverlywood Realty**, 2800 South Robertson Boulevard, Los Angeles, 310-836-8321
- **Condit Real Estate**, 830 Palm Avenue, West Hollywood, 90069, 310-659-1272, www.loop.com/~condit
- **Cushman Realty Corp.**, 2121 Avenue of the Stars, Los Angeles, 310-394-4492
- **Fred Sands Realtors, West Los Angeles**, 2999 Overland Avenue, West LA, 310-838-1600
- **Prudential**, West Hollywood, 8687 Melrose Avenue, West Hollywood, 310-855-0100
- **Regal Properties**, 9301 Wilshire Boulevard, Beverly Hills, 90210, 310-275-8888 www.regalproperties.com
- **Roque & Mark Co., Inc.**, 2802 Santa Monica Boulevard, Santa Monica, 90404, 310-828-7525, www.roque-mark.com
- **Sotheby's Realty Beverly Hills Brokerage**, 9665 Wilshire Boulevard, Beverly Hills, 90212, 310-724-7000, http://beverlyhills. sothebysrealty.com
- **Westside Estate Agency**, 202 North Canon Drive, Beverly Hills, 90210, 310-247-7770, www.w-e-agency.com
- **Westside Realty,** 914 Westwood Boulevard, Westwood, 90024, www.losangelesproperty.com
- **Vogue Properties**, 8901 West Sunset Boulevard, West Hollywood, 310-659-6935

BEACH CITIES (MARINA DEL REY, MANHATTAN BEACH, ETC.)

- **Coldwell Banker, Venice/Playa del Rey**, 450 Washington Boulevard, Marina del Rey, 90292, 310-448-5961, www.sandyberens.com
- **Coldwell Banker, Venice**, 11900 Olympic Boulevard Suite 100, Los Angeles, 90064, 310-477-9966, www.ronwynn.com
- **CJ & Jay Cole at Venice Properties**, 310-832-3129, www.cjcole.com
- **Fred Sands Realtors, Malibu**, 23676 Malibu Road, Malibu, 310-456-3638
- **Fred Sands Realtors, Marina Del Rey/Venice**, 4832 Lincoln Boulevard, Marina Del Rey, 310-822-6622
- **Prudential, John Aaroe & Associates**, 881 Alma Real Drive, Suite 100, Pacific Palisades, 90272, 310-230-3700
- **Re-Max, Marina Del Rey/Venice**, 155 Washington Boulevard, Marina del Rey, 90292, 310-577-5300
- **Re-Max, Santa Monica**, 2010 Wilshire Boulevard Santa Monica, 90403, 310-264-2225

CITY OF LOS ANGELES

- **A&W Realty**, 5622 West Pico Boulevard, Los Angeles, 323-964-6888
- **Century 21, Broman Realty**, 3681 Crenshaw Boulevard, Los Angeles, 90016, 800-569-8264, www.c21broman.com
- **Coldwell Banker**, 7231 West Manchester Avenue, Los Angeles, 90045, 310-670-2080, www.bobkramer.com
- **DBL Realtors, Sunset Strip Office**, 9000 Sunset Boulevard, Los Angeles, 90069, 310-205-0305, www.dbl.com
- **DBL Realtors, Los Feliz Office**, 1929 North Hillhurst Avenue, Los Angeles, 90027, 323-665-1700, www.dbl.com
- **Dilbeck Realtors**, 2251 Colorado Boulevard, Los Angeles, 323-255-8100, www.dilbeck.com
- **Dynamic Brokers Inc.**, 2901 West Beverly Boulevard, Montebello, 90640, 888-733-9626, www.dynamicbrokers.com
- **Fred Sands Realtors, Los Feliz**, 1932 Hillhurst Avenue, Los Angeles, 323-665-1121
- **Fred Sands Realtors, Hollywood Hills**, 8272 Sunset Boulevard, Los Angeles, 323-656-8400
- **Gilleran Griffin Realtors**, 1333 Westwood Boulevard, Los Angeles, 90024, www.gilran.com, 310-478-1835

- **Homeowners Realty, Inc.**, 4401 Crenshaw Boulevard, Los Angeles, 323-290-2260
- **Hollywoodland Realty Co.**, 2700 North Beachwood Drive, Hollywood, 323-469-9343
- **Kashu Realty Co.**, 3112 West Jefferson Boulevard, Los Angeles, 90018, 323-734-1153
- **Ramsey Shilling**, 3360 Barham Boulevard, Los Angeles, 90068, 323-851-5512, www.ramseyshillingassoc.com
- **Prudential**, Los Feliz, 1714 Hillhurst Avenue, Los Angeles, 323-671-1200
- **Wright Properties**, 8115 South Western Avenue, Los Angeles, 90047, 323-752-8782
- **White Diamond Realty**, 2038 West 70th Street, Los Angeles, 888-592-7653

SAN FERNANDO VALLEY, WEST

- **Hidden Hills Properties**, 18768 1/2 Ventura Boulevard, Tarzana, 818-757-7191
- **Prudential**, West Valley, 21021 Ventura Boulevard, West Hills, 818-999-1900
- **Troop Real Estate Inc.**, 9045 Corbin Avenue, 2nd Floor, Northridge, 91326, 818-713-9422, www.troop.com
- **White House Properties**, 15720 Ventura Boulevard, Encino, 818-501-7100
- **West Hills Real Estate**, 20342 Bassett Street, Canoga Park, 818-589-7988
- **Zuleta Realty**, 9029 Reseda Boulevard #209, Northridge, 91324, 818-773-1167, www.zuletarealty.com

SAN FERNANDO VALLEY, EAST (AND SURROUNDING CITIES)

- **Century 21**, 1725 East Washington Boulevard, Pasadena, 626-797-6680
- **Fred Sands First Class Real Estate,** 1033 North Hollywood Way, Burbank, 91505, 818-848-9977, www.fsfc.com
- **H.L. Palmer Realtor**, 15123 Ventura Boulevard, Sherman Oaks, 818-783-7832
- **Jim Dickson Realtors**, 336 South Lake Avenue, Pasadena, 626-795-9571, www.jimdickson.com
- **Larson Realty**, 2300 West Magnolia Boulevard, Burbank, 91505, 818-841-0330, www.c21larson.com

- **M. Cunningham Realtor**, 4105 West Magnolia Boulevard, Burbank, 818-845-7267
- **Podley Caughey & Doan Realtors**, 300 West Colorado Boulevard, Pasdena, 91105, 626-793-9291
- **Prudential Bryant Companies**, 1108 Fair Oaks Avenue, South Pasadena, 91030, 626-441-3141, www.bryantrealty.com
- **Ramsey Shilling**, 10205 Riverside Drive, Toluca Lake, 91602, 818-763-5162, www.ramseyshillingassoc.com
- **Re-Max on The Boulevard**, 12532 Ventura Boulevard, Studio City, 818-508-7117
- **Richard Odemar & Associates**, 18334 Sherman Way, Reseda, 888-669-1040

SANTA CLARITA AND SURROUNDING COMMUNITIES

- **Ana Verde Realty**, 2025 East Palmdale Boulevard, Palmdale, 93550, 661-273-8600, www.anaverderealty.com
- **Bob Boog Realty**, 23916 Lyons Avenue, Santa Clarita, 91321, 661-259-9723, www.sellinghomes1-2-3.com
- **HSB Realty**, 24458 Lyons Avenue, Santa Clarita, 91321, 661-222-3131
- **Landmark Realtors**, 433 North Camden Drive #400 Beverly Hills, 90210, 310-275-1105, www.landmark4realestate.com
- **Prestige Properties**, 27201 Tourney Road, Ste 201A, Valencia, 91355, 661-254-4600
- **Realty Executives Newhall/Valencia**, 24106 West Lyons Avenue, Santa Clarita, 91321, 661-286-8600

Of a concern to some, many real estate brokers alternate between representing a buyer or seller at different times. For those looking for an agent that represents only buyers check the service at Buyers Broker, 888-302-0001, www.HomeBuyerAssistance.com.

A recent trend of many real estate agencies is to offer concierge services. Expect an organized network of prescreened local vendors to provide every service a home buyer could need, from locksmiths to maid service to upholstery cleaning, often offered at a discount. Inquire with your realtor to see if they offer this service.

PROPERTIES

In Los Angeles, after nearly a decade of stagnation, home prices are again rising. In 1999, the median resale price for a home in Los Angeles County was nearly $200,000. This up from $175,500 in 1998. In itself, this number doesn't tell the full story since homes vary widely in price here, but the rising percentage prices, approximately 11% (second to San Francisco's 13%), are a good indicator of where the overall LA market is going. To get the most current information on what homes are going for in various Southern California communities, check out the *LA Times* web site: www.latimes.com/dataquick.

When considering buying an older home it makes good financial sense to hire a housing inspector. He/she can point out the signs of a bad fixer-upper: a house that requires a new roof, foundation repairs, re-plumbing, rewiring, heating-cooling repairs, or other major structural work. These are costly repairs, and while necessary, they will do little to increase the home's market value. Those in the market for a fixer-upper should look for the good kind: peeling paint, worn-out carpeting, out-of-fashion lighting fixtures, little to no landscaping, worn but working kitchen cabinets, and old counter tops. These items only require cosmetic repairs that can add at least $2 in market value for each $1 spent fixing it up.

A side note: a 1998 study commissioned by the *Wall Street Journal* came to the pessimistic conclusion that the cost of keeping a typical home up to current standards over 30 years is almost four times the original purchase price of the house. (In fact, the National Association of Home Builders say the biggest repair problems—air conditioning, foundations, water heaters, roofing—tend to occur when a house is between 10 and 20 years old.) Their recommendation to avoid this money-pit scenario: do home repairs yourself or move to a new home every 10 years. Not exactly practical, but something to think about.

The longer a home has been on the market, the more likely you can negotiate a discount on the purchase price. The most anxious sellers are those who have already purchased another home, they will want to get out of paying two mortgage payments as soon as possible. When negotiating, protect yourself, make your purchase offer contingent on an appraisal for financing and approval of a professional inspector. A word of warning however, sellers and their agents dislike contingencies, and in a competitive market, a contingency-free offer is the most attractive bid to the seller. However, if you as the buyer waive the financing contingency, you risk getting a property that will not be appraised for its purchase price. Consult with your agent.

Buying a home for the first time can be a financially overwhelming experience. First time buyers can turn to home buying assistance programs via local Neighborhood Housing Services for help. To contact the **Los Angeles Neighborhood Housing Services**, call 888-895-2647; the **Pasadena Neighborhood Housing Services** can be reached at 626-794-7191; and the number for the **Inglewood Neighborhood Housing Services** is 310-674-3756. The services offered include down payment and closing-cost assistance, arranging home-rehabilitation loans, and home-maintenance classes.

Another source of assistance is the **Los Angeles Housing Department's Home Ownership Assistance Department**. This department was designed specifically to help low- to moderate-income households and first-time home buyers purchase a home. They will provide assistance with locating private lenders, such as a local bank, or lower-cost developers working in your community. Call 213-847-7434 or 213-847-7476 or visit the city's web site, www.ci.ca.us for more information.

ADDITIONAL RESOURCES

Area Bookstores are filled with how-to-guides to help home buyers work their way through the complicated dance called "buying a home." One such title, Ilyce R. Glink's *100 Questions Every First-Time Home Buyer Should Ask* is useful not only to the first-timer, but for anyone in the housing market.

The non-profit FannieMae Foundation, "a private company chartered by Congress to provide funds to local lenders for home mortgages in communities all across America," produces informative pamphlets for first-time home buyers: "Opening the Door to a Home of Your Own" and "Choosing the Mortgage That's Right for You." Call them at 800-834-3377 to request copies.

For those with Internet access, you can research mortgage rates (updated every business day) via the *Los Angeles Times* web site (www.latimes.com/home/class/realest/mortgage). They also have a mortgage calculator (www.calcbuilder.com/cgi-bin/calcs/hom17-cig/latimes) that will be useful in helping figure out what you can afford. Other online mortgage and loan web sites worth checking out are www.eloan.com and www.clnet.com.

Happy house hunting!

BEFORE YOU CAN START YOUR NEW LIFE IN LOS ANGELES, YOU and your worldly possessions have to get here. How difficult that will be, depends on how much stuff you've accumulated, how much money you're willing or able to spend on the move, and where you're coming from.

TRUCK RENTALS

The first question you need to answer: am I going to move myself or will I have someone else do it for me? If you're used to doing everything yourself, you can rent a vehicle and head for the open road. Look in the Yellow Pages under "Truck Rental" and call around and compare. Below we list four national truck rental firms and their toll-free numbers. For the best information you should call a local office. Note that most truck rental companies now offer "one-way" rentals (don't forget to ask whether they have a drop off off/return location in or near your destination) as well as packing accessories and storage facilities. Of course, these extras are not free and if you're cost conscious you may want to scavenge boxes in advance of your move and make sure you have a place to store your belongings upon arrival. Also, if you're planning on moving during the peak moving months (May-September), call well in advance of when you think you'll need the vehicle. A month at least.

Once you're on the road, keep in mind that your rental truck may be a tempting target for thieves. If you must park it overnight or for an extended period (more than a couple of hours), try to find a safe place, preferably somewhere well-lit and easily observable by you, and do your best not leave anything of particular value in the cab.

- **Budget**, 800-428-7825
- **Penske**, 800-222-0277

- **Ryder**, 800-467-9337
- **Uhaul**, 800-468-4285

Not sure if you want to drive the truck yourself? Commercial freight carriers, such as Consolidated Freightways and ABF, offer an in-between service: they deliver a 28 foot trailer to your home, you pack and load as much of it as you need, and they drive the vehicle to your destination (usually with some commercial freight filling up the empty space). Available through their web sites at www.cfmovesu.com and www.upack.com.

MOVERS

Surveys show that most people find movers through the **Yellow Pages**. If that's too random for you, probably the best way to find a mover is through a personal recommendation. Absent a friend or relative who can point you to a trusted moving company, you can try the **Internet**; just type in "movers" on a search engine and you'll be directed to dozens of more or less helpful moving related sites. For long distance or interstate moves, the American Moving and Storage Association's site, www.moving.org, is useful for identifying member movers both in California and across the county. In the past, Consumer Reports (www.consumerreports.org) has published useful information on moving. Check out a recent Consumer Reports index to find any articles or surveys they may have published to aid you in your search. Members of the AAA can call their local office and receive discounted rates and service through AAA's Consumer Relocation Service.

Disagreeable moving experiences, while common, aren't obligatory. To aid you in your search for a hassle free mover, we offer a few **general recommendations**:

- Make sure any moving company you are considering hiring is licensed by the appropriate authority. For intrastate moves, the mover should have a Household Carrier Permit granted by the California Public Utilities Commission (CPUC). You can look at the CPUC web site, www.cpuc.ca.gov, to confirm a carrier's license. If yours is an interstate move, make sure the carrier has a Department of Transportation MC ("Motor Carrier") or ICC MC number that should be displayed on all advertising and promotional material as well as on the truck. If the number is absent, ask why.
- If someone recommends a mover to you, get names (the salesper-

son or estimator, the drivers, the loaders). To paraphrase the NRA, moving companies don't move people, people do.

- Before a move takes place, federal regulations require interstate movers to furnish customers with a copy of *Your Rights and Responsibilities When You Move,* prepared by the old ICC. If they don't give you a copy, ask for one.

- Once you've narrowed it down to two or three companies, ask a mover for references, particularly from customers who did moves similar to yours. If a moving company is unable or unwilling to provide such information or tells you that they can't give out names because their customers are all in the federal Witness Protection Program . . . perhaps you should consider another company.

- Check with the Better Business Bureau (www.bbb.org) to find out if there are any complaints against a prospective mover.

- Even though movers will put numbered labels on your possessions, you should make a numbered list of every box and item that is going in the truck. Detail box contents and photograph anything of particular value. Once the truck arrives on the other end, you can check off every piece and know for sure what did (or did not) make it. In case of claims, this list can be invaluable. Even after the move, keep the list; it can be surprisingly useful.

- Be aware that during the busy season (May-September), demand can exceed supply and moving may be more difficult and more expensive than during the rest of the year. If you must relocate during the peak moving months, call and book service well in advance of when you plan on moving. A month at least. If you can reserve service way in advance, say four to six months early, you may be able to lock in a lower winter rate for your summer move.

- Whatever you do, *do not* mislead a salesperson about how much and what you are moving. And make sure you tell a prospective mover about how far they'll have to transport your stuff to and from the truck as well as any stairs, driveways, obstacles or difficult vegetation, long paths or sidewalks, etc. The clearer you are with your mover, the better he or she will be able to serve you.

- You should never have to pay for an estimate and you should request a written "not to exceed" quote. This means that you will not be charged more than the guaranteed price, and if your shipment is lighter than the salesperson estimated, you may even be charged less. A caveat: if your shipment is much heavier or much more difficult than the salesperson estimated, the driver may cry foul and require an adjustment to the quote at the point of origin. If a potential problem is not taken care of at the point of origin, the delivering driver may protest the shipment and require a "back-weigh" and an adjustment to the quote on the other end. To avoid such a hassle, see the preceding recommendation.

- Remember that price, while important, isn't everything, especially when you're entrusting all of your worldly possessions to strangers. Choose a mover you feel comfortable with.
- Think about packing. Depending on the size of your move and whether or not you are packing yourself, you may need a lot of boxes, tape and packing material. Mover boxes, while not cheap, are usually sturdy and the right size. Sometimes a mover will give a customer free used boxes. It doesn't hurt to ask. Also, don't wait to pack until the last minute. If you're doing the packing, give yourself at least a week to do the job, two or more is better.
- Above all, ask questions and if you're concerned about something, ask for an explanation in writing.
- Listen to what the movers say; they are professionals and can give you expert advice about packing and preparing. Also, be ready for the truck on both ends—don't make them wait. Not only will it irritate your movers, but it may cost you. Understand, too, that things can happen on the road that are beyond a carrier's control (weather, accidents, etc.) and your belongings may not get to you at the time or on the day promised. (See note about insurance below.)
- Treat your movers well, especially the ones loading your stuff on and off the truck. Offer to buy them lunch, and tip them if they do a good job.
- Ask about insurance, the "basic" 60 cents per pound industry standard coverage is not enough. If you have homeowner or renter's insurance, check to see if it will cover your belongings during transit. If not, consider purchasing "full replacement" or "full value" coverage from the carrier for the estimated value of your shipment. Though it's the most expensive type of coverage offered, it's probably worth it. Trucks get into accidents, they catch fire, they get stolen—if such insurance seems pricey to you, ask about a $250 or $500 deductible. This can reduce your cost substantially while still giving you much better protection in the event of a catastrophic loss. Irreplaceable items such as jewelry, photographs or key work documents should be transported by yourself.
- Be prepared to pay the full moving bill upon delivery. Cash or

bank/cashier's check may be required. Some carriers will take VISA and MasterCard but it is a good idea to get it in writing that you will be permitted to pay with a credit card since the delivering driver may not be aware of this and may demand cash. Unless you routinely keep thousands of dollars of greenbacks on you, you could have a problem getting your stuff off the truck.

STORAGE

If your new pad is too small for all of your belongings or if you need a temporary place to store your stuff while you find a new home, self-storage is the answer.

Probably the easiest way to find storage is to look in the Yellow Pages. The Los Angeles phone books are full of companies. Look under "Storage-Self Service" or "Movers & Full Service Storage." Price, convenience, security, fire sprinklers, climate control and accessibility are all considerations. Ask, too, how a storage company bills and whether a deposit is required. A new wrinkle in the storage industry is the modular storage service. In Los Angeles, for example, **Door to Door Storage**, 213-955-9085, will deliver a 5' x 8' plywood container to your door, you fill it up with the belongings you want to store, and they truck the container to their climate controlled warehouse.

Keep in mind that demand for storage surges in the prime moving months (May-September) . . . so try not to wait till the last minute to rent storage. Also, if you don't care about convenience, your cheapest storage options may be outside of Los Angeles. You just have to figure out how to get your stuff there and back.

A word of warning: unless you no longer want your stored belongings, pay your storage bill and pay it on time. Storage companies may auction the contents of delinquent customers' lockers.

A few area storage companies include:

- **E-Z Self Storage**, 800-488-8880, multiple locations: Burbank, Culver City, Marina Del Rey, Santa Monica, West LA, Van Nuys
- **Mini Storage**, Encino, 818-989-5100; Sherman Oaks, 818-989-5100; Van Nuys, 818-901-8957
- **Public Storage**, 800-44-STORE, multiple locations: Beverly Hills, Burbank, Glendale, Hollywood, North Hollywood, Northridge, Sherman Oaks, Studio City, Van Nuys, Woodland Hills

On the Internet you can try www.storagelocator.com.

CHILDREN

Studies show that moving, especially frequent moving, can be hard on children. According to an American Medical Association study, children who move often are more likely to suffer from such problems as depression, worthlessness and aggression. Often their academic performance suffers as well. Aside from not moving more than is necessary, there are a few things you can do to help your children through this stressful time:

- Talk about the move with your kids. Be honest but positive. Listen to their concerns. To the extent possible, involve them in the process.
- Make sure the child has his or her favorite possessions with them on the trip; *don't* pack "blankey" in the moving van.
- Make sure you have some social life planned on the other end. Your child may feel lonely in your new home and such activities can ease the transition.
- Keep in touch with family and loved ones as much as possible. Photos and phone calls are important ways of maintaining links to the important people you have left behind.
- If your child is of school age, take the time to involve yourself in their new school and in their academic life. Don't let them fall through the cracks.

For younger children, there are dozens of good books on the topic. Just a few include, *Alexander, Who's Not (Do You Hear Me? I Mean It!) Going to Move* by Judith Viorst; *The Moving Book: A Kid's Survival Guide* by Gabriel Davis; *Goodbye/Hello* by Barbara Hazen, *The Leaving Morning* by Angela Johnson; and the *Little Monster's Moving Day* by Mercer Mayer.

For older children, try: *Amber Brown is Not a Crayon* by Paula Danziger; the *Kid in the Red Jacket* by Barbara Park; *Hold Fast to Dreams* by Andrea Davis Pinkney; *Flip Flop Girl* by Katherine Paterson and *My Fabulous New Life* by Sheila Greenwald.

A moving kit recommended by the Parents Choice Foundation in 1998, "Goodbye-Hello: Everything You Need to Help Your Child When Your Family Moves" might be particularly useful for those with children in the 4-12 age group. In addition to a booklet for parents, the kit includes a child's wall calendar, change of address post cards, a moving journal, markers and more. Call 888-2PPACKS to order, the cost is $19.95 plus shipping.

For general guidance, read *Smart Moves: Your Guide through the Emotional Maze of Relocation* by Nadia Jensen, Audrey McCollum and Stuart Copans (Smith & Krauss).

CONSUMER COMPLAINTS

If you have a problem with your mover that you haven't been able to resolve directly, you can file a complaint with the **California Public Utilities Commission** at 800-366-4782 or 213-576-7000. If yours was an interstate move, your options are limited in terms of government help. Once upon a time, the Interstate Commerce Commission would log complaints against interstate movers. Today, you're pretty much on your own. You can try contacting the Department of Transportation's new **Federal Motor Carrier Safety Administration** in Sacramento at 916-498-5050, but their mandate does not appear to include arbitrating consumer disputes. If satisfaction eludes you, file a complaint with the Better Business Bureau, and start a letter writing campaign: to the state Attorney General, to your Congressional representative, to the newspaper, the sky's the limit. Of course, if the dispute is worth it, you can hire a lawyer and seek redress the all-American way.

TAXES

If your move is work-related, some or all of your moving expenses may be tax-deductible—so you may want to keep those receipts. Though eligibility varies, depending for example, on whether you have a job or are self-employed, generally, the cost of moving yourself, your family and your belongings is tax deductible, even if you don't itemize. IRS rules with respect to moving are complicated, however, and you should probably consult a tax expert for guidance in this area. If you're a confident soul, get a copy of IRS Form 3903 (www.irs.gov) and try figuring it out yourself!

ONLINE RESOURCES

- **www.firstbooks.com**, relocation resources and information on moving to Atlanta, Boston, Chicago, Minneapolis-St. Paul, Los Angeles, New York, Philadelphia, San Francisco and the Bay Area, Seattle, Washington, DC, as well as London, England
- **www.homefair.com**, realty listings, moving tips, and more
- **www.usps.gov**, relocation information from the United States Postal Service
- **www.moving-guide.com**, movers and moving services
- **www.springstreet.com**, apartment rentals, moving tips, movers, and more

- **www.moving.org**, members of the American Moving and Storage Association
- **www.rent.net**, apartment rentals, movers, relocation advice and more
- **www.erc.org**, the Employee Relocation Council, a professional organization, offers members specialized reports on the relocation and moving industries
- **www.moverquotes.com**, comparison shop for mover quotes

O NE OF THE FIRST THINGS YOU WILL NEED TO DO IN LOS ANGELES is settle your banking and other financial needs. Most major national and many international financial institutions have branches in Los Angeles, so shop around for what suits your needs.

BANKING

Many banks have branches all over the city, so while your bank may be near your home, there is likely to be a branch ATM near your office, or vice-versa. **Bank of America**, 800-792-0808, www.bankamerica.com, and **Wells Fargo**, 800-869-3557, www.wellsfargo.com, are the two largest banks on the West Coast, and the numerous branches each bank offers can be convenient. However, with these large institutions, the days of knowing your teller and receiving personalized service may seem a thing of the past. Then again, with the advent of direct deposit paychecks, ATMs, and computerized telephone systems for checking your balance and finding out when your checks clear, some bank customers never actually need personal service. Most banks, especially the biggies, now offer online banking capabilities making every bank transaction possible in the convenience of your own home—except withdrawing cash. More and more people are paying bills, balancing checkbooks, and transferring funds using their home computers.

Many smaller institutions such as **Santa Monica Bank**, 310-394-9611, **Union Bank of California**, 800-238-4486, **Washington Mutual**, 800-756-8000, www.washingtonmutual.com, and **California Federal Bank,** 800-CAL-FED4, are trying to compete with the giants by offering no or fewer fees, free checks, and other customer services. The primary trade-offs: fewer branches, a limited number of ATMs, and your chosen bank may end up merging with the very bank you were trying to avoid. The best advice is to look around before you settle on a financial institution. To research the best rates for savings, CDs, money markets, mortgages and other loans, go to www.bankrate.com for a wealth of information and side-by-side comparisons on thousands of financial institutions.

A word about **credit unions**. Most people who can get into one, elect to join. Credit unions offer nearly the same services as regular banks, but these nonprofit cooperatives typically offer lower fees, higher interest rates, and possibly, better service. They frequently offer discount coupons for movies, theme parks and other entertainment options for their members. The catch, not everybody can join a credit union. Membership generally is limited to a specific group or employee association, the **LA Federal Credit Union,** 818-242-8640, for example, is limited to Los Angeles city employees and their families.

Internet banking is the new wave of banking. Telebank, **www.telebank.com,** and NetBank, **www.netbank.com,** conduct all of their business via the Internet, advertising significantly higher interest rates than their so-called "brick and mortar" competitors. While this form of banking is not for those who love the service and physical presence of a traditional bank, the Internet age has arrived, and many are embracing what's sure to become banking's future.

CHECKING AND SAVINGS ACCOUNTS

Many establishments will not take your check unless it is local and imprinted with your name, address and telephone number. Needless to say, it helps to get your checking (and savings) accounts set up as soon as possible. A minimum deposit (amounts vary by bank) is required to open an account, you'll also need to bring a photo ID and your new address.

Account services, fees and interest payments vary according to your account balance, required services, and how many accounts you open with the bank.

Popular with consumers and retailers alike, **debit cards** can be used to purchase goods and services almost everywhere. And you can get cash back without incurring a fee. Similar in appearance to a credit card, a debit card automatically withdraws the cost of your goods from your checking account. Be sure to ask about this service when setting up your account.

If you have moved to Los Angeles from another US city and previously banked with a large national institution with LA offices, chances are you can simply transfer your account with greater ease than starting a new account at another bank.

CREDIT CARDS

Credit card applications are available in most stores and banks, or you can call to obtain one:

- **American Express** offers both traditional "charge cards," wherein there is no credit extended and you must pay your entire bill each month, as well as actual credit cards. To apply for an American Express Card, call 800-528-4800.
- **Diner's Club Card** costs $80, and is designed for people who travel a great deal, either for business or pleasure. They have a generous frequent flier mileage program. To apply for a Diner's Club Card, call 800-234-6377.
- **Discover Card** can be obtained by calling 800-347-2683. There is no annual fee for the Discover Card.
- **MasterCards and VISA Cards** can be obtained through banks, university alumni associations, credit unions, and other financial institutions. Many people are choosing to align their MasterCard or VISA with a charity or airline frequent traveler program, whereby every dollar charged gives either a percentage to that charity, or points toward free travel.
- **Department Stores** in Los Angeles also offer their own store credit cards, although most department stores will take local personal checks with proper identification or major credit cards. The advantages of having a store credit card include advance notice of sales and often no annual fee.

ADDITIONAL CREDIT CARD RESOURCES

A list of low rate card issuers can be found on the Internet at www.card-web.com or by calling CardTrack at 800-344-7714. The Consumer Action site, www.consumer-action.org, may prove useful as well.

If you don't like wasting hours dialing 800 numbers after a credit card loss, register your cards with an agency that will cancel them for you. The Hotline Credit Card Bureau of America, for example, 800-327-1284, charges a yearly fee to guarantee card replacement. Major banks offer a similar service to their VISA and MasterCard customers for an annual fee.

Those interested in seeing their personal credit reports can go to www.icreditreport.com. At this site you can receive a copy (for $8) of your credit report from the three main credit bureaus.

INCOME TAXES

There is no city income tax for residents of Los Angeles, Beverly Hills, Burbank, Culver City, Glendale, West Hollywood, Malibu or Santa Monica.

FEDERAL INCOME TAX

Federal income tax forms may be obtained in the lobby of the **Federal Building,** 11000 Wilshire Boulevard, Westwood, 310-235-7110, or at your local post office or library (the Beverly Hills Library frequently has the most complete selection of forms). You may also download forms and research tax questions via the IRS's web site: www.irs.gov.

STATE INCOME TAX

State income tax forms can be obtained from the state **Franchise Tax Board** office, 300 South Spring Street, downtown LA, or by calling 800-852-5711, or check their web site: www.ftb.ca.gov. The Franchise Tax Board office is open from 8 a.m. to 5 p.m., Monday-Friday. As with federal forms, your local post office or library may have state forms, as well.

ELECTRONIC INCOME TAX FILING

Both the Franchise Tax Board and IRS accept electronic filing of your taxes. This can be done with the proper software and an online service, or through an accredited agency for a much quicker return. Web sites worth looking into for those considering filing online are: www.securetax.com, www.turbotax.com, and www.onetax.com.

The IRS's e-file site, www.irs.ustreas.gov, includes such features as convenient payment options or direct deposit for those expecting a return. This site also will direct you to IRS accepted software brands.

For some qualified individuals (singles or married couples below a certain income level), the IRS accepts electronic filing over the telephone, call 800-829-5166 for more details.

ONLINE TAX ASSISTANCE

The Internet savvy may want to visit the following web sites for tax advice:

- **Controlling Your Taxes**, www.toolkit.cch.com; a comprehensive site that addresses federal, state, and local taxes that apply to you and your business, including tips for saving on taxes. The site, run by a tax software provider, is particularly geared toward small business owners.

- **e.Smart Tax Forms**, www.etaxforms.com; income tax forms can be downloaded for free in less than one minute.
- **TaxHelp Online**, www.taxhelponline.com; free general advice on ways to lower your taxes, survive an audit, solve collection problems, and other tax payer issues—answers supplied by a tax litigation consultant.
- **Tax Resources**, www.taxresources.com; a legal research site packed with links to anything you'd ever want to know about tax and the law.
- **Tax Links**, www.taxlinks.com; another good site for those researching tax information.
- **Frequently Asked Tax Questions & Answers**, www.irs.ustreas.gov; go to this section in the official IRS web site, it answers all of the commonly asked questions received by the IRS. You'd be amazed at how "normal" your questions are when looking here!

SALES TAX

In Los Angeles, a sales tax is imposed on retail sales or consumption of personal property (fast-food, snacks, etc.). The statewide sales tax is 7.25%, but LA County tacks on an additional 1% for the Metropolitan Transit Authority. Here's how it breaks down:

State General Fund:	5.5%
Public Safety Augmentation:	.5%
County:	.25%
City:	1%
MTA:	1%
Total:	**8.25%**

O KAY. YOU'VE FOUND A PLACE TO LIVE, PERHAPS BOUGHT A CAR, and established a checking account. Here are some of the folks to whom you will be writing those first checks. The following covers most of the services you will need to start up the necessities in your home: light, water, gas, telephone, online services and that modern almost-necessity, cable television. There is also automobile-related information here, as well as doctor, newspaper and local magazine subscription details, information about owning a pet in the greater LA area and finally some hints about personal safety.

Note: for those of you needing to dig in your yard—say for a garden, call **Under Ground Service Alert**, 800-227-2600, at least two days before. This non-profit organization will notify the water, phone, cable, and electric companies who will then send representatives to your place to mark their lines.

UTILITIES

Upon moving into your Los Angeles apartment or home, your landlord/building manager or real estate agent will be able to provide you with a list of numbers for setting up utilities. For those establishing these accounts from afar, you'll need to have your new address handy when dialing these numbers:

GAS

- **Southern California Gas Company (So Cal Gas)**, 800-427-2200, www.socalgas.com

(Those of you with all-electric houses can skip this section.) Many places have gas cooking ranges and some rentals have gas heat and/or gas fireplaces. Nearly everybody in greater LA County, including Santa Clarita, is covered by So Cal Gas. A service establishment fee of $25 is required to set up an account. A deposit, based on previous occupant usage (which, while unlikely, can range above $1000), is required when setting up service. The deposit will be refunded after one year of timely payments.

If you have only a gas cooking range, you can expect your monthly bill to hover around $10. If you have gas heat, your bills will be slightly higher during the winter, but remember, temperatures seldom drop below 45 degrees here, so your heating bills will not be a major part of your budget.

ELECTRICITY AND WATER

- **Los Angeles Department of Water and Power**, www.ladwp.com
  Metropolitan LA: 213-481-5411
  San Fernando Valley: 818-342-5397
  Other areas: 800-342-5397

Commonly called the DWP, this municipal service serves electricity and water to the majority of Los Angeles. A deposit is not required if you have good credit. Those with a poor credit record (and they'll be able to tell you who you are) will have to fork over a $300 deposit for a house and $205 for an apartment. For most apartment rentals, water is paid for by the landlord, the renter only has to cover electricity. As of the winter of 1999, the DWP began a three-year water fluoridation program. However, this being the land of Perrier and Evian, most Angelenos opt to buy bottled water rather than drink from the tap. Questions regarding LA's water quality (see below) should be directed to the DWP Water Quality Customer Service line, 213-367-3182.

(For an interesting fictionalized account of the history of this powerful government office, view the movie "Chinatown," with Jack Nicholson. It tells the story of how early Los Angeles officials secured water rights for the city during its boom years. The main character, "Hollis Mulwray," is a thinly-veiled reference to William Mulholland, a turn-of-the-century water engineer who is now immortalized by the 22-mile skyline Mulholland Highway on the crest of the Santa Monica Mountains.)

- **Southern California Edison,** 800-655-4555, provides electricity to areas not covered by the DWP, such as Santa Clarita, Culver City,

Santa Monica, South Pasadena, Inglewood, and portions of Marina del Rey and Manhattan Beach. Residents of the beach communities will find less need for air conditioners (and may not need to have one at all) than those further east or in the Valley.

Electricity bills vary depending on usage. The big energy-users during the summer are air conditioners, so beware.

• **Southern California Water Company**, 310-838-2143, services other parts of Los Angeles not covered by the DWP, including Culver City, El Segundo, Hawthorne, Redondo Beach, and Inglewood.

If you do not reside within the City of Los Angeles check with your municipality about utility service:

• **Burbank** has its own water and power company, **Public Service, City of Burbank**, 818-238-3700. They require a $40 deposit to set up service, which is refunded after one year of timely payments.
• **Glendale** residents should call **Public Service, City of Glendale**, 818-548-3300.
• **Long Beach** has its own water and power companies, the **Long Beach Water Department**, 562-570-2300, and the **Long Beach Gas & Electric Department**, 562-570-2000.
• **Malibu** is served by the **Las Virgenes Municipal Water Company**, 818-880-4110, and the **Los Angeles County Water District #29**, 310-456-6621.
• **Pasadena** has its own water and power company, **Pasadena Water and Power**, call 626-744-4409 for general information, or 626-744-4005 to set up service.
• **South Pasadena** has its own water company, **City of South Pasadena Water**, 626-403-7200.
• **Santa Clarita** has a number of water companies, by county: **Santa Clarita Water Company**, 661-259-2737; **Valencia Water Company**, 661-294-0828; **Newhall County Water District**, 661-259-3610; **Castiac Lake Water Agency**, 661-257-6024.
• **Santa Monica** has its own water department, the **City of Santa Monica Water Department**, 310-458-8224.

WATER QUALITY

In California, chemical additives are mixed in with gasoline to make it burn cleaner for better air quality. However, scientists have discovered that one of these additives, MTBE, can contaminate groundwater, and is not as readily removable as other contaminates. The state department of health services has temporarily established a limit for MTBE within tap water at 35 ppb while they investigate the health consequences of this new water pollutant and try to determine what amount is safe for public exposure. Two California cities have detected excessive MTBE levels in their water supply, one is the City of Santa Monica. In response, the city has shut down the contaminated source (two drinking water well fields) and is buying replacement water from another utility. Visit the California Department of Health Services web site at www.dhs.cahwnet.gov to read their report "MTBE in Drinking Water." For additional information about LA area water quality, there are a number of departments to contact: City of Santa Monica Water Department, 310-458-8224; Los Angeles County Department of Health Services, Public Health Programs, Water Pollution Department, 213-881-4140, www.phps.dhs.co.la.ca.us; LA Regional Water Quality Control Board, 213-576-6600, www.scwrb.ca.gov.

TELEPHONE

Pacific Bell, 800-310-2355, www.pacbell.com, is the primary telephone provider in all of LA except for the Westside. Assuming you have an established credit history with a telephone company, you will not be required to pay a deposit if you have not had your service temporarily or completely disconnected in the last year for non-payment, and you have paid all previous "final" bills older than 45 days. In addition, there is a one-time charge of $34.75 to activate your service. Pacific Bell offers all kinds of extra services for fees, including voice mail, call waiting, call blocking, repeat dialing, and number referral services. For a complete list of the services available, check the front white pages of the Pacific Bell phone book or call for a brochure.

For directory assistance calls, the first five of which are free each month (after that they cost 25 cents), dial 411 within your area code (outside of your area code, dial 1, the area code, and 555-1212); repair service is 611. For the correct time, dial 853 and any four digits—there is no charge.

If you find yourself doing a lot of business with companies outside your calling area it's a good idea to collect phone books from the different sections of LA (Beverly Hills & Santa Monica make up one directory, as does Greater Los Angeles, the San Fernando Valley East, the San Fernando Valley West, and Burbank & Glendale). There is a fee (from $10.75 to $47.40) if you want to order an additional white or yellow pages phone book from Pacific Bell, call 800-248-2800, or ask friends and co-workers if they have an extra one. The phone company provides one phone book for every telephone line, and since many households have multiple lines, it's likely that someone you know will have an extra phone book lying around.

The western portions of Los Angeles receive local telephone service via **GTE**, 800-483-4000, www.gte.net, (though, there's continued talk that local service in Los Angeles will be opened to competition in the near future). GTE serves Malibu, Mar Vista, Marina del Rey, Pacific Palisades, Playa del Rey, Santa Monica, Topanga, Venice and portions of Brentwood and Culver City.

To activate new service, there is a one-time charge of $46. For a complete listing of services, check the front of the GTE Everything Pages or call for a brochure.

LOCAL LONG DISTANCE

Because GTE and Pac Bell define their "local" calling areas differently from each other, it's possible for a Westside resident to have to pay for certain calls outside the 310 area code (GTE's turf) even though, distance-wise, it's only a few blocks away to 323 (Pac Bell territory). On the other hand, a different area code does not always mean an extra charge even though you're dialing from 818 to 213—in this scenario, an extra charge is dependent on the prefix you are dialing. To determine what calls are outside your local calling area and will cost extra, look in the front part of your white pages, under "Local and Nearby Calling."

TEN DIGIT DIALING

Due to the high volume of telephone usage in the LA area (i.e., new phones, faxes, modems, and cellulars), phone numbers under existing area codes are running out, causing the frequent formation of new area codes. Residents and businesses always oppose the introduction of a new code because it means a potentially costly update of personalized stationery, business cards, address books, notices, etc. In response to this problem, the California Public Utilities Commission (CPUC) introduced an "overlay" area code in early 1999. In an overlay area, you have to dial 10 digits, that is, dial a 1, the area code, then the phone number, even if you are dialing within your own area code. The plan: instead of switching all residents to a new area code, a new area code would be given only to residents setting up new phone lines. The Westside was the first location where an overlay was attempted. Here current residents with established phone lines were able to keep their 310 area code, but newcomers were to be given the new 424 area code. The Valley is the next candidate for the overlay. However, given the negative response to mandatory ten-digit dialing created by an overlay, in December of 1999 the California Public Utilities Commission decided to indefinitely suspended existing and planned use of the overlay area codes in all of California, including Los Angeles. Instead, the CPUC implemented "number conservation" to make existing area codes last longer, thus deferring the eventuality of adding new area codes. This means that newcomers settling into the Westside or the Valley may have escaped the overlay, but should be prepared for a possible area code change in the future. For now standard dialing rules apply—when calling outside your area code, dial a 1, the area code, then the phone number; when calling within your area code, just dial the number. To keep abreast of developments on this issue, contact your local phone carrier for details or visit the CPUC web site at www.cpuc.ca.gov.

LONG DISTANCE TELEPHONE CARRIERS

At the time you install your telephone service, you will be asked to name a long-distance carrier. Most long-distance carriers now bill through your local carrier, so you will receive only one telephone bill. The largest carriers are **AT&T,** 800-222-0300, **MCI/WorldCom,** 800-888-8000, and **US Sprint,** 800-877-7746. Other up and comers: **GTE Long Distance,** 800-343-2092, **Cable & Wireless,** 888-454-4264. Currently some of the lowest per/minute rates are offered by MCI and AT&T via the Internet. In any case, if you think you could be getting a better deal elsewhere but really don't want to switch companies, call your long-distance provider and ask if they'll match a competitor's rates.

CELLULAR PHONES AND PAGERS

For some Angelenos, especially actors waiting for a call back, a cellular phone or pager is an absolute must. The cellular phone industry is so big here that the manufacturers and service providers frequently have their own storefronts (see phone numbers below to call for locations). In addition, many electronics stores sell a variety of cellular phones too. When you buy a cellular phone, you will need to set up service, typically a minimum one-year contract. Depending on the service contract you select, the cost of your cell phone may be refunded to you, making the cell phone itself free.

The largest cellular service operators are **Pacific Bell Pure Digital PCS,** 800-574-7000, **AirTouch Cellular,** 800-247-8682, **AT&T Wireless Voice Services,** 800-888-7600, and **Sprint PCS,** 800-724-2613.

Other cellular phone service options include the prepaid purchase of a block of airtime for your cell phone. No 12 month contract is required, but a monthly access fee is payable if you do not use your phone every month—and the prepaid airtime does not roll over. While a big hit in Europe, prepaid service has yet to catch on in LA.

If the monthly charges for a cellular phone are too rich for your blood (and airtime is where it all adds up), a pager is a more cost-efficient, though less glamorous, option. Like cellular phones, you can find whole stores devoted to selling pagers (**J&J Beepers,** 818-761-2000, gained popularity in LA with the owner's over-the-top "I'm JJ and I'M THE KING OF BEEP-ERS!" radio ad campaign). And similar to a cell phone, a pager can end up costing you next to nothing if you sign onto the right contract. There are a buffet of paging services in the phone book, the big names: **AirTouch Paging,** 800-6-AIRTOUCH, **PageNet,** 800-762-7243, **SkyTel,** 818-760-7838, and **MobileComm,** 800-866-2770. A typical contract for your basic numeric beeper runs a minimum of 6 months at $8.95 per month and you are allotted 400 pages each month, local coverage. If monthly bills don't thrill you, there's yet another option. **Source One** at 800-664-3438 offers 35 cent paging that's billed to the person beeping you. Their "forever page" service is good for the life of the company and works only in conjunction with pagers you purchase from the company.

ONLINE SERVICES

Many in LA are cruising the virtual highway (when not sitting on an LA freeway). If you already are with a national ISP (Internet Service Provider), they'll have service here in Los Angeles. The popular ones here are **American Online,** 800-827-6364, **CompuServe,** 800-848-8199, **Earthlink,** 800-511-2041, and **Pac Bell,** 800-708-INET. Pick up free Internet access software at any retailer that sells computers.

The cheapest Internet service is one that is entirely advertiser sup-ported. The online service they offer is free of charge, in exchange, you must be willing to provide some demographic information about yourself upon signing up (this is for directed advertising) and give up a small por-tion of your computer screen space for ad banners while online. Some experts believe this is the direction in which ISPs are headed. **Net Zero,** www.netzero.com, 805-418-2000 is one such advertiser-supported ISP.

CONSUMER PROTECTION – UTILITY COMPLAINTS

There are a number of agencies available to report problems with your utilities. **The State of California Public Utilities Commission** at 320 West 4th Street, 213-676-7000, is the place to go with inquiries and complaints about electric, gas, water, and telephone services. The **Consumer Affairs Department of California**, 800-952-5210, is another source for help.

With the proliferation of long distance telephone service providers have come the inevitable scamsters. If you look at your phone bill and think you've been "slammed" (your long distance provider was changed without your approval), you should call 700-555-4141 to verify your long distance company. If you have been slammed, notify your original provider, you have the right to be returned to your original service provider at no charge. If you think you have been "crammed" (calls you didn't make were added to your bill), your local service provider can help you. In addition, you can report the slam or cram to the **Federal Communications Commission**, 888-225-5322 and get assistance.

GARBAGE AND RECYCLING

Apartment dwellers don't have to worry about arranging garbage collection because that's the building owner/manager's responsibility. Homeowners need to make arrangements for refuse collection by contacting the **Sanitation District of Los Angeles County** at 323-685-5217. In Santa Clarita, contact the **Waste Management division** at 661-286-4098.

Recycling is a way of life in Los Angeles. Some neighborhoods have curbside pickup right alongside their regular refuse collection, others have drop-off points. For recycling, contact the **LA County Department of Public Works, Recycling and Household Hazardous Waste Program** at 800-552-5218 to locate the recycling center nearest you.

DRIVER'S LICENSES, AUTOMOBILE REGISTRATION AND STATE IDS

California residents who drive motor vehicles on public highways must have a valid California driver's license. When you make your home in the state, you must apply for a California driver's license within 10 days. If you don't drive, you still need to get a California ID at the Department of Motor Vehicles (DMV), see below under **Automobile Registration** for addresses.

New residents who come from out of state need to register vehicles in California within 20 days. Take your most recently issued registration, smog certificate and purchase information to your nearest DMV office. (A smog certificate is required by the state, the certificate itself is $8.25, but a smog test must be performed to get the certificate and the cost varies from shop to shop. See your Yellow Pages under "Automobile Repairing & Service" for ones that conduct smog checks or look for repair garages in your neighborhood that hang a sign with a red check mark, indicating smog check service.)

Unfortunately, DMVs are notorious for their long lines. In some instances, you can make an appointment, so do try. (Or, if you have AAA membership, you can walk into your AAA office to renew your registration.) Following are the DMV offices in the Los Angeles area:

- **Culver City**, 11400 Washington Boulevard, 310-271-4585
- **Glendale**, 1335 West Glenoaks Boulevard, 818-242-3245
- **Hollywood**, 803 North Cole Avenue, 213-736-3101
- **Inglewood**, 621 North La Brea Avenue, 310-412-6186
- **North Hollywood**, 14920 Vanowen, 818-766-0004
- **Northridge**, 14920 Vanowen, 818-701-6982
- **Santa Monica**, 2235 Colorado Avenue, 310-453-5513
- **Van Nuys**, 14920 Vanowen, 818-901-5500

AUTOMOBILE INSURANCE

In the state of California it is illegal to drive an uninsured automobile. Now for the bad news: Los Angeles has some of the highest automobile insurance rates in the state. In fact, according to a 1998 survey conducted by a cost of living analysis service (Runzheimer International, 800-558-1702, www.runzheimer.com), LA ranked as *the* most expensive metropolitan area in the US in which to own and operate a car, with LA's insurance rates being the largest contributing factor.

For most auto-related information, including insurance, emergency road service, DMV registration renewal, and travel services (including great free maps), you may find it worth the $43 annual membership fee (plus a one-time $20 initiation fee) to join the **Automobile Club of Southern California**, the regional branch of **AAA**, 800-222-8794, www.aaa-calif.com; their offices are located at:

- **Burbank**, 1111 West Alameda Street, 818-843-2833
- **Culver City**, 4512 Sepulveda Boulevard, 310-390-9866

- **Glendale**, 1233 East Broadway Street, 818-240-2200
- **Hollywood**, 5550 Wilshire Boulevard, Suite 101, 323-525-0018
- **Inglewood**, 1234 Centinela Avenue, 310-673-5170
- **Long Beach**, 4800 Airport Plaza Drive, 562-496-4130
- **Los Angeles**, 4825 Venice Boulevard, 323-634-8680
- **Los Angeles**, 2601 South Figueroa Street, 213-741-3686
- **Los Angeles**, 9621 South Vermont Avenue, 323-754-2831
- **Los Angeles**, 1900 South Sepulveda Boulevard, 310-914-8500
- **Manhattan Beach**, 700 South Aviation Boulevard, 310-376-0521
- **Northridge**, 9440 Reseda Boulevard, 818-993-1616
- **Pasadena**, 801 East Union Street, 626-795-0601
- **Santa Clarita**, 23770 Valencia Boulevard, 661-259-6222
- **Van Nuys**, 6725 Kester Avenue, 818-997-6230
- **Woodland Hills**, 22708 Victory Boulevard, 818-883-2660

PURCHASING AN AUTOMOBILE

The experience of purchasing a car is both exciting and a hassle, and always a big expense. It pays to conduct research beforehand to determine the worth of the car you're thinking of purchasing. For used cars, check out the Kelly Blue Book site at www.bluebook.com. To research dealer invoice prices for new cars, check www.autovantage.com. AAA offers a walk-in vehicle pricing report service to members and non-members for a nominal fee. Also, *Consumer Reports* offers a low-cost auto pricing information service, available via their web site: www.consumerreports.org.

Many local automobile dealers publish advertised specials of new and used vehicles in the automotive classifieds of the *Los Angeles Times* and run Internet specials on their web pages. Used cars also can be purchased through the classified advertisements in local newspapers. Or, visit your local newsstand for a free copy of the *Auto Trader*, 800-395-SELL, or *Recycler Auto Buys*, 323-660-5116 or 818-988-3647. Beware that while the prices in ads placed by private individuals may look cheaper than through dealers, warranties are probably not part of the package. It's a good idea to pay for an auto mechanic's evaluation of any used vehicle you are considering buying.

PARKING

Parking regulations vary from neighborhood to neighborhood. Some areas require residents to display a parking permit to park on the street in front of their apartment building, others, particularly ones that are close to shopping and business districts, allow only two-hour parking, unless you have a residential parking permit. Parts of Beverly Hills and Burbank allow no overnight parking on the street. Certain parts of the Westside, particularly Santa Monica and Westwood, have some of the quickest ticket writing meter maids in the county.

Most residential streets get cleaned by sweepers once a week and there is usually a two-hour block of time when cars may not park; look for signs posting the day and hours. If you forget about your car on street sweeping day, you're likely to find a ticket on it afterwards. Be especially aware of restricted parking on high-traffic streets, effective during certain parts of the day, usually at rush hour. Tow truck operators are known to lie in wait for the minute they can begin towing offending cars.

Do not be lax about paying parking tickets. After five unpaid tickets, a meter maid will "boot" your car. This immobilizes the vehicle and if your booted car is parked in restricted parking, your car will be ticketed for continued parking violations where it sits. A large sticker on your vehicle will give you the parking violation division's phone number, the place you'll need to contact to pay off all unpaid tickets plus an additional $40 for the boot removal.

The best advice is to read carefully the signs in your neighborhood. If permits are required for on-street parking, contact the permit department in your local city hall. The following are direct numbers for obtaining residential parking permits where they are required:

- **Beverly Hills**, 310-285-2551
- **Los Angeles**, 213-485-9543
- **Santa Monica**, 310-458-8291
- **West Hollywood**, 323-848-6392

TOWED AUTOMOBILES

When an automobile is impounded, the lot will release the car only after collecting storage and tow fees. Since this is the lot's primary means of income, LA tow truck operators are quite energetic in their pursuit of illegally parked vehicles.

If you find yourself chasing after a tow truck that's taking your car off into the sunset, don't panic. You'll need to call the traffic division of the police department for the area where your car was originally parked (see neighborhood profiles for the phone number). They will then direct you to the impound lot where your car is being held. An impounded car will only be released to the car's registered owner or to the person bearing a notarized letter of authorization from the car's registered owner. The unfortunate owner looking to claim his/her car should expect to pay approximately $120 in tow fees and $15 to $70 per day for storage fees. Many impound lots are in unsavory parts of town, best to bring a friend along. The process it not a fun one.

STOLEN AUTOMOBILES

If your car has been stolen, contact the police department as soon as possible. The police will need your driver's license, the car's year, make, model and color as well as the vehicle identification number. Once you file a report, the police department will notify you as soon as your car has been located. If you have engraved a unique identification number on your car radio, car phone and other accessories, the police can better identify those items should they be recovered.

ANTI THEFT

Newcomers to Los Angeles are often struck by the frequent din of car alarms. Unfortunately, these annoying devices are felt to be a necessity by many residents, since LA is a global hot spot for car theft. The reasons are many. For starters, Los Angelenos' cars are known to be a little nicer and more well-kept than those in other parts of the country, and there are simply more cars per capita here than in other regions. Also, proximity to an international border and a major port means that stolen vehicles can be disposed of more quickly than in other regions.

For these reasons, the Automobile Club of Southern California recommends anti-theft devices. The general feeling is that although few mechanisms will stop a professional car thief determined to take your car, devices do thwart amateurs. If you decide to buy an anti-theft device, be sure to tell your automobile insurer, as they often offer discounts for car owners who have them on their vehicles.

Steering wheel locks, like the Club, are one of the cheapest ways to go. While a pro can break through them with ease (in about 15 seconds), they may be a deterrent to the thief looking for an easy target. Some locks go around the steering column only, while others hook around the gas pedal to the steering wheel. Audible **car alarms** can scare amateurs, and the blinking light inside your car that accompanies many of these systems may be enough to make a thief choose someone else's car to steal. However, sometimes these alarms are set too sensitively and can off easily. The California Vehicle Code allows police to tow and impound an unattended vehicle after its siren has blared for 45 minutes. These systems range in cost from $100 to $500, and are sold at car dealers, or auto parts and electronics shops. **Kill switches** can be installed to shut down your car's starter, fuel pump, or ignition, unless the switch is first disengaged by the motorist. Auto parts stores sell the devices, and a mechanic will have to install it for you. Those truly serious about anti-theft devices should consider having a tracking transmitter installed, offered by **Lojack** and **Teletrac**. Lojack systems are tracked by police cars with homing devices, while Teletrac does the tracking itself and then tells police where to look for your vehicle. Both systems have excellent recovery rates (about 90%) and cost about $500-$600 for installation. Finally, here's a free option that can be effective. More than 100 Southern California cities offer a system called **Combat Auto Theft** (CAT) through local police departments. A CAT decal on your car authorizes police to stop your vehicle for no other reason than seeing the decal if the car is on the streets between the hours of 1 and 5 a.m. So far, the program has been a successful theft deterrent.

VOTER REGISTRATION

Before you can vote, or sign a petition for that matter, you must be registered to vote. For those wanting to take part in an upcoming election, registration must occur 29 days prior to election day. Voter registration forms can be obtained at post offices and through **The Los Angeles County Registrar of Voters**, 562-466-1323. As an election approaches, you will see volunteers from Democratic and Republican parties registering voters at public places like shopping malls and grocery stores.

After the Registrar processes your registration, you will be mailed a voting guide which lists the candidates and propositions on the ballot. Every guide also contains an application to request an absentee ballot by mail. A request for an absentee ballot must be filed with the Registrar at least seven days prior to the election.

If you elect to vote in person, look in your voting guide for the address of the polling location nearest your mailing address. Or call the Registrar for alternate locations. The county is in constant need of volunteer precinct officers (bi-lingual, especially) and locations for polling. If you want to help or volunteer your place of residence or business for polling, call 562-466-1373.

The **State of California Voter's Assistance Hot Line**, 800-345-8683, is a good resource for a variety of voting issues, such as reporting voter fraud, requesting absentee ballots, learning the names of your elected representatives, and finding your polling locations. The **LA County Democratic Party** is at 323-654-4626, www.lacdp.org. The **South Bay Republican Headquarters** can be reached at 310-316-7937, www.cagop.org. For the local **League of Women's Voters**, call 818-247-2407, www.cwire.com/lwv or www.lwv.org. The **American Independent Party**, headquartered in San Bernardino, can be reached at 1-800-2-VETO-IRS, www.aipca.org. **Project Vote Smart**, 888-VOTE-SMART, www.vote-smart.org, provides information on state and national candidates and voting issues. Other online sites offering pertinent details on upcoming election issues include: www.politics1.com, www.womenvote.org and the state secretary's voting web site, www.ss.ca.gov/elections.htm.

PASSPORTS

You can apply for a passport at the Federal Building, 11000 Wilshire Boulevard, Room 13100, Westwood. For passport information, call 310-575-7070. Office hours are from 9 a.m. to 4 p.m. Since Los Angeles is a port of immigration, lines for the passport room typically start forming hours beforehand. Many passport renewals can be handled by mail or at one of the city's main post offices—call ahead to find out. You can also visit the **California's Passport Services'** web site at http://travel.state.gov to receive a passport application and information. You should allow three weeks between the time you turn in your application and the time you receive your passport. If you're in a hurry you can apply for expedited service (add $35), you should receive your passport in 7 to 10 business days. If you need it even sooner, **Travisa,** at 800-222-2589, www.travisa.com, is a private service that promises to process an emergency passport application with a one- to two-day turnaround.

LIBRARIES

You can apply for a library card at any local library (check **Neighborhoods** for the one nearest you). LA's Central Library is located downtown, 630 West Fifth Street, 213-228-7000, www.lapl.org, and is the mother of all libraries for Los Angeles County. Its hours are 10 a.m.

to 8 p.m., Monday-Saturday, and 1 p.m. to 5 p.m. on Sunday. To renew a checked out book by phone, call 888-577-5275.

Aside from the local city and county libraries, non-students can access libraries at many colleges and universities in the Los Angeles area. If you want to be able to check out books, but are not a student, you may have to pay a fee. For more information, call the following public schools:

- **California State University Los Angeles,** 323-343-3000
- **California State University Northridge,** 818-885-1200
- **Los Angeles City College,** 323-953-4000
- **Santa Monica College,** 310-450-5150
- **University of California Los Angeles,** 310-825-4321
- **West Los Angeles College,** 310-287-4200

There are numerous specialty libraries in LA, some of the ones open to the public:

- **Academy of Motion Pictures Arts & Sciences Library,** 310-247-3020
- **Frances-Henry Library of Hebrew Union College,** 213-749-3424
- **LA County Law Library,** 310-288-1269
- **Norris Medical Library,** 323-442-1111
- **University of Southern California,** 213-740-2311, the campus houses several specialized subject libraries including: architecture, education, philosophy, music, science, social work, and East Asian collections.

TELEVISION STATIONS

Heaven forbid you should miss an episode of your favorite TV show! The large local stations are KTLA - 5 and KCAL - 9. Here is where you can find the major television network affiliates in Los Angeles:

- **ABC** - 7
- **CBS** - 2
- **FOX** - 11
- **KCOP** - 13
- **NBC** - 4
- **PBS** - 28

CABLE COMPANIES

Aside from offering nearly 100 stations, cable also provides better reception in some areas. Since there are several cable companies in Los Angeles, the City of Los Angeles has an **Information Technology Agency**, 213-485-2751, that will help direct you to your cable company. The monthly fee for basic cable ranges from $30 to $45.

- **Buena Vision,** 323-269-0656: East Los Angeles
- **Charter Communications,** 626-300-8228: Norwalk, West Covina, Alhambra, Pasadena, Altadena, Monterey Park, Artesia, Cerritos, LA County of Covina, Arcadia, and Long Beach
- **Century Communications,** 800-626-6299: Bell Air, Beverly Hills, Brentwood, Century City, Eagle Rock, San Fernando Valley south of Ventura Boulevard, Santa Monica, Sherman Oaks, West LA, and Westwood
- **Falcon Cablevision,** 800-964-4844 (merged with Charter Communications in the spring of 2000): Thousand Oaks, Calabasas, Topanga Canyon, and Malibu
- **Marcus Cable,** 818 295-3000: Burbank and Glendale
- **Media One,** 213-993-8200: Hollywood-Wilshire, South Central, Sylmar, Sunland-Tujunga, Harbor, Whittier; in Santa Clarita: Valencia and Newhall
- **TCI,** 800-482-4669: North Hollywood, Sherman Oaks, Studio City, and Van Nuys
- **Time Warner Communications,** 818-700-6500: Northridge, Encino, Woodland Hills, and Van Nuys. Also, South Pasadena, parts of Santa Clarita

RADIO STATIONS

Gotta make sure your car radio works for all those times you're sitting on the freeway. Both AM stations 980 and 1070 give frequent and regular traffic reports (every 6 minutes for 1070 and "on the one's," 9:01, 9:11, etc., for 980) that will help you avoid traffic jams—hopefully.

AM

- **KABC** 790 Talk Radio
- **KFI** 690 Talk Radio

- **KDIS** 710 Disney Radio
- **KFWB** 980 News
- **KLAC** 570 Swing
- **KNX** 1070 News
- **KRLA** 1110 Talk Radio
- **KXTA** 1150 Sports

FM

- **KACE** 103.9 Motown
- **KBIG** 104.3 Adult Contemporary
- **KCBS** 93 Rock & Roll Classics
- **KIIS** 102.7 Contemporary Top 40
- **KKBT** 92.3 Urban
- **KLOS** 95.5 Album Oriented Rock
- **KOST** 103.5 Soft Rock
- **KROQ** 106.7 Rock
- **KRTH** 101.1 Oldies
- **KTWV** 94.7 Smooth Jazz
- **KYSR** 98.7 Modern Adult Contemporary
- **KZLA** 93.9 Country

NEWSPAPERS AND MAGAZINES

Neighborhood publications that focus on community issues include:

- *Arcadia Weekly,* 626-294-1090, www.arcadiaweekly.com
- *Argonaut,* 310-822-1629, www.marinadelreyargonaut.com
- *Beverly Hills Courier,* 310-278-1322
- *Brentwood News,* 310-873-0226, www.brentwoodnews.com
- *Burbank Leader,* 818-843-8700
- *Culver City News,* 310-313-6727, www.culvercityonline.com
- *Daily Breeze,* 310-540-5511, www.dailybreeze.com (Torrance)
- *Downtown Gazette,* 562-433-2000, www.gazettes.com (Long Beach)
- *Downtown News,* 213-481-1448, www.losangelesdowntown.com
- *Glendale News Press,* 818-241-4141
- *Malibu Times,* 310-456-5507, www.malibutimes.com
- *NoHo News,* 818-769-8414, www.nohonews.com (North Hollywood)

- **Pasadena Weekly,** 626-795-0149, www.pasadenaweekly.com
- **Santa Monica Outlook,** 310-829-0411
- **Signal,** 661-259-1234, www.the-signal.com (Santa Clarita)
- **Tolucan Times,** 818-762-2171 (Toluca Lake)
- **Vanguard News,** 805-269-2030, www.vanguardnews.com (Acton)
- **Westside Weekly,** 310-314-1297

City-wide publications include:

- **Los Angeles Times,** 888-565-2323, www.latimes.com
  The primary newspaper in LA, it publishes a separate but similar edition for the Valley. Its Sunday edition (available as early as Saturday morning at convenience stores and newsstands) makes for hefty weekend reading.
- **Daily News,** 818-713-3000
  A daily newspaper based in the Valley and wannabe competitor to the *Los Angeles Times*.
- **LA Weekly,** 323-465-9909, www.laweekly.com
  This alternative paper is what many Angelenos turn to for information on movies, clubs and fun (wholesome and not-so-wholesome) in LA. Their often provocative personal ads are a hoot. The paper is free for the taking at newsstands, supermarkets, coffeehouses, convenience stores, etc. If you want a home-delivered subscription, you'll have to pay.
- **New Times,** 310-477-0403, www.newtimesla.com
  Another alternative paper that's not quite as thick or as shocking as the *Weekly*, it's also free and found in the same places.
- **Los Angeles Magazine,** 800-876-5222
  Nice glossy spread covering the hip and happening in the LA scene, some fashion and food as well.

FINDING A PHYSICIAN

Whether you're going for a nose job, boob job or, oh right, a medical check-up, you'll need a doctor you can trust. If you're covered by an HMO or PPO, contact your provider for a list of physicians in your area. If you're looking to switch physicians, talk to your co-workers or friends for a recommendation. The Yellow Pages contains a list of docs in its "Physicians & Surgeons, MD" section.

Here are some popular physician referral lines:

- **American Board of Medical Specialties,** 800-766-2378
- **Cedars-Sinai Physician Referral Line,** 800-CEDARS-1
- **Doctor Finder - Glendale Memorial Hospital,** 818-502-2378
- **UCLA Medical Group,** 800-UCLA-MD1
- **West Hills Hospital & Medical Center Physician Referral,** 800-265-8624

For those wanting to know if their doctor is board certified in a specialty area, check with the American Board of Medical Specialists, 800-776-2378, www.certifieddoctor.org/verify/html. Other medical sites that may be of interest are Mayo Clinic's www.mayo.edu, and the federal government's comprehensive www.healthfinder.gov.

PET LAWS & SERVICES

Now that you're all settled into your new digs, it's time to settle Rover and Kitty in too. Resident dogs, not cats, of the City of Los Angeles are required to be licensed. Licenses are available at shelters, through veterinarians or by mail; write to the Department of Animal Regulation, 419 South Spring Street, Room 1400, Los Angeles, CA 90013 or call 888-452-7381. Licenses returned by mail require six to eight weeks to process. If the application is submitted in person to any departmental office (see below), processing takes only minutes. The annual fee for dogs (four months or older) is $30 if unsterilized, or $10 if sterilized. Free licenses for sterilized dog are available to seniors (62 years or older) who meet financial requirements and to disabled persons who own a guide dog or service dog.

The centers listed below offer spaying and neutering services. The City of Los Angeles Sterilization Fund provides free spaying and neutering for dogs and cats owned by qualified persons living within the city of Los Angeles. (Persons meeting the criteria for a free dog license may have their pets altered free as well.) Contributions to the Animal Sterilization Fund may be sent to the City of Los Angeles, Department of Animal Regulation (see above for address).

All dogs over the age of four months must be vaccinated against rabies. A dog license is valid only when the required rabies vaccination certificate, issued by a licensed veterinarian, is provided and only as long as the rabies vaccination is current.

Here are a list of LA County Animal Care and Control Centers:

- **Burbank Animal Control**, 818-238-3340, 1150 North Victory Place, Burbank

- **East Valley Animal Care And Control Center,** 888-452-7381 13131 Sherman Way, North Hollywood
- **Harbor Animal Care And Control Center,** 888-452-7381 735 Battery Street, San Pedro
- **Long Beach Animal Control,** 562-570-7387, 3001 East Willow, Long Beach
- **North Central Animal Care And Control Center,** 888-452-7381, 3201 Lacy Street, Los Angeles
- **Santa Monica Animal Shelter,** 310-458-8594, 1640 9th Street, Santa Monica
- **South Central Animal Care And Control Center,** 888-452-7381, 3320 West 36th Street, Los Angeles
- **Southeast Area Animal Control Center,** 562-803-3301, 9777 Seaca Street, Downey
- **West Los Angeles Animal Care And Control Center,** 888-452-7381, 11950 Missouri Avenue, Los Angeles
- **West Valley Animal Care And Control Center,** 888-452-7381 20655 Plummer Street, Chatsworth

VETS, GROOMERS & DAY CARE

There are no shortage of veterinary hospitals, pet groomers and dog/cat day-care centers in la-la land. Flip through the Yellow Pages and look under "Veterinary Hospitals," "Dog & Cat Grooming," and "Dog & Cat Kennels" for one near you. Or give the Southern California Veterinary Medical Association a call at 562-948-4979 for vet referral assistance. If you're seeking medical coverage for your pet, try Veterinary Pet Insurance, 800-872-7387 or Pet Assure, a pet HMO, 888-789-7387, www.petassure.com.

Pet day care centers are all the rage in LA, and are especially popular among professionals who don't want to leave their pet home alone while they work during the day. Fees vary, but expect to pay a minimum of $25 for a half-day and $40 for a full day. Top of the line day care offers limousine shuttles (for Puddles, not you) and air-conditioned, cage-less day of TLC, snacks, games and even television—expect to pay a premium for such service.

Los Angeles pet lovers of a spiritual bent can have their pets blessed. Every March, on the Saturday before Easter, there is the Blessing of the Animals festival. Pet lovers from throughout LA unite, bringing their furry and feathered friends to be blessed by a Catholic priest at the historic landmark, El Pueblo de los Angeles, 125 Paseo de la Plaza, downtown. Call 213-628-7833 for details.

DOG PARKS

Off-leash canine parks are popular in this dog-loving city with its zero tolerance policy for off-leash dogs. Some of the dog parks listed below are outfitted with doggie drinking fountains and free scoop-the-poop baggies. While obviously popular with Fido, dog parks have become a hot spot for meeting friends or even a significant other.

- **Calabasas**, Calabasas Bark Park
  4232 Las Virgines Road, across from A.E. Wright Middle School
- **Encino**, Sepulveda Basin Recreation Area
  White Oak and Victory Boulevard
- **Hollywood**, Laurel Canyon Park
  Mulholland Drive just off Laurel Canyon; open after 3:00 p.m.
- **Hollywood**, Runyon Canyon Park
  Top of Fuller Avenue (the north end of Fuller - west of La Brea, north of Franklin Avenue)
- **Long Beach**, Long Beach Dog Park
  7th and Park, Long Beach. CA
- **Los Angeles**, Silverlake Dog Park
  Silverlake Boulevard at Easterly Terrace, Los Angeles
- **Pasadena**, Brookside Park
  360 North Arroyo Boulevard
- **West Los Angeles**, Westminster Park
  1234 Pacific Avenue on east side of Westminster Park

One final note for pet lovers who want their best friend to accompany them on vacation, get a copy of *Vacationing with your Pet* by Eileen Barish. It lists over 23,000 hotels, motels, B&Bs, etc. that welcome guests with pets.

SAFETY AND CRIME

Every city has its higher crime and lower crime areas, and Los Angeles is certainly no exception. Check out prospective communities when trying to determine how comfortable and secure you might feel. Observe. Is there a lot of graffiti? Litter? Loiterers? Security bars? All these are indicators that should not be ignored.

Big city rules apply here in LA; don't be stupid. Be pro-active when it comes to your safety and use common sense:

- Keep your doors and windows locked. If you like fresh air and want to keep your windows open a crack, take extra precautions and buy a window lock (available at hardware stores) that prevents the window from being slid further open or wedge it with a stick. Upper level apartments are not as easy targets to thieves as street level apartments.
- Walk with a purpose, trust your instincts, and keep clear of abandoned areas, especially at night. Be particularly cautious in South Central.
- When taking public transportation, ride toward the front of the bus, next to the driver. On the Metro, sit in a populated car.
- Be extra aware of your surroundings in unfamiliar areas. Once you get a feel for the level of precautions needed for your personal comfort level in your neighborhood, you'll fall right in with the pace of the city and, like most Angelenos, go about your days with no incident.

AUTO SAFETY

Safety experts say that with the advent of car alarms and other anti-theft devices, autos are getting more difficult to steal. Unfortunately, thieves who formerly would steal unattended parked cars have learned that violent confrontation, i.e. car-jacking, may be the only way to get the cars they want. Here are some guidelines for auto safety:

- Know how to get to where you are going. Study your route ahead of time to eliminate the need to look at a map while driving.
- Keep your car doors locked while driving, and keep windows up in unfamiliar areas. If it is hot and you have no air conditioning, roll down the window enough to get air in the car, but not enough for an arm to get in.
- Keep your wallet or purse hidden, either under the seat or in the trunk.
- Park in well-lit areas. If you need to use a pay phone or purchase gasoline, stop where the attendants can see you. While more costly, having someone pump gas for you is safer than getting out of your car and paying yourself. Avoid parking in alleys, their low visibility makes them a favorite for thieves.

- Do not be tricked into getting out of your car. If you are rear-ended in a remote or dark area and feel uneasy about getting out of your car to exchange insurance information, motion to the other driver to follow you to a police or fire station, or a 24-hour store.
- Do not stop for flashing white lights. Law enforcement vehicles use red flashers or blue and white ones.
- Drive in the middle lane if you feel insecure in a certain area. Try not to get into a lane where you can easily be cut off. If a car blocks you intentionally, honk repeatedly for help, but do not get out of your car.
- Most importantly, if you are confronted, give up your car, your jewelry, your wallet or purse. Often violence occurs when citizens resist a car-jacking or mugging. No possession is more valuable than your life.

In general, driving in and around Los Angeles is not a dangerous proposition. Millions of people do it every day, without confrontation or even a hint of danger. *Just stay alert, and be defensive.*

C AN'T QUITE AFFORD ALL THE FURNITURE YOU NEED? NEED A HAIR cut? Can't quite muster the energy to clean-up your new place and need to hire help? Here are some services that may be useful as you settle into your new home. Check the Yellow Pages for additional listings.

RENTAL SERVICES

Just about anything you need can be rented in Los Angeles. It's just a matter of hunting it down.

APPLIANCE RENTAL

In LA, it is common to find apartments that do not come with a refrigerator or other appliances. Some places that rent major appliances:

- **Anthony Rents**, 11012 Ventura Boulevard, Studio City, 818-980-1001 or 323-650-7060
- **Rent-A-Center,** 12735 Van Nuys Boulevard, Van Nuys, 818-890-3000
- **Renters Choice**, 6112 Lankershim Boulevard, North Hollywood, 818-769-6000
- **Wil-Quip Appliance Rentals,** 23705 Crenshaw Boulevard, Torrence, 818-509-0053

FURNITURE RENTAL

If you're just getting settled and haven't had time to buy furniture yet, or perhaps you want some time to shop around for just the right pieces, here are some places where you can rent furniture, for both the office and home. Most places offer free pick-up and delivery with purchase options.

- **Brook Furniture Leasing & Sales**, www.bfr.com
  Beverly Hills, 8549 Wilshire Boulevard, 310-652-6795
  Marina Del Rey, 13400 West Washington Boulevard, 310-306-2131
  Sherman Oaks, 15125 Ventura Boulevard, 818-386-2158
  Los Angeles, 655 South Hope Street, 213-624-1202
- **Cort Furniture Rental**, www.cort1.com
  Beverly Hills, 8484 Wilshire Boulevard, 310-652-2678
  Marina Del Rey, 4161 Lincoln Boulevard, 310-301-2577
  Sherman Oaks, 14140 Ventura Boulevard, 818-907-5496

COMPUTER RENTALS AND LEASES

Every **Kinko's Copies** store has PCs and Macs, plus laser and color print-
ers, for rent by the hour. You'll find a Kinko's in just about every neighborhood in Los Angeles and in the cities outside of LA County, many offering
24 hour service. Check your phone book for locations. If you prefer working at home, you can rent or lease a computer through these companies:

- **Complete Computer Cure Valley**, 15122 Ventura Boulevard,
  Sherman Oaks, 818-986-8770
- **Computer Rental Center**, 975 North Michillinda, Pasadena, 626-
  351-5310
- **Hi-Tech Computer Rental**, 172 West Verdugo Avenue, Burbank,
  818-841-0677
- **Micro Rent,** 888-499-4311, www.microrent.com
- **PC Rental,** 888 PC-LEASING
- **Personal Computer Rentals,** 818-781-0600 or 800-4-RENT-PC
- **We-Rent-Computers,** 800-RENT-PCS

DOMESTIC SERVICES

For all you multi-taskers who could use some help around the house, the
following services may be of interest.

DIAPER SERVICES

Service throughout most of LA County:

- **Bare Bottoms Diaper Service**, 800-606-8800
- **Dy-Dee Diaper Service**, 800-803-9333, www.dy-dee.com

DRY CLEANING DELIVERY

There seems to be a dry cleaner on every other street corner in LA, which must explain why so few offer delivery service. Nonetheless, here are some that will pick-up and deliver:

- **Dickie Dobins Cleaners**, 8387 Beverly Boulevard, Los Angeles, 323-685-6830
- **Effrey's**, 8917 Melrose Avenue, Beverly Hills, 310-858-7400; 8302 Wilshire Boulevard, Beverly Hills, 323-653-0525
- **Encino Dry Cleaners**, 16946 Ventura Boulevard, Encino, 818-986-8464
- **Merry Go Round**, 8550 West Third Street, Los Angeles, 310-275-1782
- **Regal Cleaners,** 12154 Ventura Place, Studio City, 818-762-4350; 17471 Ventura Boulevard, Encino, 818-986-9105; 11335 Camarillo, North Hollywood, 818-762-2456
- **The Shirt Shuttle**, 2515 South Barrington Avenue, West Los Angeles, 310-822-8771

HOUSE CLEANING SERVICES

For those who want the luxury of maid service there are plenty of options. Check the telephone directory under "House Cleaning" for a complete listing of agencies near you. If you choose a service, make sure it's bonded and insured. Also, since many house cleaning personnel in Los Angeles are Spanish-speaking, you might find the Spanish phrase book, *Spanish-English Housekeeping* by Ruth M. Dietz, to be a worthwhile investment.

- **Betty's Maid Service,** 800-877-MAID
- **Dana's Housekeeping Personnel Service,** 310-329-2901, 818-342-3930, 661-255-1988
- **Dependable House Cleaning,** 310-838-1427
- **Fresh Beginnings,** 310-274-4439, 310-829-7759
- **Golden Maid Agency,** 818-783-7777
- **M&M Cleaning,** 818-705-6336
- **Merry Maids,** 818-508-7411, 818-609-8570
- **Oriental Lady Cleaning,** 800-358-4258
- **Queen of Clean,** 800-805-8395

HAIRCUTS

LA's beautiful people have elevated the haircut to an art form. Any stylist who snips the bangs of a celebrity becomes a coveted stylist who then commands fees in the hundreds—that is, assuming you've got the clout to even get an appointment. Choices for salonists in LA run the gamut from Beverly Hills' high-priced chic ones, e.g. President Clinton's famous $200 trim by **Cristophe**, 310-274-0851, and famous stylist **Jose Eber's** own salon, 310-278-7646, to the budget-minded **SuperCuts**, a nationwide chain with multiple locations. Check your phone book under "Barbers" or "Beauty Salons" for a mind-boggling array of choices. If you want to avoid a salon with attitude—and there are a lot of them—call the shop beforehand to see how friendly they are. By the way, the hip hair cutter of the moment is Jonathan Antin of **Jonathan** in West Hollywood, 310-855-0225, he trims the locks of Ricky Martin, Drew Barrymore and Jewel.

MAIL SERVICES

Renting a post box at a mail receiving center is a good option for those still on the hunt for a house, for people frequently out of town, or for those who work from home but don't want to use their residence address for business. Aside from mailbox companies, mailboxes can also be rented at your local post office—however, these typically have a waiting list of three months or more.

The difference between a post office mailbox and a private mailbox is that holders of a private mailbox can write their address as if it were an actual street address, which can give the impression that one resides or works at that address. In other words, a person who lives in Hollywood can "purchase" the use of a Beverly Hills address. (There is no mistaking a post office mailbox address.)

- **Beverly Hills Postal Center**, Beverly Hills, 310-274-7265
- **Mail Boxes Etc**. has multiple locations in Los Angeles, hours and days of operation vary. Call 800-789-4MBE or visit www.mbe.com for a complete list of locations.
- **PostNet:** Encino, 17328 Ventura Boulevard, 818-789-6500; Northridge, 9135 Reseda Boulevard #A, 818-341-7591
- **United Mail Boxes**, Beverly Hills, 310-652-7522

JUNK MAIL

If your mailbox is drowning in junk mail, there is a way to curtail the volume of ads, circulars, and flyers. Write a note, including your name and address, asking to be purged from the Direct Marketing Association's list (Direct Marketing Association's Mail Preference Service, P.O. Box 9008, Farmingdale, NY 11735). Some catalog companies need to be contacted directly to be removed from their mailing lists. Another option is to call the "Opt-out" line at 888-567-8688 and request that the main credit bureaus not release your name and address to marketing companies.

MAIL DELIVERY

Mail delivery within the city is fast and efficient. The only time you have to worry about your mail is once it hits your mailbox where theft can be a problem depending on your neighbors and the security of your mailbox. If you are experiencing stolen or missing mail, speak to someone at your local post office or contact the US Post Office's Consumer Affairs at 800-275-8777.

TELEPHONE ANSWERING SERVICES

These services offer options such as call-forwarding, paging, wake-up calls, and voice mail, whatever suits your needs. (Some private mailbox offices also offer answering services.) For a complete listing, check your Yellow Pages under "Answering Bureaus" or try one of these:

- **Answer California**, 213-251-3800, 310-281-5959
- **Around the Clock Call Center**, 818-904-3435
- **Community Answering**, 818-508-6001
- **Concorde Communications**, 800-800-4411
- **Professional Communications Network**, 800-627-4235
- **Signius**, 800-677-7699
- **Telecom Communications Center**, 800-897-2600

SHIPPING SERVICES

Couldn't get everything to fit in the moving truck? You can always ship it via one of these services:

- **Airborne Express (AirEx)**, 800-247-2676
- **DHL Worldwide Express**, 800-225-5345
- **Federal Express (Fed Ex)**, 800-463-3339
- **Roadway Package Systems**, 800-762-3725
- **United Parcel Service**, 800-742-5877
- **US Postal Service Express Mail**, 800-222-1811

SERVICES FOR PEOPLE WITH DISABILITIES

Los Angeles has a variety of resources for people with special needs. Many public, private and commercial facilities provide for sight, hearing, or mobility impaired people. Public transit alone provides various types of assistance to the elderly and disabled. Major crosswalks equipped with audio signals and ramps are most common in the LA neighborhoods where colleges and universities are located. Here is a list of some available services and agencies that can offer referrals and assistance:

- **Braille Institute,** 800-272-4553, serves anyone with reading difficulties due to visual impairment or physical disability. Their Books on Tape program, 800-808-2555, is very popular.
- **California Assistive Technology System** (**CATS**), 800-390-2699; TTY, 800-900-0706, provides information on obtaining assistive devices and services.
- **California Association of the Physically Handicapped** (**CAPH**), 310-391-5703, provides information on recreational events and advocates for the rights of people with disabilities.
- **California Department of Rehabilitation,** 310-582-8900; TTY, 310-528-8927
- **Center for the Partially Sighted,** 310-458-3501, provides counseling, equipment and rehabilitative programs for independent living.
- **Computer Access Center,** 310-338-1597, provides access and information on assistive technology for people with disabilities.
- **Crisis Line for the Handicapped,** 800-426-4363; a 24-hour support and information line.
- **Driving Systems, Inc.,** 818-782-6793, develops customized adaptive driving devices.
- **Easter Seal Society,** 818-996-9902, gives infant-care education, adult day programs and referrals to rehabilitation services.
- **Greater Los Angeles Council on Deafness** (**GLAD**), 323-478-

8000; TTY, 323-478-8000, offers counseling, job development, translation, and information for the hearing-impaired.

- **Goodwill Industries of Southern California,** 323-223-1211, offers counseling, job placement, and educational services.
- **Independent Living Center of Southern California,** 818-988-9525; TTY, 818-988-3533
- **Jay Nolan Community Services,** 818-361-6400, serves people with developmental disabilities, including autism.
- **Los Angeles Caregiver Resource Center,** 213-740-8711, 800-540-4442, is a resource for caregivers of brain-impaired adults.
- **Los Angeles County Adult Protective Services,** 213-251-5401, 800-992-1660; report abuse of dependent adults to this number.
- **Los Angeles County Commission on Disabilities,** 213-974-1053; TDD, 213-974-1707
- **LA Unified School District Parent Resource Network Hotline,** 800-933-8133, provides information and referrals to special education programs.
- **North Los Angeles County Regional Center,** 818-788-1900, serves people with developmental disabilities.
- **Recording for the Blind and Dyslexic,** 800-499-5525, www.lafn.org/community/rfbd, records over 3,000 new books each year on audio cassettes for loan to students and adults who cannot read standard print because of a visual, perceptual or physical disability: Los Angeles, 323-664-5525; El Segundo, 310-414-6506; West Hills, 818-226-6055
- **Social Security and Medicare Eligibility Information,** 800-772-1213; TTY, 800-288-7185
- **Spinal Cord Injury Network International,** 800-548-2673, is an information network and video library for people with spinal cord injuries.
- **Venice Skills Center,** 310-392-4153, offers free rehabilitation services for people with disabilities, such as sign language interpreters for the hearing impaired, readers for the blind, and job placement assistance and counseling.
- **Westside Regional Center for Independent Living,** 310-258-4000, offers a variety of services, from counseling to living skills, for seniors and people with developmental disabilities.
- **West Hollywood Disability Services,** 323-851-6746; TTY, 323-848-6496; the city provides free assistance to persons with disabili-

ties, including counseling, advocacy and referrals, job placement, transportation, and medical services.

GETTING AROUND

Contact your local **DMV** for handicapped licenses, TTY, 800-368-4327. If you need a blue curb painted at your residence contact **The Department of Transportation Bureau of Parking Management and Regulations Analysis Section** at 213-913-4603. Expect about two weeks for completion. For those who need other forms of special transportation, these are some options:

- **Access Services** provides curb to curb transportation for disabled residents of LA County, 800-827-0829; TTY, 800-827-1359.
- **Cityride** provides curb to curb transportation for seniors and mobility impaired residents of the San Fernando Valley and LA, 818-908-1901.
- **Culver City Bus,** 310-253-6500; TTY, 310-253-6548
- **Lift Van Program,** 323-761-8810, provides inexpensive lift van transportation for wheelchair-bound residents to any destination within an eight-mile radius of the user's departure point (within West Hollywood and Beverly Hills only).
- **Medi-Ride, Inc.** provides non-emergency medical transportation service for Valley and Los Angeles residents, 818-989-1111.
- **Metrolink,** 800-371-5465; TTY, 800-698-4833
- **MTA,** 800-266-6883; TTY, 800-252-9040; **Disabled Riders Emergency Hotline,** 800-621-7828
- **Paratransit Information Referral Service** is a clearinghouse of transportation services for seniors and mobility-impaired residents of LA County, 800-431-7882; TTY: 800-431-9731.
- **Santa Monica Municipal Bus Lines,** 310-451-5444; TTY, 310-395-6024
- **Taxi Coupons,** 323-761-8810; this program allows persons age 65 and older, and residents of any age who are wheelchair-users or blind, to purchase one book of discounted taxi coupons per month.

COMMUNICATION

Telephone relay service for the hearing/speech impaired is available free of charge via the **California Relay Service** (**CRS**). They will relay phone calls between TTY and voice callers. There is no charge for the service itself, however, regular toll and long-distance fees apply: TTY to voice, 800-735-2929; voice to TTY, 800-735-2922

Special adaptive telecommunications equipment can be purchased from **Pacific Bell Accessibility Resources,** 800-772-3140, or **GTE Special Needs Center,** 800-821-2585.

OTHER RESOURCES

The **Los Angeles Housing Department** sponsors a Handyworker program, providing minor repairs to low- and moderate-income homeowners who are physically disabled, or to senior citizens 62 years and older, free of charge. Repairs can take place anywhere from two weeks to nine months after a request, depending upon the required repair and the demand for services in your area. There is currently a waiting list for service in some communities. Call 213-367-9228 or 800-994-4444 for more information.

The **Los Angeles City Fire Department** offers a Fire Safety, and a Safety and Earthquake Program for the disabled. Contact the Disaster Preparedness Section at 818-756-9672.

The **Bet Tzedek Legal Services** 323-939-0506, provides free legal services to low- and moderate-income residents, the disabled, and the frail elderly in the areas of nursing home law, conservatorship, power of attorney and other health issues.

The **Western Law Center for the Handicapped** at Loyola Law School, 213-736-1031, offers legal advocacy on disability rights issues.

The **Partners Adult Day Healthcare Center,** 323-883-0330, sponsored by the city of West Hollywood, is for the frail elderly, younger disabled adults and persons with AIDS.

GAY AND LESBIAN LIFE

When you're in Los Angeles, especially around West Hollywood and Los Feliz, the joke about that cute single man probably being gay is often true. In fact, the city of West Hollywood is *the* openly gay and lesbian enclave, offering a Domestic Partnership Ordinance to its residents. This ordinance officially recognizes domestic partnerships between two adults (regardless of sexual orientation) if they are each other's sole partner and are responsible for each other's welfare. Contact the Domestic Partnerships Department at 323-848-6332 for information on how to apply for a Certificate of Domestic Partnership (a $20 fee applies).

Much of the night scene is focused on a long stretch of Santa Monica Boulevard in West Hollywood, from La Brea Avenue to La Cienega Boulevard, where bars, restaurants and clubs are packed shoulder to shoulder on weekend nights. It is on this same street where the Gay Pride Parade is held in June. On Halloween night it seems as though all of LA (of every persuasion) converges on the Boulevard in costume. The main event at this wild street party are the drag queens who pull out all the stops, strutting up and down the Boulevard in outrageous clothing. For a more complete introduction to gay and lesbian life in LA, check out *Gay USA: Where the Babes Go* by Lori Hobkirk.

Following is a list of some local organizations that specialize in gay and lesbian issues:

- **AIDS Project Los Angeles,** 323-993-1600, provides comprehensive assistance to persons living with HIV/AIDS, and an AIDS information hotline.
- **American Civil Liberties Union** (**ACLU**), 213-977-9500, provides civil liberties litigation and legal referrals.
- **Anti-Gay-Bashing Resources,** 323-848-6414
- **GLAAD,** Los Angeles chapter, 323-658-6775
- **Gay & Lesbian Association of Santa Clarita,** 661-288-2814
- **Gay & Lesbian Counseling Center,** 323-936-7500, 818-765-4447
- **Gay & Lesbian Youth Talk Line,** 818-508-1802
- **Los Angeles Gay & Lesbian Center,** 323-993-7400, www-gay-lesbian-center.org; provides a variety of social and health services.
- **West Hollywood Cares,** 310-659-4840
- **Progressive Health Services & Holistic Health for Women,** 323-650-1508; this organization offers a variety of health services including lesbian and gay healthcare.

LOCAL GAY PUBLICATIONS

- *The Advocate,* 323-871-1225, www.advocate.com
- *Edge Magazine,* 323-962-6994
- *Frontiers,* 323-848-2222
- *The Lesbian News,* 310-787-8658, www.lesbiannews.com
- *West Hollywood Independent,* 323-932-6397

CONSUMER PROTECTION

"Buyer beware" may be a cliché, but it is the best line of defense against fraud and consumer victimization. Sometimes, even the most cautious of us can be hoodwinked by an unscrupulous business. Here are some agencies that can help on your quest for justice:

- **Automotive Repair Bureau, Department of Consumer Affairs,** 818-596-4400, 800-952-5210
- **California Attorney General's Office,** 800-952-5225
- **California Department of Consumer Affairs,** 800-952-5210
- **California Department of Insurance,** 213-897-8921
- **Los Angeles Better Business Bureau,** 213-251-9696, 818-386-5510, www.bbb.org
- **Los Angeles County Bar Association,** 213-627-2727, operates an attorney referral line and the Smart Law information line which has several pre-recorded messages providing basic information about hundreds of areas of law. To reach the Smart Law hotline, call 213-243-1500.
- **Los Angeles County Department of Consumer Affairs,** 213-974-1452
- **US Consumer Product Safety Commission,** 800-638-2772

L IKE MOST MAJOR US CITIES, FINDING GOOD DAY CARE CAN BE A problem, and waiting lists abound for day care centers that come highly recommended.

Los Angeles has 12,885 licensed child care centers and 36,390 licensed family child care providers. The quality varies enormously, so careful screening is advised. The state requires a license for any child care provider who cares for the children of more than one family. To check if your childcare provider's license is up to date, or to investigate any filed complaints against the provider, call the **Department of Social Services Community Care Licensing Offices,** 310-337-4333 or 323-981-3350. If your day care provider is exempt from licensing, you can contact the **Trust Line,** 800-822-8490, for a $24 fee they will conduct a background check on the provider.

Other resources for parents include the **National Parent Information Network,** 800-583-4135, www.npin.org, and the **National Resource Center for Health, Safety, and Child Care,** 800-598-KIDS, http://nrc.uchsc.edu On the Internet, visit **www.parentrover.com**, their site has a bulletin board for LA parents where information can be exchanged, from the going rate for a teen-age baby-sitter, to determining when your youngster is ready for kindergarten.

Whether you hire a nanny, a baby-sitter, or decide on group day care, during your screening, be sure to examine how the caretaker interacts with your child. The following checklist may be helpful. Determine for yourself if a prospective day care provider:

- Seems friendly and patient
- Is someone you think your child will enjoy being with

- Seems to feel good about himself or herself and the job
- Displays child-rearing attitudes and methods that are similar to your own
- Understands child development, and has a good supply of age-appropriate materials
- Encourages good habits: healthy snacks, hand washing, etc.
- Exhibits respect for little ones
- Provides a routine and rules the children can understand and follow
- Accepts and respects your family's cultural values
- Has previous experience or training in working with children

DAY CARE

When seeking quality day care, begin with referrals from friends, family, and co-workers. A nationwide online directory of day care providers can be found at **www.careguide.com**. Touted as the Internet's number one child and elder care resource, this non-profit site assists those searching for care for either their children or elderly relatives. The following organizations offer resources and referrals for day care and cover everything from high-end centers to financially assisted options, such as Head Start Programs, and subsidized day care.

- **Cedars-Sinai WARM Line,** West Hollywood, 310-855-3500; information hotline, sponsored by Cedars-Sinai Hospital, for a variety of questions on child rearing.
- **Child and Family Services,** Echo Park, 213-427-2700; this non-profit organization provides information and referrals to licensed child care providers, Head Start programs, subsidized day care, family day care providers, and developmental programs for children with disabilities, as well as training for prospective daycare providers and information about child development.
- **Child Care Resource Center,** Van Nuys, 818-756-3360, refers parents to child day care and family day care centers.
- **Connections for Children:** Santa Monica, 310-452-3202; West Los Angeles, 310-322-1877
- **Crystal Stairs**, Los Angeles, 213-399-0199; subsidized child care for low-income families.
- **The Help Company,** Santa Monica, 310-828-4111; a child care referral service.
- **Home Safe Child Care,** Los Angeles, 323-934-7979, offers low-

income and homeless families a comprehensive range of child care services including subsidized child care.

- **YWCA,** Los Angeles, 213-365-2991, offers child care and support services for parents.

BABY-SITTERS

The best source for baby-sitting is to ask around—friends, neighbors, co-workers, if you're lucky they may give up a name from their list. Membership in a church or synagogue can be a good source for referrals. Another possible source to tap is the local hospitals. A notice posted on the staff bulletin board may bring in a nurse looking to subsidize her income. Also, check out the "Baby-Sitters" and "Nurses & Nurses Registries" section of your Yellow Pages. The **LA Baby Sitters Guild,** 323-658-8792, 6399 Wilshire Boulevard, Suite 812, Los Angeles, CA 90048, offers referrals. An on-call service (with a four-hour minimum), the Guild may be able to point you to someone who will provide regular sittings.

Junior has woken with a fever, you've got a big presentation at work, and you normally don't use a baby-sitter or day care. What to do? **Child Sick Care, Inc.**, 818-846-0118, www.childsickcare.com, offers in-home care services for mildly ill children. They will send a caregiver (bonded and trained in first-aid) to your home. Their hourly fee is $16, with a four-hour minimum. Though their offices are in Burbank, they service all of Los Angeles, including the Valley, the Westside, Pasadena, and Santa Clarita.

NANNIES

Need a sitter on a more permanent basis? Tired of toting the kids off to day care? A nanny may be the right choice for you. Can't quite afford a nanny? Consider doing a nanny-share with another family, thereby splitting the cost. Where to find a nanny? Nanny referral agencies offer the benefit of prescreening applicants for you, but they will cost slightly more than if you located one yourself. A "Help Wanted" posting in the *Los Angeles Times* or a local parenting magazine may work. Or see the resources in **Baby-sitters** for more ideas. The following companies offer a range of domestic care. For a full listing check the Yellow Pages under "Nannies."

- **ABC Nannies,** 310-246-1640
- **Another You**, 818-776-0444

- **Buckingham Nannies,** 310-247-1877
- **Elite Nannies Agency,** 310-203-3069
- **Family Care Services, Inc.,** 800-741-4800, www.familycareser-vices.com
- **Golden Maid Agency,** 818-981-4444
- **Jewish Nanny Connection Agency,** 818-780-2418
- **Nannies Unlimited,** 310-551-0303
- **Next Best Thing to Mom Inc.,** 310-553-9669
- **The Nanny Exchange,** 310-440-1088
- **TeachCare,** 888-TEACH-76, www.teachercare.com
- **Tender Care Agency,** 310-274-8322, 818-366-6718

AU PAIRS

If you land the right applicant, an au pair (typically, a young woman— 18 to 25—from abroad who will take care of your child and do light housekeeping in exchange for room, board and a weekly stipend) may be a better alternative than a nanny. However, an au pair will likely not have the extended experience of a professional nanny and usually only works for one year. The US Information Agency oversees and approves organizations that offer this service. The national agencies below can match your family with an au pair:

- **American Heritage/Au Pair International,** 800-654-2051
- **American Institute for Foreign Study/Au Pair in America,** 800-928-7247
- **Au Pair Care,** 800-482-7247
- **Educational Foundation for Foreign Students/Au Pair EF,** 800-333-6056
- **Euraupair International/Au Pair Care,** 800-333-3804
- **Exploring Cultural and Educational Learning/Au Pair Registry,** 800-547-8889
- **InterExchange/Au Pair USA,** 800-287-2477

SCHOOLS

PARENT RESOURCES

Newcomers with school-aged children may find it helpful to obtain a list-ing of schools in LA County when beginning their research. The *Los Angeles*

Times web site lists addresses and phone numbers of all the public and private schools in LA County: www.latimes.com/communities/schools.cgi. You may also purchase the *Public Schools Directory*, a hard-copy listing of all public school districts and their schools within LA County, from the **LA County Office of Education (LACOE)**, by calling or writing them at 562-922-6111, www.lacoe.edu, LA County Education Center, 9300 Imperial Highway, Downey, CA 90242-2890. The LACOE also offers a separate Private Schools Directory.

Parents researching an appropriate school for their child have a number of resources at their disposal. Comprehensive web sites to investigate public and private school scores and standings include www.schoolwisepress.com/latimes and the **California Department of Education's** web site, www.cde.ca.gov. The **Ed-Data Education Partnership** posts the latest fiscal, demographic and performance data to public schools at www.ed-data.k12.ca.us. Also, the **LA Learning Exchange's** web site www.lalc.k12.ca.us has dozens of links to LA schools and educational resource sites.

Researching schools takes a considerable time investment. If you want to leave the footwork of finding the right school for your child to someone else, **School Match,** 800-992-5323, www.schoolmatch.com will research the neighborhood and rank the top 15 schools, public or private, for you. The fee for this service is just under $100. They also offer more basic reports for a lower fee. **The School Report** provides a report consisting mainly of statistics (total enrollment, student to teacher ratio, etc.) for any school district of your choice at www.theschoolreport.com. The web site is advertiser supported, so the service is free, provided you fill out a brief survey. (This web site also offers a free comparative report between cities specified by the user.) Another web site offering free school district stats is **www.2001beyond.com**. This site is aimed at real estate agents, but you don't have to be an agent to get their "school snapshot" report. Another site widely used by real estate agents, which "helps parents get smart about schools" is **School Wise Press,** www.schoolwisepress.com. The site offers school rankings and profiles, as well as school related news articles. More in-depth reports are available for a fee.

Often, a parent's involvement in their child's education does not end once the child has enrolled in a school, it's usually just the beginning. Parent groups that may be useful to you include the **Parent Teacher Association** (**PTA**), 213-620-1100, www.capta.org, a united forum of parents, teachers, and school administrators to address education issues;

Parents for Unity (PFU), 323-734-9353, which provides assistance with grievance resolution within LA Unified School District; and the **California Association for the Gifted**, 310-215-1898, www.cagift-ed.org, which provides support for the academically advanced child. And finally, those who educate their children at home can rely on the **Home School Association of California**, 805-462-0726, www.hsc.org, and **Alternative Schools of California**, 818-846-8990 for assistance.

PUBLIC SCHOOLS

LA Unified School District has the second largest student population in the nation. In the fall of 1999, it reached an all time high of over 700,000 students. Enrollment of this magnitude places a huge financial burden on public schools, especially those in lower income areas. As with most metropolitan areas in the US, student test scores are higher in the wealthier neighborhoods, and vice versa. Beverly Hills Unified School District is lauded as one of the best school districts in LA County. Within LA Unified, the Westside and the San Fernando Valley are home to some of the more highly regarded schools. However, student achievement scores don't tell the whole story. A school's overall test scores may be affected by immigrant students who have yet to achieve English proficiency. And, of course, parental involvement, not just income, has a lot to do with an individual student's performance.

Individual neighborhood districts within LA Unified are broken into "clusters." When considering a prospective neighborhood, you might want to call LA Unified to find out which cluster/district your child would be attending, and whether bussing (used to ease overcrowding in certain schools) is utilized there. To register your child in LA Unified, you must show proof of immunization for polio, diphtheria, tetanus, hepatitis B, whooping cough, measles, rubella, and mumps. Call 800-933-8133 for enrollment information. Some schools within LA Unified are year-around, but most follow traditional schedules.

LA Unified offers an **open enrollment** program that's both popular and straightforward: a student who resides in one cluster can petition to attend a school outside of their cluster. However, the number of seats available to students who want to take advantage of this program are fast dwindling, for a variety of reasons, including the rise in immigration to Los Angeles. State law requires that a school accommodate students from its neighborhoods before offering open enrollments. And, the ambitious class size reduction program (mandating a maximum of 20 students to one teacher in kindergarten through third grades and some ninth grade classes) is another contributing factor.

Within Los Angeles there are over 100 **magnet schools,** those that offer an emphasis in a specialty area, such as mathematics and science, performing arts, and science. Contact your prospective district for specific information on their magnet programs.

- **Antelope Valley Union High School District,** 44811 Sierra Highway, Lancaster, 93534, www.avdistrict.org
- **Beverly Hills Unified School District,** 255 South Lasky Drive, 310-277-5900
- **Burbank Unified School District,** 330 North Buena Vista Street, 818-558-4600, www.burbank.k12.ca.us
- **Culver City Unified School District,** 4034 Irving Place, www.ccusd.k12.ca.us
- **Downey Unified School District,** 11627 Brookshire Avenue, 562-904-3500
- **El Segundo Unified School District,** 641 Sheldon Street, 310-615-2650
- **Glendale Unified School District,** 223 North Jackson Street, 818-241-3111
- **Inglewood Unified School District,** 401 South Inglewood Avenue, 310-419-2500
- **La Canada Unified School District,** 5039 Palm Drive, La Canada Flintridge, www.lcusd.k-12.ca.us
- **Lancaster School District,** 44711 North Cedar Avenue, wwwlancaster.k12.ca.us
- **LA Unified School District,** 634 Cesar E. Chavez, LA, 800-933-8133; www.lausd.k12.ca.us
- **Manhattan Beach Unified School District,** 1230 Rosecrans Avenue, 310-725-9050, www.manhattan.k12.ca.us
- **Newhall School District,** 25375 Orchard Village Road, Valencia, www.newhall.k12.ca.us
- **Norwalk-La Mirada Unified School District,** 12820 Pioneer Boulevard, Norwalk, California 90650-2894, 562-868-0431 ext. 2122
- **Palmdale School District,** 39139-49 10th Street East, www.psd.k12.ca.us
- **Pasadena Unified School District,** 351 South Hudson Avenue, 626-441-5700, www.pasadena.k-12.ca.us
- **San Marino Unified School District,** 1665 West Drive, 626-299-7000, www.san-marino.k-12.ca.us

- **Santa Monica-Malibu Unified School District,** 1651 16th Street, www.smmusd.org
- **Saugus Union School District,** 24930 Avenue Stanford, Santa Clarita, www.saugus.k12.ca.us
- **South Pasadena Unified School District,** 1020 El Centro Street, 626-441-5700, www.spusd.k-12.ca.us
- **William S. Hart Union High School District,** 21515 Redview Drive, Santa Clarita, www.hart.k12.ca.us

PRIVATE SCHOOLS

If you are considering private schooling for your child, there are many options in greater LA. Many parents choose private schooling because of the lower teacher to student ratio and higher quality education. However, it doesn't come cheap. Entrance requirements vary from school to school, so get details when you contact them. For a list of all the private schools within LA, call the city's **Human Services Department** at 323-848-6510 or the LACOE, 562-922-6111. The following list is a sample of what you'll find, check **Parent Resources** (see above) for tips to research the best school for your family:

- **Academy of Princeton College Preparatory** (6-12), 818-761-2931
- **Bethel Lutheran Elementary** (K-6), 17500 Burbank Boulevard, Encino, 818-788-2663
- **Beverly Hills Prep** (7-12), 310-276-0151, 9250 Olympic Boulevard, Beverly Hills, 90212-4659
- **Burbank Montessori Academy,** 217 North Hollywood Way, Burbank, 818-848-8226
- **Fairfield School** (K-8), 16945 Sherman Way, Van Nuys, 818-996-4560
- **Harvard-Westlake School** (7-12), 3700 Coldwater Canyon, Studio City, 818-980-6692
- **Hillel Hebrew Academy** (K-8), 9120 West Olympic Boulevard, Beverly Hills, 310-276-6135
- **Laurel Hall** (K-8), 11919 Oxnard Street, North Hollywood, 818-763-5434
- **Los Angeles Lutheran Junior-Senior High School** (7-12), 13570 Eldridge Avenue, Sylmar, 818-362-5861
- **Montessori Learning Center** (K-6), 11363 Washington Boulevard, Culver City, 310-391-7004

- **Montessori School Santa Monica** (K-9), 1909 Colorado Avenue, Santa Monica, 310-829-3551
- **New World Montessori School** (K-6), 10520 Regent Street, West LA, 310-838-4044
- **Saint Monica's Catholic High School** (9-12), 1030 Lincoln Blvd., Santa Monica, 310-394-3701
- **Summit View School** (K-12), 6455 Coldwater Canyon Avenue, 818-779-5262
- **Venture School** (9-12), 5333 South Sepulveda Boulevard, Culver City, 310-559-2678
- **West LA Baptist** (7-12), 1609 South Barrington Avenue, West LA, 310-826-2050

COLLEGES AND UNIVERSITIES

Los Angeles is blessed with a number of first-rate institutions offering a wide range of higher education options. In addition to offering degree programs, local schools offer concerts, plays, lecture series and many other cultural opportunities to the public. Call the campus or visit their web site for more information.

- **Art Center College of Design,** 1700 Lida Street, Pasadena, 626-396-2200; a four-year college known for its classes in both fine and applied arts.
- **California Institute of Technology,** 1201 East California Boulevard, Pasadena, 626-395-6811, www.caltech.edu, is a small, highly regarded school devoted to the study of science and mathematics, and the place where news cameras turn for information after local earthquakes.
- **California Institute of the Arts,** 24700 West McBean Parkway, Valencia, 661-255-1050; referred to as Cal Arts, this avant-garde school focuses on visual, theatrical, and written arts. Now sponsored by Disney Studios.
- **Loyola Marymount University,** 7101 West 80th Street, Westchester, 310-338-2700, www.lmu.edu; this Catholic University is located near the Los Angeles airport.
- **California State University Long Beach,** 1250 Bellflower Boulevard, Long Beach, 562-985-4111, www.csulb.edu; offers degrees in business, education, engineering, health, and liberal arts. CSULB's blue Pyramid is a popular venue for concerts and events.

- **Los Angeles City College,** 855 North Vermont Avenue, Los Angeles, 323-953-4000, www.lacc.cc.ca.us, is a large, two-year community college with an ethnically mixed student body in an urban environment.
- **Los Angeles Valley College**, 5800 Fulton Avenue, Van Nuys, 818-781-1200; a small two-year college with a leafy campus.
- **Mount Saint Mary's College,** 12001 Chalon Road, West Los Angeles, 310-476-2237; located in the scenic hills above Brentwood with views of the city below, this Catholic school holds art gallery shows and other cultural events.
- **Pasadena City College,** 1570 East Colorado Boulevard, Pasadena, 626-585-7123; this two-year community college hosts cultural events, as well as special programs for part-time students.
- **Pepperdine University,** 24255 West Pacific Coast Highway, Malibu, 310-456-4000, www.pepperdine.edu; a marquee name and a magnificent ocean view.
- **Santa Monica College,** 1900 Pico Boulevard, Santa Monica, 310-450-5150, is a well-respected, two-year community college with a high transfer rate to UCLA.
- **University of California, Los Angeles,** 405 Hilgard Avenue, Westwood, 310-825-4321, www.ucla.edu, has the largest enrollment of all nine campuses in the UC system, with more than 35,000 students. Walking tours of the pretty, 419-acre campus are available. Don't miss the Franklin D. Murphy Sculpture Garden.
- **University of Southern California,** Exposition Boulevard between Vermont Avenue and Figueroa Street, 213-740-2311, www.usc.edu; this private school has a number of galleries and museums open to the public, as well as displays of scripts and movie memorabilia at the Cinema Special Collections Library. Their cinema, law, and dentistry schools are considered top-notch.

TO SAY THAT SHOPPING IS A POPULAR PASTTIME IN LOS ANGELES is to say the obvious—with so many people and so much money, you've got the ingredients for some of the best retail establishments in the world.

Below is a list of full-service department stores where you can do a good portion of your shopping, followed by specialty stores, a list of second-hand shopping districts, and finally food—or maybe food should be first? Shopping requires so much energy...

SHOPPING MALLS

From chi-chi shopping on Rodeo Drive in Beverly Hills to Pasadena's flea market-type Rose Bowl Swap Meet, LA is perfect for shopping mavens, many of whom liken it to an indoor sport.

Most of the full-service department stores like Robinson's May and Macy's can be found in the larger malls. Here are the major malls, and the big department stores that anchor them:

- **The Beverly Center,** 8500 Beverly Boulevard, Los Angeles, 310-854-0070; this mall includes Macy's and Bed, Bath & Beyond.
- **Century City Shopping Center,** 10250 Santa Monica Boulevard, Century City, 310-553-5300; Macy's and Bloomingdale's are the two major department stores here.
- **Fashion Square Sherman Oaks,** 14006 Riverside Drive, Sherman Oaks, 818-783-0550, is anchored by Bloomingdale's and Macy's.
- **Fox Hills Mall,** Slauson and Sepulveda Boulevards, Culver City,

310-397-3146; major department stores include Robinson's May, and JC Penny.

- **Glendale Galleria,** South Central Avenue and West Colorado Street, Glendale, 818-240-9481; major department stores include Nordstroms and Macy's.
- **Northridge Fashion Center,** 9301 Tampa Avenue, Northridge, 818-701-7051; features Macy's and Robinson's May.
- **Media City Center,** East Magnolia Boulevard and North San Fernando Boulevard, Burbank, 818-566-8617, is anchored by Macy's, Sears and AMC Theaters.
- **Santa Monica Place,** 395 Santa Monica Place, Santa Monica, 310-394-1049; Robinson's May and Macy's anchor this mall.
- **Sunset Plaza,** 8623 West Sunset Boulevard, West Hollywood, 310-652-2622; is a chic outdoor strip lined with designer clothiers and trendy sidewalk cafes.
- **Topanga Plaza Shopping Center,** 6600 Topanga Canyon Boulevard, Canoga Park, 818-594-8740; featuring Nordstroms and Robinson's May.
- **Two Rodeo,** 9480 Dayton Way, Beverly Hills, 310-247-7040, is a beautiful cobblestone street of upscale stores, anchored by Tiffany's.
- **The Plaza Pasadena,** East Colorado Boulevard and South Los Roble Avenue, Pasadena, 626-449-5667
- **The Promenade Mall,** 6100 Topanga Canyon Boulevard, Woodland Hills, 818-884-7069
- **The Westside Pavillion,** 10800 West Pico Boulevard, West Los Angeles, 310-474-5940; major department stores include Nordstroms and Robinson's May.
- **Valencia Town Center,** McBean Parkway and Magic Mountain Parkway, Santa Clarita, 661- 287-9050, is anchored by Robinson's May and Sears.

DEPARTMENT STORES

The city's biggest department stores typically anchor the malls they're in. Many chains tailor their wares to specific regions, so fashions and selections offered sometimes vary from store to store.

- **Bloomingdales,** a higher-end store with nice selections in clothing, jewelry, and make-up.
- **JC Penny,** affordable chain with your standard department store

selections, good variety in children's clothing.

- **Macy's,** nice department store with big selection of clothing, a respectable household goods and bedding department. A solid, all-around department store that won't break the bank.
- **Nordstroms,** upscale store with a reputation for outstanding, you-gotta-hear-what-they-did-for-me customer service. Clothing, shoes, jewelry, make-up and home decorations too. Pricey, but worth every penny.
- **Robinson's May,** another chain that carries just about anything you'd need for your home, clothing, furniture, household goods, and electronics.

SHOPPING DISTRICTS

For the area's choicest department stores head to, where else, **Beverly Hills**. Along Wilshire Boulevard, west of **Rodeo Drive** is Tiffany's, Neiman-Marcus, Sak's Fifth Avenue, Barney's, and Bloomingdales. Go north on Rodeo Drive and you can check out the likes of Cartier, Bang and Olufsen, and the Giorgio Armani Boutique.

Downtown is *the* place to go when you want to buy directly from the wholesaler, often at a significant discount. The flower, produce, toy, textiles and fabrics, and jewelry districts are clustered here. These are wholesalers, some of whom happen to sell to the public, so don't expect much in the way of presentation: fresh **flowers** are available at Wall and Seventh Street; the **garment** section is centered at East Olympic Boulevard and Los Angeles Street; **produce** dominates along Central Avenue between 8th and 9th streets; **textiles & fabrics** are at Wall and Eighth Street; **toys** can be found along 3rd Street between South San Pedro and Los Angeles streets; and finally, **jewelry** is located on Hill Street between 6th and 7th streets.

Melrose Avenue, between La Brea Avenue and Doheny Drive in Los Angeles is still *the* place to go for funky fashions and food.

Old Town Pasadena is a lovely shopping district where modern stores like Sur La Table, Gap, and Restoration Hardware are housed in well preserved, historical buildings. It is a 20-block area located on Colorado Boulevard, between Pasadena Avenue on the west, and Arroyo Parkway on the east, Walnut Street on the north, and Del Mar on the south. Upscale shopping district **South Lake Avenue** is on Lake Avenue between Colorado and California Boulevards.

Santa Monica's **Third Street Promenade,** permanently closed to cars between Broadway and Wilshire Boulevard, offers three city blocks of shopping and strolling.

DISCOUNT DEPARTMENT STORES

- **99 Cent Only Stores,** food, toiletries, household goods, all for under a dollar, found throughout greater LA.
- **Fed Co,** 800-283-3883, a members-only no-frills discount department store and food market: Los Angeles, 3535 South La Cienega Boulevard, 310-837-4481; Pasadena, 3111 East Colorado Boulevard, 626-449-8620; Van Nuys, 14920 Raymer Street, 818-786-6863
- **Kmart** or **Big K,** the budget chain is refining its image with the Big K moniker and not doing too bad a job at it. Numerous locations throughout the county, check your phone book.
- **Target,** 800-800-8800; www.target.com, all around chain for clothing, household goods, food, and furniture. Numerous locations throughout the county.

BOOKSTORES

Bookstores have become popular places to meet people throughout the country, and Los Angeles is no exception. The big chains that dot the area are **Barnes & Noble**, **Borders** and **Bookstar**. In most of the Barnes & Noble stores, you'll find a Starbucks inside, along with sofas and chairs. Borders has a cafe section and seating areas. All three chains are well organized and stocked with large selections of books and magazines. Check your phone directory for the one near you. Or browse online bookstores like www.amazon.com, www.borders.com or www.barnesandnoble.com.

If you're seeking a non-chain or specialty bookstore, for example, cooking, political science, or mysteries, try the following:

- **A-Z Technical Bookstore,** 1025 North Sycamore Avenue, Los Angeles, 800-903-4567
- **A Different Light Bookstore,** 8853 Santa Monica Boulevard, Los Angeles, 310-854-6601, specializes in gay and lesbian literature.
- **Autobooks,** 3524 West Magnolia, Burbank, 818-845-0707, also features aviation literature.
- **Builders Book Inc., Bookstore,** 8001 Canoga Avenue, Woodland Hills, 818-887-7828

- **Book'Em Mysteries,** 1118 Mission, South Pasadena, 626-799-9600
- **Children's Book World,** 10580 3/4 West Pico Boulevard, West LA, 310-559-BOOK
- **Cook's Library,** 8373 West Third Street, Los Angeles, 323-655-3141
- **Le Cite Des Livres French Books,** 2306 Westwood Boulevard, Los Angeles, 310-475-0658
- **Dutton's Brentwood Books,** 11975 San Vicente Boulevard, Brentwood, 310-476-6263; downtown in the Arco Plaza (5th and Flower), 213-683-1100, and in Burbank, 3806 West Magnolia Boulevard, 818-840-8003
- **The Legal Bookstore,** 316 West Third Street, Los Angeles, 310-777-0404
- **Hennesse & Ingalls Art & Architecture Books,** 1254 Third Street Promenade, Santa Monica, 310-458-9074
- **Medical Tech Book Center,** 8001 Canoga Avenue, Woodland Hills, 818-887-7828
- **Midnight Special Bookstore,** 1318 Third Street Promenade, Santa Monica, 310-393-2923; specializes in political and social science, and world history.
- **The Mysterious Bookshop,** Los Angeles, 8763 Beverly Boulevard, 310-659-2959
- **Oriental Bookstore,** 1713 East Colorado Boulevard, Pasadena, 626-577-2413
- **Russian Books,** 13757 Victory Boulevard, Van Nuys, 818-781-7533
- **Samuel French's Theatre & Film Bookshops,** 7623 Sunset Boulevard, Los Angeles, 323-876-0570; 11963 Ventura Boulevard, Studio City, 818-762-0535
- **Shalom House Jewish Store,** 19740 Ventura Boulevard, Woodland Hills, 818-704-7100
- **Spanish and European Bookstore,** 3102 Wilshire Boulevard, Los Angeles, 213-739-8899
- **Storyopolis Children's Bookstore,** 116 North Robertson Boulevard, Los Angeles, 310-358-2500
- **Traveler's Bookcase,** 8375 West third Street, Los Angeles, 323-655-0575
- **Valley Book & Bible Stores,** 20936 Roscoe Boulevard, Woodland Hills, 818-709-5610; 6502 Van Nuys Boulevard, Van Nuys, 818-782-6101

Used and rare booksellers are numerous here as well, check your Yellow Pages under "Books-Used & Rare" for a complete listing. The most well-known second-hand bookstore in LA is **Duttons Books** in North Hollywood, 5146 Laurel Canyon Boulevard, 818-769-3866. They're famous for their friendly service, esoteric selection, and amazing ability to locate the rarest of books.

HOUSEHOLD SHOPPING

COMPUTERS, ELECTRONICS & APPLIANCES

In addition to the following chains, many department, office supply, and wholesale stores also sell computers and household electronics and appliances.

- **Best Buy,** West LA, 11301 West Pico Boulevard, 310-268-9190; Woodland Hills, 21601 Victory Boulevard, 818-713-1007
- **Circuit City,** www.circuitcity.com: Burbank, 401 North First Street, 818-558-1172; Culver City, 5660 Sepulveda Boulevard, 310-313-6002; Glendale, 200 East Broadway Street, 818-247-0410; Hollywood, 4400 Sunset Boulevard, 213-663-6033; Los Angeles, 1839 La Cienega Boulevard, 310-280-0700; West Los Angeles, 3115 Sepulveda Boulevard, 310-391-3144; Westwood, 1145 Gayle Avenue, 310-208-6885; Valencia, 25610 North The Old Road, 661-260-3751; Van Nuys, 13630 Victory Boulevard, 818-782-3355; Woodland Hills, 6401 Canoga Avenue, 818-888-3233
- **CompUSA,** 761 North San Fernando Boulevard, Burbank, 818-848-8588; 11441 Jefferson Boulevard, Culver City, 310-390-9993; 2150 North Bellflower Boulevard, Long Beach, 562-598-1992
- **Fry's Electronics,** Burbank, 2311 North Hollywood Way, 818-526-8100; Manhattan Beach, 3600 Sepulveda Boulevard, 310-364-FRYS; Woodland Hills, 6100 Canoga Avenue, 818-227-1000
- **The Good Guys,** Glendale, 142 South Brand boulevard, 818-409-1400; Los Angeles, 100 North La Cienega, 310-659-6500, open 24 hours; Marina del Rey, 13450 Maxella Avenue, 310-574-1810; Pasadena, 310 South Lake, 626-577-5300; Santa Clarita, 24840 Pico Canyon Road, 661-222-3100; Studio City, 12050 Ventura Boulevard, 818-754-6250; West LA, 10831 West Pico Boulevard, 310-441-4600

BEDS, BEDDING & BATH

There is a large selection of mattress dealers in LA. If you don't mind buying a mattress sight unseen, try shopping online at www.dialabed.com, or by calling 800-345-2337. If you want to jump on the mattress to test it first, you'll have to walk into one of these stores:

- **Beautyrest Mattress Gallery**, call 800-99-GALLERY, or check www.beautyrestgallery.com for a location near you.
- **Beds Plus,** 7052 Van Nuys Boulevard, Van Nuys, 818-994-9461
- **Discount Mattress Depot,** Northridge, 8974 Tampa Avenue, 818-700-5320; Woodland Hills, 20829 Ventura Boulevard, 818-716-5516
- **The Mattress Store,** West LA, 10545 West Pico Boulevard, 310-441-1997
- **Mattress Central,** Glendale, 111 North Central Avenue, 818-550-9211; Northridge, 8732 Tampa Avenue, 818-772-4330; Valencia, 25660 North The Old Road, 661-255-9988
- **Mattress Discounters,** call 800-BUY-A-BED for a location near you.
- **Ortho Mattress,** Los Angeles, 6205 Wilshire Boulevard, 323-933-9503; Marina Del Rey, 2570 South Lincoln Boulevard, 310-823-0268; North Hollywood, 6321 Laurel Canyon Boulevard, 818-760-4163; West LA, 10672 West Pico Boulevard, 310-839-0274
- **Sit'n Sleep,** 3824 Culver Center, Culver City, 800-319-3192

For one-stop shopping for bedding, towels and other linens, try one of these chains:

- **Bed, Bath & Beyond,** Los Angeles, 11801 West Olympic Boulevard, 310-478-5767, 142 South San Vicente Boulevard, 310-652-1380; Studio City, 1255 Ventura Boulevard, 818-980-0260; Woodland Hills, 19836 Ventura Boulevard, 818-702-9301
- **Linens 'N Things,** Northridge, 19500 Plummer, 818-882-3377; Sherman Oaks, 13730 Riverside Drive, 818-461-0770
- **Strouds,** Encino, 17230 Ventura Boulevard, 818-981-3033; Los Angeles, Strouds Clearance Center, 100 North La Cienega, 310-657-2422; Santa Monica, 3202 Wilshire Boulevard, 310-586-0020; Studio City, 12160 Ventura Boulevard, 818-752-2660

CARPETS & RUGS

- **Carpet Depot,** 13451 Sherman Way, North Hollywood, 800-640-6595, 818-765-3622
- **Carpet Market Outlet,** 5900 Kester Avenue, Van Nuys, 818-989-0940
- **Carpet One Carpet Factory,** 5836 Sepulveda Boulevard, Sherman Oaks, 818-780-4044
- **The Carpet Showcase,** 1430 Lincoln Boulevard, Santa Monica, 310-395-4575
- **Close Out Carpets,** 1446 South Robertson Boulevard, West LA, 310-273-1464
- **Culver Carpet Center,** 4026 South Sepulveda Boulevard, Culver City, 310-391-5286, 323-870-5797
- **IKEA,** 600 North San Fernando Boulevard, Burbank, 818-842-4532
- **Pier 1 Imports,** locations throughout the city.

FURNITURE

In recent years, upscale houseware and furniture stores have sprouted up all over Los Angeles. Serious interior design shoppers may want to check out the Pacific Design Center and neighboring areas in West Hollywood, the interior design mecca of greater Los Angeles. Browse your telephone book or keep your eyes open in the local papers for additional furniture stores. Here are some of the biggies:

- **Cost Plus World Market,** locations throughout the city.
- **Crate & Barrel,** locations throughout the city.
- **Ethan Allen Home Interiors,** locations throughout the city.
- **IKEA,** 600 North San Fernando Boulevard, Burbank, 818-842-4532
- **Pier 1 Imports,** locations throughout the city.
- **Plummers Home and Office Interiors,** North Hollywood, 12240 Sherman Way, 818-765-0401; West LA, 8876 Venice Boulevard, 310-837-0138; Woodland Hills, 21725 Erwin Street, 818-888-9474
- **Restoration Hardware,** locations throughout the city.
- **Target,** locations throughout the city, 800-800-8800; www.target.com
- **Expo Design Center,** Huntington Drive and May Flower Avenue, Monrovia, 626-599-3400
- **Z Gallerie,** locations throughout the city.

LAMPS & LIGHTING

- **IKEA,** 600 North San Fernando Boulevard, Burbank, 818-842-4532
- **Lamps Plus,** www.lampsplus.com, Glendale, 200 South Brand Boulevard, 818-247-3005; Los Angeles, 200 South La Brea Avenue, 323-931-1438; North Hollywood, 12206 Sherman Way, 818-764-2666; West Los Angeles, 2012 Bundy Drive, 310-820-7567
- **Light Bulbs Unlimited,** Los Angeles, 8383 Beverly Boulevard, 323-651-0330; Santa Monica, 2309 Wilshire Boulevard, 310-829-7400; Sherman Oaks, 14446 Ventura Boulevard., 818-501-3492
- **Lightwave Lighting,** Los Angeles, 8211 Melrose Avenue, 323-658-6888; Woodland Hills, 21732 Ventura Boulevard, 818-610-0600

HARDWARE, PAINTS & WALLPAPER, GARDEN CENTERS

- **Armstrong's Garden Centers,** Glendale, 5816 San Fernando Road, 818-243-4227, Santa Monica, 3232 Wilshire Boulevard, 310-829-6766; Sherman Oaks, 12920 Magnolia Boulevard, 323-877-2394, 818-761-1522
- **B&B Hardware,** 12450 Washington Boulevard, Los Angeles, 310-390-9413
- **Burkard Nurseries,** 690 North Orange Grove Boulevard, Pasadena, 626-796-4355
- **Do-It Center,** 3221 West Magnolia Boulevard, Burbank, 818-845-8301
- **HomeBase,** Los Angeles, 4925 West Slauson Avenue, 323-398-1155; North Hollywood, 12727 Sherman Way, 818-503-9082
- **Home Depot,** Glendale, 5040 San Fernando Road; Hollywood, 5600 Sunset Boulevard, Los Angeles, 12975 West Jefferson Boulevard; North Hollywood, 11600 Sherman Way, Santa Clarita, 20642 Golden Triangle Road; Van Nuys, 16810 Roscoe Boulevard; Woodland Hills, 6345 Variel Avenue
- **Marina del Rey Garden Center,** 13198 Mindanao Way, Marina del Rey, 310-823-5956

HOUSEWARES

Most houseware chain stores are located within malls. Refer to the **Shopping District/Mall** section in this chapter for a specific address and phone number.

- **Crate & Barrel,** Topanga Plaza, Century City Mall, and Old Town Pasadena
- **Pottery Barn,** Beverly Center, Century City Mall, Glendale Galleria, Santa Monica Place, Sherman Oaks Fashion Square, and at 6600 Topanga Canyon Boulevard, Woodland Hills
- **Restoration Hardware,** 6600 Topanga Canyon Boulevard, Woodland Hills; 1219 Third Street Promenade, Santa Monica; 127 West Colorado Boulevard, Pasadena; 141 North La Cienega Boulevard, Los Angeles; Sherman Oaks Fashion Square
- **Williams Sonoma,** Glendale Galleria, Glendale; 339 North Beverly Drive, Beverly Hills; The Promenade Mall, and Sherman Oaks Fashion Square

SPORTING GOODS

- **Adventure 16,** 11161 West Pico Boulevard, Los Angeles, 310-473-4574
- **Big 5 Sporting Goods,** Encino, 17019 Ventura Boulevard, 818-905-7213; Los Angeles, 6601 Wilshire Boulevard, 323-651-2909; Santa Monica, 3121 Wilshire Boulevard, 310-453-1747; Studio City, 12033 Ventura Place, 818-769-5526; Woodland Hills, 7000 Topanga Canyon Boulevard, 818-346-3355; Van Nuys, 7250 Van Nuys Boulevard, 818-785-3773
- **Niketown,** 95660 Wilshire Boulevard, Beverly Hills, 310-275-9998
- **Patagonia,** 2936 Main Street, Santa Monica, 310-314-1776
- **Play It Again Sports,** Santa Monica, 1231 Wilshire Boulevard, 310-395-8229; Studio City, 12038 Ventura Boulevard, 818-752-9123
- **Sport Chalet,** Burbank, 201 East Magnolia Boulevard, 818-558-3500; Los Angeles, 100 North La Cienega Boulevard, 310-657-3210
- **Sportmart,** 1919 South Sepulveda Boulevard, Los Angeles, 310-312-9600

SECOND-HAND SHOPPING

A popular and inexpensive way to shop for furniture, clothes and jewelry is in second-hand stores. Merchandise runs the gamut from trendy to tacky to vintage to designer cast-offs from the costume departments of the local film and TV industries. Check your telephone directory under "Clothing-Used" for listings in your area or try one of the following:

- **All American Hero,** 314 Santa Monica Boulevard, Santa Monica, 310-395-4452
- **Couture Exchange,** 12402 Ventura Boulevard, Studio City, 818-752-6040
- **Junk for Joy Halloween and Vintage,** 3314 West Magnolia Boulevard, Burbank, 818-569-4903
- **Out of the Closet Thrift Store,** all purchases made at this thrift store are tax deductible, the money benefits the AIDS Healthcare Foundation: Fairfax District, 360 North Fairfax Avenue, 323-934-1956; Hollywood, 1408 North Vine Street, 323-466-0747; Los Angeles, 4136 Beverly Boulevard, 213-380-8955; North Hollywood, 6241 Laurel Canyon Boulevard, 818-769-0503; Santa Monica, 1908 Lincoln Boulevard, 310-664-9036; West Hollywood, 8224 Santa Monica Boulevard, 310-473-7787; West Los Angeles, 1608 Sawtelle Boulevard, 310-473-7787; Woodland Hills, 21703 Sherman Way, 818-676-0105
- **The Paperbag Princess,** 883 Westbourne Drive, West Hollywood, 310-360-1343
- **Past Perfect,** 12616 Ventura Boulevard, Studio City, 818-760-8872
- **Polkadots & Moonbeams,** 8367 West Third Street, Fairfax District, 323-651-1746
- **Supply Sergeant,** Los Angeles, 6664 Hollywood Boulevard, 323-463-4730; Santa Monica, 1431 Lincoln Boulevard, 310-458-4166; Burbank, 503 North Victory Boulevard, 818-845-9433
- **Screamin' Kings,** 4850 Vineland Avenue, North Hollywood, 818-769-3170

Also, the **Rose Bowl Swap Meet,** held in the Rose Bowl Stadium parking lot, is one of the largest flea markets in the Los Angeles area. It is held on the second Sunday of every month from 9 a.m. to 3 p.m., and there is a charge for admission. Some of the hip Los Angeles furniture retailers shop here, and after some touch-up work on their swap meet purchases, resell them in their stores. Another big swap meet is the **Valley Indoor Swap Meet**, 6701 Variel Avenue, Woodland Hills, 818-884-6430. Another smart source for used goods is *The Recycler*, a newspaper that comes out each Thursday and is available at most convenience stores.

GROCERIES

The major **supermarket** chains that operate here: **Ralphs** (the biggest and most successful chain in Southern California), **Vons** (the oldest chain in Southern California and big-time rival to Ralphs), and the new-comer, **Albertsons**. All three are your everyday neighborhood grocery stores that also offer member discounts (to join just fill out a club card application form at the store). Many Ralphs and Vons stores, always competing to be number-one in California, have been recently remod-eled. There is also **Pavilions Place**, an upscale version of Vons. **Gelson's** and **Bristol Farms** are gourmet market chains with premium prices, but first-rate service. **Trader Joe's** is known for its specialty foods and wine sections at bargain prices. **Cost Plus World Market** is simi-lar to Trader Joe's, but concentrates on imported, packaged foods and wine. **Whole Foods** is an upscale health food grocery chain with a large selection of fresh and prepared foods. Check your phone directory for locations nearest you.

WAREHOUSE STORES

- **Food 4 Less,** a bulk-item grocery store with no-frills presentation, no membership required.
  Hollywood, 5420 West Sunset Boulevard, 323-871-8011
  Los Angeles, 1717 South Western Avenue, 323-731-0164
  South Pasadena, 4910 Huntington Drive, 626-222-2659
  Woodland Hills, 20155 Saticoy, 818-998-8074
  Van Nuys, 16530 Sherman Way, 818-997-0170
- **CostCo,** a members-only warehouse sized store that sells food, clothing, appliances, etc. in bulk.
  Burbank, 10950 Sherman Way, 818-840-8115
  Inglewood, 3560 West Century Boulevard, 310-672-1296
  Northridge, 8810 Tampa Avenue, 818-775-1322
  Norwalk, 12324 Hoxie Avenue, 562-029-0826
  Woodland Hills, 21300 Roscoe Boulevard, 818-884-8982
  Van Nuys, 6100 North Sepulveda Boulevard, 818-989-5256
- **Smart and Final,** a warehouse sized store that sells groceries and office products in bulk, no membership required.
  Burbank, 1320 West Magnolia Boulevard, 818-845-4544
  Encino, 16847 Ventura Boulevard, 818-789-0242
  Glendale, 210 North Verdugo Road, 818-243-4239

Hollywood, 939 North Western Avenue, 323-466-9289
Los Angeles, 12210 Santa Monica Boulevard, 310-207-8688
Los Angeles, 7720 Melrose Avenue, 323-655-2211
North Hollywood, 6601 Laurel Canyon Boulevard, 818-769-2292
Pasadena, 1382 Locust Street, 626-793-2195
West Hollywood, 1041 Fuller Avenue, 323-876-0421
West LA, 12210 Santa Monica Boulevard, 310-207-8688
Woodland Hills, 19718 Sherman Way, 818-996-1331
Van Nuys, 7817 Van Nuys Boulevard, 818-780-7222
Venice, 604 Lincoln Boulevard, 310-392-4954

HEALTH FOOD STORES

Here are some local foodstuff outlets to keep you in "the zone," on your macrobiotic diet, or other health-conscious regime:

- **Erewhon Natural Food Market,** 7660 Beverly Boulevard, Los Angeles, 323-937-0777; well stocked and has a busy juice bar/deli.
- **Nowhere Natural Foods Market & Deli,** 8001 Beverly Boulevard, Los Angeles, 323-658-6506; an organic grocery that features a great selection of vitamins.
- **Whole Foods,** top quality, selection and presentation. Multiple locations, call 888-746-7936 for a location near you.
- **Wild Oats,** multiple locations; well stocked, picture-perfect presentation.
  Pasadena, 603 South Lake Avenue, 626-792-1778
  Santa Monica, 1425 Montana Avenue, 310-576-4707
  West Hollywood, 8611 Santa Monica Boulevard, 310-854 6927
  West LA, 3476 Centinela Avenue, 310-545-1300
- **Windward Farms,** 105 Windward Avenue, Venice, 310-392-3566; countrified organic market.

COMMUNITY GARDENS

So you live in an apartment, but yearn to grow your own fruits, vegetables, or flowers? There are a few small plots of land that have been set aside for urban farmers to till. Contact the **Los Angeles Recreation Services and Farmer's Market Division,** 323-848-6502, about obtaining gardening space at one of the following community gardens: 417 Norwich Avenue; 1351 Havenhurst Drive; 1257 North Detroit Street.

FARMER'S MARKETS

There are numerous popular farmers' markets throughout the city, including the famous, permanent Farmer's Market at Third and Fairfax, which offers the adventurous shopper gorgeous seasonal produce stalls, butchers, and tourist-oriented shops. Below are some of the many neighborhood outdoor farmer's markets that sell fruits, eggs, fish, vegetables, honey, nuts, cut flowers, plants, and more—usually for less than you would find at supermarkets. Many stalls feature organically grown produce, but be sure to ask, or look for the certified organic sign, if that's important to you.

- **Beverly Hills,** North Canon Drive between Clifton and Dayton Ways, Sundays, 9 a.m. to 1 p.m., 310-285-1048
- **Brentwood,** 11600 block of Chayote Street, between Barrington Place and Sunset Boulevard, Wednesdays, 3:30 to 7 p.m. during daylight saving time, 3:30 to 6 p.m. during standard time.
- **Burbank,** Orange Grove Avenue and 3rd Street, Fridays, 8 a.m. to 12:30 p.m.
- **Calabasas,** 23504 Calabasas Road at El Canon Avenue, Saturdays, 8 a.m. to 1 p.m.
- **Culver City,** Media Park, Culver Boulevard and Canfield Avenue, Tuesdays, 3 to 7 p.m., 310-253-5775
- **El Segundo,** Main Street between Grand and Holly avenues, Thursdays, 3 to 7 p.m.
- **Encino,** 17400 Victory Boulevard between Balboa Boulevard and White Oak Avenue, Sundays, 8 a.m. to 1 p.m.
- **Glendale,** Brand Boulevard between Broadway and Wilson Avenue, Thursdays, 9:30 a.m. to 1 p.m.
- **Hollywood,** Ivar Avenue between Sunset and Hollywood boulevards, Sundays, 8:30 a.m. to 1 p.m., 323-463-3171
- **Los Angeles,** St. Agnes Church, 1432 West Adams Boulevard, Wednesdays, June through August, 1 to 6 p.m.; September through May, 2 to 6 p.m.; Seventh Market Place, 735 South Figueroa Street, Thursdays, noon to 4 p.m.
- **Norwalk,** Alondra Boulevard, west of Pioneer Boulevard, Tuesdays, 9 a.m. to 1 p.m.
- **Pasadena,** Villa Park, 363 East Villa Street, at Garfield Avenue, Tuesdays, 9 a.m. to 1 p.m.; Victory Park, 2800 block of North Sierra Madre Boulevard, between Paloma and Washington Avenues, Saturdays, 8:30 a.m. to 1 p.m.

- **Santa Clarita,** College of the Canyons lot 8, Valencia Boulevard and Rockwell Canyon Road, Sundays, 8:30 a.m. to noon.
- **Santa Monica,** Arizona Avenue between 2nd and 3rd streets, Wednesdays, 9 a.m. to 2 p.m., Saturdays, 8:30 a.m. to 1 p.m.; Pico Boulevard at Cloverfield Avenue, Saturdays, 8 a.m. to 1 p.m.; 2640 Main Street at Ocean Park Boulevard, Sundays, 9:30 a.m. to 1 p.m.; California Heritage Museum Farmers Market, 2612 Main Street, Sundays, 10:00 a.m. to 4:00 p.m., 310-392-8537
- **Studio City,** Ventura Place between Ventura and Laurel Canyon Boulevards, Sundays, 8 a.m. to 1 p.m.
- **South Pasadena,** Meridian Avenue at Mission Street, Thursdays, 4 to 8 p.m.
- **Venice,** Venice Boulevard at Venice Way, Fridays, 7 to 11 a.m.
- **West Hollywood,** Plummer Park, 7377 Santa Monica Boulevard, Mondays, 9 a.m. to 2 p.m.
- **Westwood,** Weyburn Avenue at Westwood Boulevard, Thursdays, 2 to 7 p.m.

ETHNIC FOOD

As one of the biggest melting pots in the nation, LA's large Middle-Eastern, Hispanic, Jewish, and Asian populations mean plenty of stores to go to if you need to stock up on ghee, kreplach, or kimchi. Many of the markets listed below are located within their respective ethnic communities.

LA's Chinatown has experienced a decline lately. Much of its thunder has been stolen by the community of Monterey Park, nicknamed "Little Hong Kong" because of its huge Chinese population, many recently immigrated from Hong Kong. **Chinese** groceries, restaurants and goods can be found in this bustling neighborhood. Or try **99 Ranch Market,** 800-600-TAWA, www.99ranch.com, Monterey Park, 771 West Garvey Avenue, 626-458-3399; Van Nuys, 6450 North Sepulveda Boulevard, 818-988-7899.

For sturdy **English** or **German** fare, try: **Tudor House,** 1403-1409 Second Street, Santa Monica, 310-451-4107 or **Van Nuys German Deli,** 16155 Roscoe Boulevard, Van Nuys, 818-892-2212 (respectively).

Those in need of a matzo should head down to the Fairfax District on North Fairfax Avenue between Melrose Avenue and Beverly Boulevard for mom and pop stores that carry kosher food and other supplies. **Jewish** delis like **Jerry's Deli** are dotted throughout LA, so you'll never be far from some good matzo ball soup.

Many know about Koreatown in Los Angeles (Western Avenue between Olympic and Beverly Boulevard), but there is also a large **Korean** population in Northridge, just look for the Korean script on signage and you'll know you're there, or try **HK Korean Supermarket,** Los Angeles, 124 North Western Avenue, 213-469-8934; Van Nuys, 17634 Sherman Way, 818-708-7396; **Koreatown Plaza Market,** 928 South Western Avenue, Koreatown, 213-385-1100.

Meticulously clean Little Tokyo (between First, 4th, San Pedro and Alameda streets) really does bring a little bit of **Japan** into LA. The **Yaohan Market,** 333 South Alameda Street, Little Tokyo, 213-687-6699 can supply all of your ingredients for the perfect California roll.

Need some spice in your life—say a bite of vindaloo? Try the **Indian Bharat Bazaar,** 11510 West Washington Boulevard, Culver City, 310-398-6766 or **India Sweets and Spices,** Culver City, 9409 Venice Boulevard, 310-837-5286; Woodland Hills, 22011 Sherman Way, 818-887-0868.

For pasta aficionados looking for the perfect **Italian** ingredients, try **Bay Cities Importing Co.,** 1517 Lincoln Boulevard, Santa Monica, 310-395-8279.

Though many parts of LA show a strong **Mexican** influence, Boyle Heights (along First Street and Cesar E. Chavez Avenue) is largely Mexican. The best place for a taste of Mexico City is said to be **El Gallo Giro,** a combination bakery, meat market, and cake shop in one: East LA, 5686 East Whittier Boulevard, 213-726-1246; El Monte, 11912 Valley Boulevard, 626-575-1244; Huntington Park, 7148 Pacific Avenue, 213-585-4433. Another popular place for Mexican foodstuffs is at the **Grand Central Market,** 317 South Broadway, downtown, 213-624-2378.

A mix of Persian, Israeli, and Greek populations reside along the western border of Los Angeles. In addition, the city of Glendale has a large **Middle-Eastern** population; drive through the neighborhood to browse the restaurants and bakeries. If you're in Pasadena, check out Allen and Washington boulevards. Or try these favorites: **Elat Market,** 8730 West Pico Boulevard, Los Angeles, 310-659-7070; **Good Food,** 1864 East Washington Boulevard, Pasadena, 626-79-5367.

Borscht anyone? Russian fare can be found at: **Royal Gourmet,** 8151 Santa Monica Boulevard, West Hollywood, 213-650-5001; **Tatiana,** 8205 Santa Monica Boulevard, West Hollywood, 213-656-7500.

A S HOME TO THE ENTERTAINMENT INDUSTRY, AS WELL AS TO thousands of artists, musicians and writers, there seems to be an infinite number of things to do in LA to occupy your leisure time. Whatever your interests, from music to theater to visual art, Los Angeles has not only a wide variety of cultural offerings, but some of the finest in the world as well.

If you want to find out what's going on this week or this month, check out the following publications:

- **LA Weekly** is the largest and most well-read free weekly newspaper in Los Angeles. Editorial coverage includes social and political issues, as well as extensive film, art, music and restaurant critiques. Each week, the "Calendar" section lists some fifty pages of events—everything from coffeehouse folk performances to Latin dance clubs to political symposiums. (And don't forget the personal ads, they offer entertainment unto themselves!)

- **Entertainment Today** is a free weekly offering entertainment listings, it comes out every Friday.

- **New Times** is another entertainment listings option.

- **Los Angeles Times** publishes a daily "Calendar" section that covers a variety of cultural and entertainment options throughout LA, check on Thursdays for a list of upcoming weekend events, and on Sundays for a detailed pull-out version.

- **Los Angeles,** a monthly city magazine; check the back section for entertainment listings.

- **Buzz,** the challenger to *Los Angeles*, also publishes an entertainment guide.

- The **LA Cultural Affairs Department**, 213-485-4581, is another resource for events. For 24-hour, seven-days-a-week access to the latest information about music, art, dance, theater, special events, and festivals going on throughout Los Angeles or check out www.theater-la.org, www.artscenecal.com or www.lacountyarts.org.

Tickets to many events can be purchased through **Ticketmaster,** 213-365-3500, www.ticketmaster.com. A smaller ticket venue, **Tickets LA**, 323-655-8587, sells seats to local concerts, sporting events, theater, benefits, etc. Half-price theater tickets are available to Tickets LA club members ($25 annual fee).

FOOD

In Philly it's cheesesteaks, Chicago, deep-dish pizza—ask an Angeleno about Los Angeles' equivalent fast food fame and they'll rave to you about **LA chili-cheeseburgers.** Perhaps it is the exquisite meeting of the Latino-origined chili with the red, white and blue standard hamburger; whatever the reason, the chili-cheeseburgers here are justifiably famous, and everyone swears by their favorite burger joint. Dine around for your favorite, just don't forget the Tums!

- **The Apple Pan,** 10801 Pico Boulevard, Westwood, 310-475-3585. This Westwood institution is known for its burgers and for its pies.
- **Carney's,** 12601 Ventura Boulevard, Studio City, 818-761-8300; housed in an old train car, Carney's aficionados swear by the chili-burgers and chili-fries.
- **Fatburger,** various locations citywide. These spots stay open late, perfect for those midnight cravings.
- **In-N-Out Burger,** various locations citywide. For the one nearest you, call 800-786-1000.
- **Marty's Hamburger Stand,** 10558 West Pico Boulevard, West Los Angeles, 310-836-6944; this is the original Marty's.
- **Marty's Hamburger Stand,** 1255 La Cienega Boulevard, Los Angeles, 310-652-8047; the brave here go for "the combo," a chili-cheeseburger with a sliced hot-dog on top.
- **Pink's,** 709 North La Brea Boulevard, Los Angeles 213-931-4223; a favorite late night chili-dog stop, open 'till 2 a.m. during the week and 3 a.m. on weekends.
- **Tail o' the Pup,** 329 North San Vicente, West Hollywood, 310-652-4517; architecturally famous—the stand is in the shape of a hot-dog.
- **Tito's Tacos,** 11222 Washington Place, Culver City, 310-391-5780; don't be daunted by the line out front, it moves fast.

- **Tommy's**, various locations citywide. A popular burger joint with imitators all over the city.

MUSIC

For a complete listing of the week's musical offerings, check out the *LA Weekly*, which offers the most comprehensive guide to the vast Los Angeles music scene. What follows is a glimpse of what's available musically.

CLASSICAL

Led by Esa-Pekka Salonen and recognized as one of the best orchestras in the world, the **Los Angeles Philharmonic Orchestra**, 213-972-7300, www.laphil.org, presents a variety of concerts, recitals, and special programs at the Dorothy Chandler Pavilion in The Music Center and at the Hollywood Bowl. For information call **The Music Center**, 135 North Grand Avenue, downtown, 213-202-2200 or 213-972-7211.

The **Beverly Hills Symphony,** in existence since 1993 and led by conductor Bogidar Avramov, can be reached at 310-276-8385. Their summer series is held outdoors at Greystone Park on the grounds of the historic mansion there; the winter series is held at various civic sites in Beverly Hills. The 50-year-old **Santa Monica Symphony Orchestra,** conducted by Allen Robert Gross, can be reached at 310-996-3260. Other orchestral choices include the **Pasadena Symphony**, 626-793-7172, www.pasadenasymphony.org, **Glendale Symphony,** 818-500-8720, **Burbank Symphony,** 818-846-5981, **Brentwood-Westwood Symphony,** 310-450-2407, **Marina Del Rey-Westchester Symphony,** 310-837-5757, **Symphony in the Glen,** 800-440-4536 (summers only), and the **Hollywood Bowl Orchestra,** 323-850-2000 (summers only).

CHORUSES

- **Angeles Chorale**, 818-888-6293, as large as the LA Master Chorale, but entirely composed of volunteer community members, the chorus performs at Royce Hall on UCLA campus. Their conductor, Donald Neuen, is also chair of Chorale Music at UCLA.
- **Gay Men's Chorus of Los Angeles**, 800-MEN-SING, directed by Jon Bailey, tickets for this popular and talented group may be purchased through Telecharge at 800-233-3123. They perform primarily in the Alex Theater in Glendale.

- **Los Angeles Master Chorale,** 213-972-7282; this 120-voice professional symphonic chorus, conducted by Paul Salamunovich, performs its subscription series at the Dorothy Chandler Pavilion at The Music Center.
- **Los Angeles Children's Chorus,** 626-793-4231; most popular during the Christmas season.

OPERA

The world-class **Los Angeles Opera** performs from September through June in The Music Center in the Dorothy Chandler Pavilion, 135 North Grand Avenue, downtown, 213-972-7211. Tickets may be purchased in person at The Music Center box office, or by calling Ticketmaster, 213-480-3232. And let's not forget the **Santa Monica Civic Light Opera** at 310-458-5939.

COFFEEHOUSE PERFORMANCES

This relaxing, semi-Bohemian alternative to clubs and restaurants offers afficionados food, music, socializing and, of course, coffee and tea. Here are a few local coffeehouses that offer music and other performances on a regular basis, as well an alternative to the omni-present Starbucks.

- **Anastasia's Asylum,** 1028 Wilshire Boulevard, Santa Monica, 310-394-7113
- **Cobalt Cafe,** 22047 Sherman Way, Woodland Hills, 818-348-3789
- **Cow's End,** 34 Washington Boulevard, Venice, 310-574-1080
- **Highland Grounds,** 742 North Highland Avenue, Hollywood, 323-466-1507
- **Insomnia,** 7286 Beverly Boulevard, Fairfax District, 213-931-4943
- **Kings Road Cafe,** 8361 Beverly Boulevard, Fairfax District, 323-655-9044
- **Lulu's Beehive,** 13203 Ventura Boulevard, Studio City, 818-986-2233
- **Novel Cafe,** 212 Pier Avenue, Santa Monica, 310-396-8566
- **Opus,** 38 East Colorado Boulevard, Pasadena, 626-685-2800
- **Tsunami Coffeehouse,** 4019 Sunset Boulevard, Silverlake, 213-661-7771
- **Un-urban Coffeehouse,** 3301 Pico Boulevard, Santa Monica, 310-315-0056

CONCERT FACILITIES

Tickets can be obtained by standing in line at the venue itself, or through Ticketmaster, 213-365-3500, www.ticketmaster.com.

- **Great Western Forum,** 3900 West Manchester Boulevard, Inglewood, 310-419-3100
- **Greek Theater,** 2700 North Vermont Avenue, Los Feliz, 323-665-1927
- **Hollywood Bowl,** 2301 North Highland Avenue, Hollywood, 323-850-2000
- **John Anson Ford Amphitheatre,** 2580 East Cahuenga Boulevard, Los Angeles, 323-461-3673
- **Los Angeles Sports Arena,** 3939 South Figueroa Street, downtown, 213-748-6136
- **Shrine Auditorium,** 665 West Jefferson Boulevard, downtown, 213-749-5123
- **Staples Center,** 1111 South Figueroa Street, downtown, 877-5-ACT-NOW
- **UCLA's Royce Hall,** 405 Hilgard Avenue, Westwood, 310-825-4401
- **Universal Amphitheatre,** 100 Universal City Plaza, Universal City, 818-622-4440
- **Wiltern Theatre,** 3790 Wilshire Boulevard, Los Angeles, 213-380-5005

NIGHT CLUBS

There are many, many, many nightclubs in LA. Cover charge varies by venue and day. Here is a sampling of the most well known, refer to other music genres in this chapter for more choices, or check out the *LA Weekly* for the complete guide:

- **House Of Blues,** 8430 Sunset Boulevard, West Hollywood, 323-848-5100; the dance floor is close enough to the stage that your favorite blues singer might even climb down to boogie with you. Excellent sight lines and sound system for live bands despite it being a restaurant too.
- **Key Club,** 9039 Sunset Boulevard, West Hollywood, 310-274-5800; two-level showcase featuring a variety of acts. Three full bars

feature a "tequila library."

• **Mayan Theatre,** 1038 South Hill Street, Los Angeles, 213-746-4674; normally an LA nightclub, its cool, gothic building makes it irresistible as a concert venue.

JAZZ & R&B

• **Atlas Bar & Grill,** 3760 Wilshire Boulevard, Los Angeles, 213-380-8400; this jazz club/restaurant is located inside the landmark Wiltern Theater.

• **Babe & Ricky's Inn,** 5259 South Central Avenue, Los Angeles, 213-235-4866; this is LA's longest running blues club, located on Central Avenue, which in the 1950s was the heart of the city's African American music community.

• **The Baked Potato,** 3787 Cahuenga Boulevard, North Hollywood, 818-980-1615; a small, well-known jazz spot that serves 38 kinds of baked potatoes. Cover charge: $5-$8.

• **The Baked Potato,** 26 East Colorado Boulevard, Pasadena, 626-564-1122; the second location.

• **B.B. King's Blues Club,** 1000 Universal Center Drive, Universal City, 818-622-5464; sister to the flagship club in Memphis, this large dinner club features all kinds of live blues performances.

• **Catalina Bar & Grill,** 1640 North Cahuenga Boulevard, Los Angeles, 323-466-2210; an upscale jazz supper club, often with big-name acts on the bill.

• **Harvelle's,** 1432 Fourth Street, Santa Monica, 310-395-1676; funky, small blues spot that gets very crowded.

• **House of Blues,** 430 Sunset Boulevard, West Hollywood, 323-848-5100; the restaurant's second floor overlooks the homey club below.

• **Jazz Bakery,** 3233 Helms Avenue, Culver City, 310-271-9039; a popular place to hear local and touring jazz acts.

• **St. Mark's,** 23 Winward Avenue, Venice, 310-452-2222; this two-story dinner and music venue is situated just up the street from the Venice Boardwalk.

LATIN, BRAZILIAN & SPANISH CLUBS

• **El Floridita,** 1253 Vine Street, Hollywood, 323-871-8612, offers Cuban music and food.

• **Cha, Cha, Cha,** 17499 Ventura Boulevard, Encino, 818-789-3600; Caribbean restaurant with a Latin beat.

- **Grand Avenue,** 1024 South Grand Avenue, downtown, 213-747-0999; for all kinds of Latin dance sounds.
- **La Masia,** 9077 Santa Monica Boulevard, West Hollywood, 310-273-7066, a supper club featuring the cuisine of Northeastern Spain, plus live salsa and merengue music.
- **Zabumba,** 10717 Venice Boulevard, West Los Angeles, 310-841-6525; for Brazilian food, music, and fun.

ALTERNATIVE, ROCK, HIP-HOP, & POP

- **Al's Bar,** 305 South Newitt Street, downtown, 213-625-9703; a gritty, trendy downtown standard.
- **Alligator Lounge,** 3321 Pico Boulevard, Santa Monica, 310-449-1844; this westside club is a popular place with the alternative music scene.
- **Coconut Teaszer,** 8121 Sunset Boulevard, Hollywood, 323-654-4773; several bands play nightly.
- **14 Below,** 1348 14th Street, Santa Monica, 310-451-5040; live music and dancing every night, plus pool, darts, and lots of beer on tap.
- **Molly Malone's Irish Pub,** 575 South Fairfax Avenue, Fairfax District, 323-935-1577; for Irish (and other) rock, folk, and R & B.
- **The Palace,** 1735 North Vine Street, Hollywood, 323-462-3000; a legendary club with a dance floor, balcony seating, and a patio.
- **Roxy Theatre,** 9009 Sunset Boulevard, West Hollywood, 310-276-2222; this venue often serves as a showcase for the music industry's newest signs. Cover charge: $8 - $15.
- **The Troubadour,** 9081 Santa Monica Boulevard, West Hollywood, 310-276-6168; a tried and true venue for live nightly live performances.
- **The Viper Room,** 8852 Sunset Boulevard, West Hollywood, 310-358-1880; this is the dark, smoky place now notorious as the site of River Phoenix's overdose.
- **Whiskey-a-Go-Go,** 8901 Sunset Boulevard, West Hollywood, 310-652-4202; for years a popular rock-and-roll club, the Whiskey now features mostly heavy metal.

ACOUSTIC PERFORMANCES

- **Genghis Cohen,** 740 North Fairfax Avenue, Fairfax District, 323-653-0640; this place is half Chinese restaurant, half music den.
- **Luna Park,** 665 Robertson Boulevard, West Hollywood, 310-652-

0611; this restaurant/music hang-out plays host to a variety of acts, from folk to Brazilian pop.

- **McCabe's Guitar Shop,** 3101 Pico Boulevard, Santa Monica, 310-828-4497; yes it's a guitar store, but there's a back room that features fine acoustic performances.

COUNTRY

- **The Cowboy Palace Saloon,** 21635 Devonshire Street, Chatsworth, 818-341-0166; live country music and dancing seven nights a week.
- **Culver Saloon,** 11513 Washington Boulevard, Culver City, 310-391-1519; a country nightclub featuring local acts.
- **Country Star,** 1000 Universal Center Drive, Universal City, 818-762-3939, is a Valley country restaurant and club.

REGGAE

Unfortunately, LA's only full-time reggae venue, Kingston 12, is no longer in operation. Other clubs offer reggae on selected nights including: **Domenico's/Billy's Dugout,** 82 North Fair Oaks Avenue, Pasadena, 626-449-1948/1736; on Friday nights try the **Seaport Marina Hotel,** 6400 East Pacific Coast Highway, Long Beach, 562-493-9059; the **Reggae Lounge** presents live music every Wednesday evening at **St. Mark's,** 23 Windward Avenue, Venice, 310-452-2222; and **The West End,** 1305 Fifth Street, Santa Monica, 310-394-4647, has live reggae every Wednesday night.

FREE CONCERTS

In addition to all of the above, there are often free concerts throughout the city, especially during the summer months. The city of Santa Monica sponsors the **Twilight Dance Series** on Thursday nights from 7:30 to 9:30 p.m., located at the Santa Monica Pier. Featured musicians include jazz, rock, blues, salsa, gospel, and international artists. For more information, call 310-458-8900. The LA Cultural Affairs Department sponsors **Sundays at Four,** a free chamber music series during the spring in the Bing Theater, 5905 Wilshire Boulevard, 213-485-6873 or 213-485-9572. And, the **Los Angeles County Museum of Art** features a variety of free concerts, including live jazz in the museum's outdoor plaza every Friday night from 5:30 to 8:30 p.m., chamber music concerts in a museum auditorium on Sunday afternoons at 4:00 p.m., and big band concerts on selected Sunday afternoons throughout the summer. For more information, call 323-857-6000.

Local colleges and universities offer many cultural and educational opportunities, from extension classes to concerts to lecture series. See **Child Care and Education** for a listing of some of the institutions of higher learning in the Los Angeles area.

DANCE

- **Golden West Ballet Theater,** 310-202-7005
- **Joffrey Ballet,** 213-487-8677
- **Los Angeles Classical Ballet,** 310-427-5206
- **Los Angeles Contemporary Dance Theater,** 213-932-8500
- **Los Angeles Modern Dance and Ballet,** 213-655-6812
- **Lula Washington Dance Theatre,** 323-936-6591
- **Pasadena Civic Ballet,** 626-792-0873
- **Pasadena Dance Theatre Conservatory of Performing Arts,** 626-683-3459
- **West Coast Classical Ballet,** 310-477-6414

THEATER

There are dozens of fine productions going on in Los Angeles each week. Check one of the weekly newspapers (listed at the beginning of this chapter) for a full listing. Below are some of the larger and/or better-known theaters in Los Angeles.

- **Beverly Hills Playhouse,** 254 South Robertson, Beverly Hills, 310-855-1556
- **Canon Theatre,** 205 North Canon Drive, Beverly Hills, 310-859-2830
- **Doolittle Theatre,** 1615 North Vine Street, Hollywood, 323-972-7372
- **Glendale Central Theatre,** 324 North Orange Street, Glendale, 818-244-8481
- **Will Geer Theatricum Botanicum,** 1419 North Topanga Canyon Boulevard, Topanga Canyon, 310-455-3723; features Shakespeare and more, in a rustic, outdoor amphitheater.
- **Geffen Playhouse,** 10886 Le Conte Avenue, Westwood, 310-208-5454; formerly the Westwood Playhouse, renamed after receiving a generous donation from entertainment mogul David Geffen.

- **The Music Center** (Dorothy Chandler Pavilion, Mark Taper Forum, and Ahmanson Theatre) 135 North Grand Avenue, downtown, 213-972-7211 or 213-628-2772
- **Odyssey Theatre Ensemble,** 2055 South Sepulveda Boulevard, West Los Angeles, 310-477-2055
- **Pantages Theatre,** 6233 Hollywood Boulevard, Hollywood, 323-468-1700
- **The Pasadena Playhouse,** 39 South El Molino Avenue, Pasadena, 800-233-3123
- **Santa Monica Playhouse,** 1211 4th Street, 310-394-9779
- **Shubert Theatre,** 2020 Avenue of the Stars, Century City, 800-447-7400
- **Tiffany Theatres,** 8532 Sunset Boulevard, West Hollywood, 310-289-2999

COMMUNITY THEATER

With so many actors in LA, there seem to be community theaters hidden in buildings throughout Los Angeles. Many of them are clustered, where else, in Hollywood. Browse through one of the weekly newspapers for a more complete list, and make sure you call first—the founding members may have all gotten jobs on daytime television and the theater may be no more.

- **Actors' Gang El Centro,** 6201 Santa Monica Boulevard, Hollywood, 323-655-TKTS
- **Celebration Theater,** 7051 Santa Monica Boulevard, Hollywood, 310-289-2999
- **Hollywood Court Theater** in the Hollywood Methodist Church, 6817 Franklin Avenue, Hollywood, 323-993-8505
- **Jewel Box Theater,** 1951 Cahuenga Boulevard, Hollywood, 323-469-4343
- **Theater Forty,** 241 Moreno Drive (on the Beverly Hills High School campus), Beverly Hills; 323-936-5842
- **Theater of Hope,** 11050 Magnolia Boulevard, North Hollywood, 818-766-9702
- **Theater of NOTE,** 1517 Cahuenga Boulevard, Hollywood, 323-856-8611

COMEDY

Famous comedians often show up at various clubs around LA to try out new material, so you never know when you might be in for a special treat. There are several popular comedy clubs in and around Los Angeles, including:

- **Acme Comedy Theater,** 135 North La Brea Boulevard, Los Angeles, 323-655-TKTS
- **Comedy Store,** 8433 Sunset Boulevard, West Hollywood, 323-656-6225
- **Comedy Store West,** 1000 1/2 Gayley Avenue, Westwood, 310-208-0623
- **Conga Room,** 5364 Wilshire Boulevard, Los Angeles, 323-938-1696
- **Groundlings Theatre,** 7307 Melrose Avenue, Los Angeles, 323-934-9700; this improvisational comedy troupe was the training ground for several "Saturday Night Live" veterans, such as Phil Hartman and Julia Sweeney.
- **Ice House,** 24 North Mentor Avenue, Pasadena, 626-577-1894
- **Igby's,** 11637 West Pico Boulevard, West Los Angeles, 310-477-3553
- **The Improv,** 8162 Melrose Avenue, Los Angeles, 323-651-2583
- **Improv Olympic,** 6468 Santa Monica Boulevard, Hollywood, 323-694-2935
- **LA Connection Comedy Theatre,** 13442 Ventura Boulevard, Sherman Oaks, 818-784-1868
- **Laugh Factory,** 8001 Sunset Boulevard, Hollywood, 323-656-8860
- **MICE,** West Hollywood Playhouse, 666 1/2 North Robertson Boulevard, West Hollywood, 323-656-1591
- **Upfront Comedy Club,** 123 Broadway, Santa Monica, 310-319-3477; this club was formed by some former members of "Second City."

MOVIE THEATERS

As one might expect, movies are popular and important in Los Angeles and because of the film industry, most films open here and in New York ahead of the rest of the country. You may be approached in front of theaters to attend market survey screenings, where you can watch a free movie in exchange for filling out a questionnaire at the end of the show.

While the large multi-screen theaters are everywhere (the biggies are AMC, Mann, Pacific, General, and Edwards; check the telephone directory or newspaper for the one nearest you), here are a few **alternative theaters** that feature foreign, classic, budget and/or art films.

- **Aero,** 1328 Montana Avenue, Santa Monica, 310-395-4990; six bucks (cheap here) will get you a movie that has been out for a few months and free popcorn.
- **American Cinematheque,** 6712 Hollywood Boulevard, Hollywood, 323-461-2020, screens alternative, classic, foreign and art house movies that generally can't be seen anywhere else.
- **Silent Movie,** 611 North Fairfax, Fairfax District, 323-655-2520; features only "pre-talkies," accompanied by a live band.
- **Laemmle Theatres**
  Downtown: Figueroa at Third Street, 213-617-0268; Beverly Hills: Music Hall, 9036 Wilshire Boulevard, 310-274-6869; Encino: Town Center 5, 17200 Ventura Boulevard, 818-981-9811; Pasadena: Playhouse, 667 East Colorado Boulevard, 626-844-6500; Colorado, 2588 East Colorado Boulevard, 626-796-9704; Santa Monica: Monica, 1332 2nd Street, 310-394-9741; West Hollywood: Sunset 5, 8000 Sunset Boulevard, 323-848-3500; West Los Angeles: Royal, 11523 Santa Monica Boulevard, 310-477-5581
- **Landmark Theaters**
  Beverly Hills: Cecchi Gori Fine Arts, 8556 Wilshire Boulevard, 310-652-1330; Santa Monica: NuWilshire, 1314 Wilshire Boulevard, 310-394-8099; South Pasadena: Rialto, 1023 South Fair Oaks, 626-799-9567; West Los Angeles: Nuart, 11272 Santa Monica Boulevard, 310-478-6379; Royal, 11523 Santa Monica Boulevard, 310-477-5581; Westside Pavillion, 10800 Pico Boulevard, 310-475-0202

TELEVISION TAPINGS

Live-audience TV shows are filmed during the week, rarely on weekends. Watching a sit-com taping is a guaranteed way to see a celebrity in the flesh, and mementos from shows, such as T-shirts and autographed scripts, are frequently given away to audience members. Be prepared to devote several hours to the taping and be ready to clap on demand. If you would like to be an audience member at a live TV taping, write to the Los Angeles Convention and Visitors Bureau, 633 West 5th Street #6000, Los Angeles, CA 90071 and enclose a self-addressed, stamped envelope. (Or you can contact them at 213-624-7300 with more specific questions). Write to them well ahead of time, especially if you would like to see a popular show. They tend to be booked months in advance.

A monthly calendar of television tapings is available when you send a self-addressed, stamped envelope to Audiences Unlimited, 100 Universal City Plaza, Building 153, Universal City, 91608. For a weekly listing, call 818-506-0067. A similar service is available through Audience Associates, 213-653-4105. Or, contact the network studio that carries your favorite live-taped TV show directly: CBS, 213-852-2624, NBC, 818-840-3537, Paramount Pictures, 323-956-5575. Tickets are free, but more tickets than seats are always issued, so arrive early.

MUSEUMS

If it can be exhibited, it's on display somewhere in the LA area. Many museums offer free admission once a month, contact the museum for the specific day. If you're up for an intensive day of exhibit-hopping you might want to head for what is known as "Museum Row," along Wilshire Boulevard running east from Fairfax. In these few blocks you'll find the Los Angeles County Museum of Art, Craft and Folk Art Museum, Petersen Automotive Museum, Museum of Miniatures, and the Page Museum at the La Brea Tarpits. It could make for quite an interesting outing!

- **Craft and Folk Art Museum,** 5814 Wilshire Boulevard, Fairfax District, 323-937-4230; international and American folk art are featured in the museum's new digs. Admission is $4, $2 for students and seniors, and free for children under twelve.
- **Geffen Contemporary,** 152 North Central Avenue, downtown, 213-626-6222, formerly known as the Temporary Contemporary, it began as a temporary space while MOCA was being built, but continues now as an extra exhibit space for MOCA events.
- **Huntington Library and Gardens,** 1151 Oxford Road, Pasadena, 626-405-2141; the Huntington features an extensive European art collection, a scholarly library, plus notable botanical gardens. Admission is $7.50 for adults, $6 for seniors, and $4 for children over twelve. Free admission the first Thursday of every month.
- **J. Paul Getty Center,** 1200 Getty Center Drive, Brentwood, 310-440-7300, www.gety.edu; this $1 billion, 110-acre museum "campus" opened in 1997 and houses a vast and impressive collection of art and antiquities. European paintings and sculptures, drawings,

decorative arts, and photographs are free to view, but parking is $5 and reservations are required. You should plan on booking months in advance, or try calling at the last minute to nab a cancellation. There is also a shuttle from nearby parking lots (no reservations needed), private automobile and cab drop-offs, or you can arrive via an MTA bus; call the museum for more information. The **Getty Villa** on the Malibu cliffs overlooking the Pacific Ocean, the original site of the Getty Museum, will reopen in 2001 upon completion of extensive renovations; its focus will be ancient Grecian and Roman art. Call the same number for more information.

- **Los Angeles Contemporary Exhibition** (**LACE**), 6522 Hollywood Boulevard, Hollywood, 323-957-1777, presents contemporary and experimental art.
- **Los Angeles County Museum of Art** (**LACMA**), 5905 Wilshire Boulevard, Fairfax District, 323-857-6000, www.lacma.org, houses everything from American and European art to photography to Indian and Southeast Asian art. It also has a fine film department featuring lectures and screenings. If a major traveling exhibition is coming to Los Angeles it will usually mount the show at LACMA. (For information on free musical performances held at LACMA, see the **Music** section in this chapter.) Admission is $6 for adults, $4 for students and seniors, $1 for children aged six to seventeen.
- **Museum of African-American Art,** 4005 South Crenshaw Boulevard, Third Floor, Los Angeles, 213-294-7071; permanent and rotating exhibitions by African American artists, as well as seasonal events like an annual tree lighting ceremony at Christmas. Admission is free.
- **Museum of Contemporary Art** (**MOCA**), 250 South Grand Avenue, downtown, 213-621-2766; permanent collection features painting, sculpture, live performances, and environmental work, all in a landmark building designed by Arata Isozaki. Free admission Thursdays from 5 to 8 p.m. General admission is $6, $4 for seniors and students, free admission for children under twelve.
- **Norton Simon Museum of Art,** 411 West Colorado Boulevard, Pasadena, 626-449-6840; the recently renovated museum houses a permanent collection of European art from the Renaissance to the mid-20th century. Admission is $4 for adults, $2 for seniors and students.
- **Santa Monica Museum of Art,** 2525 Michigan Avenue, 310-586-6488; this small museum features changing contemporary exhibitions. An admission donation of $4 is recommended.

- **Skirball Museum,** 2701 North Sepulveda Boulevard, Brentwood, 310-440-4500, features Jewish fine arts, archaeological artifacts, ceremonial and religious objects, photographs, and folk arts. Admission is $8 for adults, $6 for students and seniors, and free for children under twelve.
- **UCLA/Armand Hammer Museum of Art,** 10899 Wilshire Boulevard, Westwood, 310-443-7000; the permanent collection features more than five centuries worth of West European art. Admission is $4.50 for adults, $3 students and seniors, children under seventeen are free.
- **Watts Towers,** 1727 East 107th Street, Watts, 213-847-4646; though not a museum in the traditional sense, this monumental piece of folk art took artist Sam Rodia 33 years to complete. The towers are built of salvaged steel rods, dismantled pipes, bed frames and cement, and are covered with bottle fragments, ceramic tiles, china plates, and more than 70,000 seashells. The adjacent **Watts Towers Art Center** hosts visual and performing art exhibits, poetry readings and other events.

HISTORICAL, CULTURAL, SCIENCE

- **Autry Museum of Western Heritage,** 4700 Western Heritage Way, Griffith Park, 323-667-2000, www.autry-museum.org, founded by famed movie cowboy Gene Autry, this museum houses a permanent collection of art and artifacts depicting the history of the American West. Admission is $7.50 for adults, $5 for seniors and students, and $3 for children two to twelve.
- **California African-American Museum,** South Figueroa Street and State Drive, downtown, 213-744-7432, focuses on African-American achievements in science, politics, religion, athletics, and the arts. Admission is free.
- **California Heritage Museum,** 2612 Main Street, Santa Monica, 310-392-8537; admission is $2, free for children under twelve.
- **Fowler Museum of Cultural History,** UCLA, Westwood, 310-825-4361; admission is $5 for adults, $3 for students and seniors, free for children under 17, in addition to fees to park on the UCLA campus.
- **Griffith Park Observatory,** 2800 East Observatory Road, Griffith Park, 323-664-1191; admission to the astronomy exhibits is free, there is a charge of $4 to get into the planetarium and laserium shows.

- **Hollywood Wax Museum,** 6767 Hollywood Boulevard, Hollywood, 323-462-5991; admission is $8.95 for adults, $6.95 for children six to twelve.
- **Japanese-American National Museum,** 369 East First Street, downtown, 213-625-0414; this cultural center illustrates the history of Japanese immigration to the United States. Admission is $6 for adults, $5 for seniors and students, children under five are free.
- **The Carol & Barry Kaye Museum of Miniatures,** 5900 Wilshire Boulevard, Fairfax District, 323-937-6464; houses a permanent display of more than two hundred tiny fantasy worlds, located directly across the street from the Los Angeles County Museum of Art. Admission: $7.50, $6.50 for seniors, $5 for students twelve to eighteen, and $3 for children three to eleven.
- **Museum of Flying,** 2772 Donald Douglas Loop, Santa Monica, 310-392-8822, features exhibits of flyable aircraft, which, on the weekends, take off. Admission is $7 for adults, $5 for seniors, $3 for children three to seventeen.
- **Museum of Jurassic Technology,** 9341 Venice Boulevard, Culver City, 310-836-6131; it's hard to characterize this place, except to say as they do that they feature "exhibits of idiosyncratic and curious things throughout the world." No admission fee but a $4 donation is requested.
- **Latino Museum of History, Art and Culture,** 112 South Main Street, Los Angeles, 213-626-7600; free admission the first Tuesday of each month. Regular admission fees are $8 for adults, $5.50 for seniors and students, $2 for children five to twelve.
- **Los Angeles Natural History Museum,** 900 Exposition Boulevard, Los Angeles, 213-763-DINO; free admission the first Tuesday of each month. Regular admission fees are $8 for adults, $5.50 for seniors and students, $2 for children five to twelve.
- **Museum of Science and Industry,** 700 State Drive, Los Angeles, 323-724-3623; free admission.
- **Museum of Tolerance,** 9786 West Pico Boulevard, Beverly Hills, 310-553-8043, features high-technology exhibits dedicated to the promotion of understanding among people of different races and religions. Admission is $8.50 for adults, $6.50 for seniors, $5.50 for students, and $3.50 for children aged three to eleven.
- **Page Museum at the La Brea Tarpits,** 5801 Wilshire Boulevard, Fairfax District, 323-934-PAGE, features fossils from La Brea Tarpits, and other exhibits on paleontology. Admission is $6 for adults, $3.50 for students and seniors, $2 for children five to ten.

- **Pacific Asia Museum,** 46 North Los Robles Avenues, Pasadena, 626-449-2742; the only museum in the southwest dedicated to Asian and Pacific Islands art and culture. Admission is $5 for adults, $3 for students and seniors, free for kids under twelve.
- **Petersen Automotive Museum,** 6060 Wilshire Boulevard, Fairfax District, 323-930-CARS; where else, besides Detroit, would you expect to find a museum devoted to the automobile? Admission is $7 for adults, $5 for seniors and students, $3 for children five to twelve.
- **Southwest Museum,** 234 Museum Drive, Los Angeles, 323-221-2164; Los Angeles' first museum, founded in 1907, it contains an important collection of Native American art and artifacts. Admission is $6 for adults, $5 for seniors or college students, $3 for children seven to eighteen.

CULTURE FOR KIDS

Active children (or active parents) can keep busy year around in Los Angeles. Junior can be entertained by anything from a working farm to youth choruses to children's theater groups.

MUSEUMS

- **Kidspace Museum,** 390 South El Molino Avenue, Pasadena, 626-499-9144; a participatory museum with exhibits scaled for kids twelve and under.
- **LA Children's Museum,** 310 North Main Street, downtown, 213-687-8800; two levels of hands-on "edutainment" and exploring in downtown LA. Admission is $5.
- **My Jewish Discovery Place Children's Museum,** 5870 West Olympic Boulevard, Los Angeles 323-857-007; located at the Westside Jewish Community Center, the museum is open to the general public.
- **Museum of Science and Industry,** 700 State Drive, Los Angeles, 323-724-3623; another hands-on kind of place that's fun for kids of all ages. And it's free too.
- **Museum of Flying,** 2772 Donald Douglas Loop N, Santa Monica, 310-392-8822; this aviation museum offers tours, model making classes, and an interactive children's area. Admission: for adults $7, $3 for children three to seventeen.

Most museums, from LACMA to the Getty, feature children's workshops. Contact the museum for more information.

PLAY/DISCOVERY FACILITIES

- **Children's Time Machine,** 14562 Ventura Boulevard, Sherman Oaks, 877-846-3622, four theme rooms (plus a time-out room) with lots of activities, all-day admission is $8 for children 2 years and older, under 2 free.
- **Create Your Own,** 3006 Wilshire Boulevard, Santa Monica, 310-453-2005; a crafts store and classroom for kids to make their own crafts projects. Costs depend on the individual project.
- **Fit for Kids,** 1106 North La Cienega Boulevard, Suite 105, 310-360-6282; a Westside children's gym, free trial classes offered.
- **Gymboree,** Burbank: 818-955-8964; Sherman Oaks, 818-905-6225; a padded, colorful playground for youngsters and music classes for kids 5 and younger. It costs $125 to participate once a week (either the gymboree or the music classes) within a 14-week session, plus a $25 registration fee.
- **Happy All Day, Inc.,** 11301 West Olympic Boulevard #110, West Los Angeles, 310-473-6090; 16101 Ventura Boulevard #242, Encino, 818-380-0373; offers classes in cooking, dancing, music, and art to keep kids twelve and under busy year round. Free trial classes offered. Also hosts birthday and slumber parties.

OUTDOOR

- **Cirque Du Soleil,** Santa Monica Pier, 800-678-5440, www.cirquedusoleil.com; this funky Montreal circus-like-no-other pitches its colorful tents at the Pier every fall.
- **Griffith Park** offers pony and wagon rides, a miniature train and old-fashioned carousel, enough to take up a full day.
- **Kids Koncerts,** Theatricum Botanicum, 1419 North Topanga Canyon Boulevard, Topanga, 310-455-2322; summer series featuring popular artists in children's music. Admission, $7.
- **Long Beach Aquarium of the Pacific,** Shoreline Drive and Aquarium Way, Long Beach, 562-590-3100, www.aquariumofthepacific.org; situated across from the Queen Mary, the aquarium shows off over 10,000 fish in 17 habitat tanks. Admission is $14.95 for adults, $7.95 for children eleven to three, $11.95 for seniors.

- **Los Angeles Zoo,** Griffith Park, 323-644-6400, www.lazoo.org, is a modest sized zoo with a petting area that recently received a bond for expansion. Admission is $8.25 for adults, $5.25 for seniors, $3.25 for children twelve to two.
- **Open House: Hollywood Bowl,** Hollywood Bowl Plaza, Highland Avenue, Hollywood, 323-850-2000; a summer series of arts and crafts workshops for kids. Fees vary.
- **Ringling Bros Barnum & Bailey Circus,** Ticketmaster: 213-480-3232, www.ringling.com; the famous traveling circus makes the rounds from the LA Sports Arena to the Great Western Forum during select weekends in the summer. Visit their web site for specific dates.
- **Universal City Walk,** 1000 Universal Center Drive, 818-622-3801; while this outdoor mall is popular among adults, it's the pulsing, interactive water fountain that kids can't resist. Free admission, but there is a fee for parking.
- **The Farm,** 8101 Tampa Avenue, Reseda 818-341-6805; an animal farm that also offers pony rides. Open weekends.
- **Green Meadows Children's Farm,** 800-393-3276, 4235 Monterey Road, Ernest Debs Park, Los Angeles; take a guided tour of a farm filled with hundreds of farm animals. Open October through June. Admission is $9.
- **Party Animal Farm at Tierra Rejada Ranch,** 3370 Moorpark Road, Moorpark 805-523-2957, another animal farm with pony rides. Open weekends. Free, except for pony rides.
- **Pierce College Animal Farm,** 6201 Winnetka Avenue, Woodland Hills, 818-703-0826; a working farm that hosts special events during the year.
- **William S. Hart Park,** 24151 North San Fernando Road, Newhall, 661-259-0855; inside the park is a barnyard animal feeding area for kids.

SCOUTS

For years, the scouts have cultivated self-esteem and civic awareness in boys and girls alike.

- **Boy Scouts of America Western LA County Council,** 16525 Sherman Way, C-8, Van Nuys, CA 91406, 818-785-8700, www.bsa.la.com; serves communities in the North and West regions of Los Angeles County.

- **Boy Scouts of America Los Angeles Area Council,** 2333 Scout Way, Los Angeles, CA 90026-4995, 213-413-4400, www.bsa.com; serves the rest of the Los Angeles County area.
- **Girl Scouts of the USA, Los Angeles Girl Scout Council,** 5057 West Adams Boulevard Los Angeles, CA 90016, 323-933-4700, www.angeles.org; serves all of greater LA.
- **Campfire Boys & Girls,** 1541 Wilshire Boulevard, Suite 516, Los Angeles, CA 90017, 213-413-5501; conducts camping and self-reliance programs to enhance the skills and social development of young people.

THEATER

The following theaters have regular performances to delight young audiences.

- **Comedy Pups,** 4378, Lankershim Boulevard, North Hollywood, 818-216-0672; young stand-up comedians as young as six perform their funny antics for free at the Kindness of Strangers Coffeehouse.
- **Serendipity Children's Theatre Company,** 818-557-0505
- **LA Connection Comedy Theatre,** 13442 Ventura Boulevard, Sherman Oaks, 818-784-1868; the same people who run the Improv, offer a "Comedy Improv for Kids" program, call for more information.
- **Occidental Children's Theater,** 1600 Campus Road, Eagle Rock, 323-259-2922
- **Puppet & Magic Center,** 1255 Second Street, Santa Monica, 310-656-0483; musical variety shows.
- **Santa Monica Playhouse,** 1211 Fourth Street, Santa Monica, 310-394-9779; regular family-oriented performances by the Playhouse Actors' Repertory Theater Company and the Young Professional's Company.
- **Ye Olde Faerytale Playhouse,** 5108 Lankershim Boulevard, North Hollywood, 818-779-0586

OTHER

- **American Youth Symphony,** 310-476-2825
- **Los Angeles Children's Chorus,** 626-793-4231
- **Pasadena Junior Philharmonic,** 626-792-0463
- **San Fernando Valley Youth Chorus,** 818-888-6293 via the Angeles Chorale
- **Toyota Symphonies for Youth,** 213-850-2000

AMUSEMENT PARKS

The Los Angeles area is home to several amusement parks, including the granddaddy of them all, Disneyland. To avoid sticker-shock, you might want to call ahead to find out the various parks' admission and parking prices, which can be steep. We list the biggies:

- **Disneyland,** 1313 Harbor Boulevard, Anaheim, 714-781-4565; this is the original theme park, and the one that still seems to be held dearest in America's heart. Other parks may be larger or have more thrilling rides, but most people agree that there is something special about bumping into Mickey Mouse as you walk down Main Street, USA. Disneyland offers 55 different rides and attractions spread throughout seven different theme areas. Open daily year-round, hours vary by season.
- **Knott's Berry Farm,** 8039 Beach Boulevard, Buena Park, 714-220-5200; stretches across 150 acres, and offers more than 160 rides and attractions, as well as live performances. A Western theme pervades the park, which is open daily except Christmas.
- **Legoland,** One Lego Drive, Carlsbad, 877-534-6526, the first of its kind in the US, the 128-acre theme park is geared for kiddies 2 to 12. There are six theme areas to the park, all clustered around a large man-made lake. Everything's made out of legos, including 500 replicas of American landmarks in Minitown. Open year-around, seasonal hours vary.
- **Raging Waters,** 111 Raging Waters Drive, San Dimas, 909-592-6453; this 44-acre water park features rides, slides, sandy beaches, chutes and lagoons, in short, all different wild ways to cool off on a hot summer day. Open daily during the summer, weekends only during May and September through mid-October.
- **Santa Monica Pier,** at Ocean and Colorado Boulevards, Santa Monica, 310-260-8744; though not really an amusement park, the Pier boasts carnival-style games and rides, a huge Ferris wheel, and a vintage carousel, all with an ocean view. Most attractions are open all day (until midnight on weekends, 9 p.m. weekdays) during the summer, and only on weekends during the rest of the year.
- **Six Flags Magic Mountain,** 26101 Magic Mountain Parkway, Valencia, 661-255-4111; this 260-acre amusement park offers an array of rides, attractions and shows. It is famous for its scary roller coasters including an intimidating looping roller coaster called the

Viper. Magic Mountain is open daily from Memorial Day to Labor Day, and school holidays and weekends during the rest of the year. Closed on Christmas.

- **Universal Studios Tour,** 100 Universal City Plaza, Universal City, 818-508-9600; offers a comprehensive tram ride tour throughout the studio grounds (with the possibility of star sightings!) and live action shows. Also at Universal City is a multiplex movie theater and Universal City Walk, a three-block long shopping mall that is a mini-replica of Los Angeles.

THE EXCELLENT YEAR-ROUND WEATHER IN LOS ANGELES MAKES IT a great place for those interested in athletics, be you a fan, participant, or both. With two professional baseball teams, two professional basketball teams, a professional ice hockey team, and excellent college athletics, sports enthusiasts can keep very busy here. True, the areas' former football teams, the Rams and the Raiders, are deserters. LA continues to lobby for an expansion team, but with all the other offerings, including great college football, the Rams and Raiders are barely missed.

PROFESSIONAL SPORTS

BASEBALL

Baseball season runs from April through October.
- **The California Angels** play at **Anaheim Stadium** (lovingly called "The Big A") in Orange County. Under Disney ownership, the Angels have had only sporadic success. Recent news of major staff changes and that the team is up for sale have shaken things up. Hopefully, under the guidance of new general manager Bill Stoneman, the young up-and-comers and key veterans will restore the Angels as contenders in the American League West. For ticket information, call 888-796-4256, or check www.angelsbaseball.com.
- **The Los Angeles Dodgers** play at **Dodger Stadium** in Chavez Ravine. The Dodgers last won the World Series in 1988 under the leadership of famous manager, eater, and dieter, Tommy Lasorda. As Fernando Valenzuela's pitching success in the early 1980s drew a new crowd of fans to the park, the pitching sensation, Hideo Nomo from Japan produced what was locally known as "Nomomania" in the early 1990s. Now, all eyes are on Raul Mondesi, an outstanding right-fielder beleaguered by fines for bad sportsmanship. Tickets for adults run from $6-$16, giving Dodger games the nickname "the cheapest ticket in town." For ticket information, call 323-224-1491.

For minor league baseball, the nearest teams are the **Lancaster Jethawks**, 805-726-5400, who play at The Hangar ballpark; the **Lake Elsinore Storm**, 909-245-4487, play at the Lake Elsinore Diamond, and the **San Bernardino Stampede**, 909-888-9922, play at The Ranch ballpark.

BASKETBALL

Basketball season picks up after baseball, and runs from October through April.

As of the fall of 1999, the **Los Angeles Clipper** (season seats, 213-745-0500, www.nba.com/clippers), are playing at the newly built **Staples Center**, near USC. In this town, used to the Laker glory days of Magic Johnson and Kareem Abdul Jabbar, the Clippers were once treated like poor second cousins. Lately though, smart trades and fresh blood on the Clippers team have brought new fans into the fold, including the requisite court-side celebrities. For ticket information call Ticketmaster, 213-365-3500, www.ticketmaster.com, or the Staples center, 877-5-ACT-NOW, www.staplescenter.com.

Like the Clippers, **The Los Angeles Lakers** (season seats, 310-419-3131, www.nba.com/lakers), have likewise moved from The Forum, in Inglewood, to the Staples Center. Although the famed seasons of Magic Johnson, Kareem Abdul Jabbar, Wilt Chamberlain, Elgin Baylor and Jerry West are no longer, the flamboyant Shaquille O'Neal and outstanding Kobe Bryant have made the game much more exciting. The hiring of Coach Phil Jackson, the 14th coach to head the franchise since its inception, has jazzed things up as well. If the game gets boring, you can always scan the audience (courtside) for the likes of Jack Nicholson. For ticket information call Ticketmaster, 213-365-3500, www.ticketmaster.com, or the Staples Center, 877-5-ACT-NOW, www.staplescenter.com.

HOCKEY

The Los Angeles Kings (season seats, 888-KINGS-LA, www.lakings.com), also play at the Staples Center. Ice hockey season begins in November and ends in March, unless as in 1993, the Kings make it to the Stanley Cup finals in June. "The Great One" Wayne Gretzky popularized hockey here in a city that only sees ice or snow on TV. As testimony to his popularity, these days you're as likely to see kids playing after-school street hockey games as sandlot baseball or touch football. Recently however, the news of the team's financial chaos and ownership changes has gotten more ink than the King's on-ice achievements. For ticket information, call Ticketmaster, 213-365-3500, www.ticketmaster.com, or the Staples Center, 877-ACT-NOW, www.staplescenter.com.

HORSE RACING

There are three race tracks in the Los Angeles area.

- **Hollywood Park,** Inglewood, 310-419-1574; races are run April through July, and November through December.
- **Los Angeles County Fairgrounds,** 909-623-3111; races are run through the fair each September.
- **Santa Anita Park,** Arcadia, 626-574-RACE; races are run October through November, and December through April.

SOCCER

Major League Soccer (MLS) is one of the legacies of the 1994 World Cup at Pasadena's Rose Bowl, and is the first attempt at a major soccer league since the NASL folded in 1993. The **LA Galaxy** is one of ten Division One franchises started across the US in the spring of 1996. With the recent nationwide captivation of the 1999 Women's World Cup Soccer at the Rose Bowl, it's easy to see just how far the sport has come along in the US. The LA Galaxy plays at the **Rose Bowl** in Pasadena. Call 626-577-3100 for tickets.

TENNIS

Each August the men's professional **Infiniti Open** is played at the Los Angeles Tennis Center at UCLA, and the women's professional **Toshiba Open** is played at the Manhattan Beach Country Club. Both events draw some of the world's top players. For more information on either of the tournaments, contact the local United States Tennis Association office at 310-208-3838.

COLLEGE SPORTS

With all the labor disputes in professional sports disrupting schedules and disillusioning fans, take heart that here in LA, fine local college games are plentiful *and* dependable. In fact, enthusiasts of college-level sports may feel that living in LA is like dying and going to heaven, as the local schools consistently boast some of the nation's finest athletes and teams.

UCLA's basketball program is legendary, producing such phenoms as Kareem Abdul-Jabbar (then Lou Alcindor), Gail Goodrich, Jamaal (then Keith) Wilkes, Bill Walton, Marcus Johnson, Ann Meyers (sister of Dave), Reggie Miller and Ed O'Bannon. The football program is no slouch either, with former players on the roster like Troy Aikman and Ken Norton, and the home field being none other than the Rose Bowl. Likewise **USC** football can usually be described as nothing short of a powerhouse, energized in the past by the likes of Mike Garrett, Charles White, Marcus Allen, Ricky Bell, Ronnie Lott, Junior Seau and yes, O.J. Simpson. Cheryl Miller, one of the greatest female basketball players ever, also was a Trojan. Other local college sports programs of note are baseball at **Cal State Fullerton, Pepperdine's** tennis and water polo, **Loyola Marymount** for basketball, **Long Beach State's** basketball, UCLA's volleyball, gymnastics, softball, and water polo, and USC's water polo.

For athletic ticket information, call the following numbers:

- **Cal State Fullerton,** 714-773-2187
- **Loyola Marymount,** 310-338-4532
- **Long Beach State,** 310-985-4949
- **Pepperdine,** 310-456-4150
- **UCLA,** 310-825-2101
- **USC,** 213-740-4672

PARTICIPANT SPORTS AND ACTIVITIES

PARKS & RECREATION DEPARTMENTS

For information on park facilities, leagues, clubs, and lessons:

- **Beverly Hills Recreation and Parks Dept.,** 310-285-2537
- **Burbank Parks and Recreation Dept.,** 818-238-5300
- **Culver City Recreation Dept.,** 310-202-5689
- **El Segundo Parks and Recreation Dept.,** 310-322-3842
- **Glendale Parks Recreation Dept.,** 818-548-2000
- **Los Angeles Recreation and Parks Dept.,** 818-756-8891, 310-837-8116, 213-738-2961

- **Long Beach Dept. of Parks, Recreation & Marine**, 562-570-3100
- **Malibu Parks and Recreation Dept.**, 310-456-2489, ext. 235
- **Manhattan Beach Recreation Dept.**, 310-545-5621, ext. 325
- **Pasadena Parks and Recreation Dept.**, 626-405-4306
- **Santa Monica Recreation Division**, 310-458-8311
- **Santa Clarita Parks and Recreation Dept.**, 661-255-4910
- **West Hollywood Recreation Dept.**, 310-854-7471

BASKETBALL

Pick-up basketball games are available all over the city, with competition ranging from friendly to fierce. The movie "White Men Can't Jump" showed off the busy pick-up basketball scene at Venice's Boardwalk. While it may seem like this is the spot with the best and flashiest players in town, there are good games to be found all over, from schoolyards to city parks. The Wooden Center's indoor courts at UCLA, 310-825-1135, are where the "big names" show up, and it's not uncommon for hot college players, former professionals, or even a current pro to drop by for a game of pick-up.

Check out www.socalhoops.com for the latest pick-up game leads. Here is a sampling of neighborhood parks and recreation centers with basketball courts:

- **Balboa Sports Center,** Burbank and Balboa Boulevards, Encino, 818-756-9642
- **Roxbury Park,** South Roxbury Drive and Olympic Boulevard, Beverly Hills, 310-550-4761
- **Reed Park,** Wilshire and Lincoln Boulevards, Santa Monica, 310-458-8974
- **Victory-Vineland Recreation Center,** Victory Boulevard and Vineland Avenue, North Hollywood, 818-985-9516
- **Venice Beach Athletic Center,** Ocean Front Walk and Winward Avenue, Venice, 310-399-2775
- **West Hollywood Park,** North San Vicente and Santa Monica Boulevards, West Hollywood, 323-848-6534
- **Westwood Recreation Complex,** South Sepulveda and Wilshire Boulevards, Westwood, 310-473-3610

BASEBALL/SOFTBALL

There are numerous baseball and softball leagues throughout Los Angeles, many of which are organized through the workplace. There is, for instance, an advertising league and a law league. For more information, ask your colleagues, call your department of parks and recreation, or contact the **US Amateur Baseball Association,** 425-776-7130, www.usaba.com. If you've got money to burn and a dream to fulfill, sign up for the **Dodgers Adult Baseball Camp,** 800-334-7529. The month-long camp provides pro-level baseball practice and coaching by the LA Dodgers staff and ex-players like Steve Garvey to anyone...with $4,000.

BICYCLING

Both tour bicycling and mountain bicycling are popular in Los Angeles. The most traveled bike path is the **coastal bike path** from **Pacific Palisades** in the north to **Torrance** in the south. The path looks like a bicycling and skating freeway during the weekends. If you don't own a bike, rentals are available at several shacks down on the beach in Marina del Rey, Venice and Santa Monica. Other popular trails include the **Ballona Creek Trail** and the **Pasadena bike trail.**

Mountain bikers enjoy the challenging trails in the **Santa Monica mountains,** including **Sullivan Canyon** along (and through) the creek bed, the **Malibu Canyon trails, Topanga State Park,** 310-455-2465, and **Sycamore Canyon.**

For more information about area routes, call the **Los Angeles County Transportation Commission** at 213-236-9555. Or visit www.xenon.stanford.edu/~rsf/mtn-bike.html for a guide to area trails. Local clubs include the **Los Angeles Wheelmen,** 310-556-7967 and the **Over The Bars Mountain Bike Club,** 818-504-4037.

For bicycling equipment and other information, here are two of the more popular cycling retailers:

- **Bikeology**
  Beverly Hills, 9006 West Pico Boulevard, 310-278-0915
  Santa Monica, 1515 Wilshire Boulevard, 310-902-1940
- **Helen's Cycles**
  Manhattan Beach, 1570 Rosecrans Avenue, 310-643-9140
  Marina del Rey, 2472 Lincoln Boulevard, 310-306-7843
  Santa Monica, 2501 Broadway, 310-829-1836
  Westwood, 1071 Gayley Avenue, 310-208-8988

BILLIARDS/POOL

Pool possibilities here run the gamut from lone tables in the middle of seedy bars, to old-fashioned smoky billiard halls, to the trendy pool halls where pagers are handed out to those waiting for a pool table. Here are a few for you to sample:

- **Gotham Hall,** 1431 Third Street Promenade, Santa Monica, 310-394-8865
- **Hollywood Athletic Club,** 6525 Sunset Boulevard, 323-962-6600; Universal City Walk, 818-505-9238
- **House of Billiards,** 1901 Wilshire Boulevard, Santa Monica.
- **LA Society Billiard Cafe,** 19626 Ventura Boulevard, Tarzana, 818-344-POOL
- **Q's Billiard Club & Restaurant,** 11835 Wilshire Boulevard, Brentwood, 310-477-7550
- **Stick & Stein Eatery and Sports Parlor,** 707 Sepulveda Boulevard, El Segundo, 310-414-9283
- **Yankee Doodles,** 1410 Third Street Promenade, Santa Monica, 310-394-4632

BOATING/SAILING/WINDSURFING

Marina del Rey is the spot for most boating and water sport activity in the Santa Monica Bay. **Redondo Beach's** King Harbor, and **Long Beach's** downtown marina, 562-570-1815, are busy with water sport enthusiasts as well. A good resource for the boating enthusiast is the **Southern California Boat Club,** 13555 Fiji Way, Marina del Rey, 310-822-0073. Aside from the private sailboats, speed boats, jet-craft and plain old yachts that are moored in a marina, many companies offer sailing lessons and rentals. However, not all water sports companies are located near a marina, check your Yellow Pages under "Boat Renting & Leasing" for a complete list.

- **Bluewater Sailing,** 13505 Bali Way, Marina del Rey, 310-823-5545
- **Pacific Sailing,** 14110 Marquesas Way, Marina del Rey, 310-823-4064
- **Rent-A-Sail,** 13719 Fiji Way, Marina del Rey, 310-822-1868
- **Offshore Water Sports,** 128 East Shoreline Village Drive, Long Beach, 562-436-1996

BOWLING

AMF operates a chain of bowling facilities in Southern California. Call 800-BOWL-AMF or visit their website, www.amf.com to locate the one nearest you. Or try:

- **Allstar Lanes,** 4459 Eagle Rock Boulevard, Los Angeles, 323-254-2579
- **Bahama Lanes,** 3545 East Foothill Boulevard, Pasadena, 626-351-8858
- **Bay Shore Bowl,** 234 Pico Boulevard, Santa Monica, 310-399-7731
- **Brunswick Bowlerland Lanes,** 7501 Van Nuys Boulevard, Van Nuys, 818-989-1610
- **Canoga Park Bowl,** 20122 Vanowen Street, Woodland Hills, 818-340-5190
- **Hollywood Star Lanes,** 5227 Santa Monica Boulevard, Hollywood, 323-665-4111; offers 24-hour bowling, and cocktails served until 2 a.m.
- **Mar Vista Bowl,** 12125 Venice Boulevard, West Los Angeles, 310-391-5288
- **Pickwick Bowling Center,** 1001 Riverside Drive, Burbank, 818-846-0035
- **Sports Center Bowl,** 12655 Ventura Boulevard, Studio City, 818-769-7600
- **Woodlake Bowl,** 23130 Ventura Boulevard, Woodland Hills, 818-225-7181
- Finally, there's the **Southern Los Angeles County Bowling Association,** in Bellflower, at 562-925-0417.

FISHING

If you are over 16 years of age, you must purchase a fishing license ($27.55 for freshwater, $18.95 for saltwater) good through the end of the year. Fishing licenses may be purchased from any bait and tackle shop, see your Yellow Pages under "Fishing Tackle Dealers" for locations. Sport fishing enthusiasts should inquire at such shops for information on fishing charters. The **California State Fish & Game Department,** located in Long Beach, 562-590-5132, can provide more information on local fishing laws.

Popular saltwater fishing spots are off the many piers along the

Westside, especially the **Santa Monica Pier**. For freshwater fishing, **Castiac Lake** is one of the most popular spots. It is just north of Santa Clarita at 32100 North Ridge Route Road in Castiac. Call 805-257-4050 for more information.

FRISBEE

An impromptu game of Frisbee can be had in any open field, especially the larger parks like **Will Rogers State Park** in the Pacific Palisades or **Sepulveda Basin Recreation Area** in Van Nuys. Contact the area parks and recreation department for references to Frisbee clubs or groups. For disc golf, check out the challenging **Oak Grove Park Disc Golf Course**, in Pasadena, 626-797-1114. Disc enthusiasts should visit www.frisbee.com for more information on the sport.

GOLF

There are more than 100 **public golf courses** in the greater Los Angeles area. The City of Los Angeles operates seven 18-hole courses, and five 9-hole courses. For information, call 213-485-5555. The County of Los Angeles operates 16 courses; for information, call 213-738-2961. Be fore-warned, golf is very popular here, so book a tee-time well in advance.

Other popular spots include, but are not limited to:

- **Eaton Canyon Golf Course**, 1150 North Sierra Madre Villa Avenue, Pasadena, 626-794-6773; this is a 30-year-old, 2,900 yard, 9-hole layout featuring two par fives.
- **Holmby Park Golf Course**, 601 Club View Drive, Westwood, 310-276-1604, is an 18-hole pony golf course, 3-par.
- **Malibu Golf Course**, 901 Encinal Canyon Road, Malibu, 818-889-6680, offers one 18-hole golf course.
- **Penmar Golf Course**, 1223 Rose Avenue, Venice, 310-396-6228, features one 9-hole course.
- **Rancho Park Golf Course**, 10460 Pico Boulevard, West Los Angeles, 310-838-7373, is billed as one of the busiest golf courses in the country. It features an 18-hole course, plus a par three 9-hole pitch-n-putt.
- **Roosevelt Golf Course**, 2650 North Vermont Avenue, Los Angeles, 213-665-2011, features one 9-hole course.
- **Sepulveda Basin Recreational Area**, Burbank and Balboa Boulevards, Encino, 310-989-8060; there are two 18-hole golf courses at this 60-acre wildlife refuge.

HIKING

The **Santa Monica** and **San Gabriel Mountains** provide miles of varied hiking trails. The following are local state parks offering hiking trails:

- **Coldwater Canyon Park,** 818-753-4600; located along the southern slope of the Santa Monica Mountains, this park offers five-plus miles of hiking trails.
- **Elysian Park,** 213-225-2044; located in Echo Park, it offers more than ten miles of hiking trails, winding through forested hills and green valleys.
- **Griffith Park,** 323-665-5188, located above Hollywood, there are 35 miles of hiking trails in this vast park.
- **Malibu Creek State Park,** 310-880-0350, has more than 15 miles of hiking trails weaving through this mostly undeveloped park.
- **Santa Monica Mountains National Recreation Area,** 818-597-1036; the Santa Monica Mountains stretch almost 50 miles across Los Angeles. This area includes **Will Rogers State Historic Park**, 310-454-8212, which includes the 31-room former ranch home of actor, humorist, and columnist Will Rogers and the miles of trails behind his house. Most of the trails in the Santa Monica Mountains are part of, or hook up to, the **Backbone Trail**.
- **Temescal Gateway Park,** 310-756-7154, is a 20-acre park that includes a trail that travels more than 12 miles north to the Backbone Trail.
- **Topanga State Park,** 310-455-2465, is a 10,000-acre park offering 32 miles of hiking trails.

The county once required that anyone using LA County nature trails purchase a $23 annual pass—this proved so unpopular that it has since been rescinded. City, state, and federal trails are free. There are about 330 miles of country trails in Los Angeles, including the following: **Frank G. Bonnell Regional Park Trail, San Dimas; Schabarum Trail,** from Whittier to Rowland Heights; **Colby Dalton Trail,** Glendora; **Altadena Crest Trail,** Altadena; **La Canada Open Space Trail,** La Canada Flintridge; **Los Angeles River Trail,** from Downey to Long Beach; **Devil's Punchbowl Nature Trail,** Antelope Valley; **Los Pinetos Trail,** Sylmar; **Coastal Slope Trail,** Malibu; and **Eaton**

Canyon Park Trail, Pasadena. For an informative guide to LA's hiking and biking trails, check out *On the Trail - Malibu to Santa Barbara* by Cathy Phillipp.

HIKING CLUBS/PROGRAMS

- **William O. Douglas Outdoor Classroom,** Sooky Goldman Nature Center, Beverly Hills, 310-858-3834, organizes hiking and picnics.
- **Mountain Recreation and Conservation Authority,** Santa Clarita, 661-255-2974
- **Nursery Nature Walks,** Santa Monica, 310-998-1151, offers walks in throughout LA geared specifically for parents and children.
- **Placerita Cyn Nature Center,** Newhall, 661-259-7721, organizes Saturday hikes.
- **Santa Monica Mountains Recreational Area,** Agoura Hills, 818-597-9192, offers numerous outdoor programs.
- **Sierra Club,** Los Angeles Headquarters, 213-387-4287; hundreds of people join their organized evening hikes through Griffith Park and other locales.
- **Trail Runners Club,** Pacific Palisades, 310-459-3757
- **Will Rogers State Historical Park,** Pacific Palisades, 310-454-8212, offers nature walks for adults and families on weekends.
- **Valley Trailers,** Northridge, 818-725-3657

HORSEBACK RIDING

Several areas offer horseback riding rentals, lessons, and/or boarding, including the following:

- **Altadena Stables,** Altadena, 626-797-2012
- **Griffith Park Circle K Riding Stable,** Burbank, 818-843-9890
- **Los Angeles Equestrian Center,** Burbank, 818-840-9063
- **Malibu Riding and Tennis Club,** Malibu, 310-457-9783
- **Mill Creek Equestrian Center,** Topanga, 310-455-1116
- **Red Barn Stables,** Malibu, 818-879-0444, or toll-free 800-300-0968, offers beach rides.
- **Sunset Ranch Hollywood Stables,** Hollywood, 213-464-9612, offers moonlight rides through Hollywood Hills and Griffith Park.

ICE SKATING

If ice skating is your sport, try one of the following rinks, which also offer lessons:

- **Culver City Ice Arena,** 4545 Sepulveda Boulevard, Culver City, 310-398-5718
- **Ice Capades Chalet,** 6100 Laurel Canyon Boulevard, North Hollywood, 818-985-5555
- **Ice'O Plex,** 8345 Hayvenhurst Place, North Hills, 818-893-1784
- **Pasadena Ice Skating Center,** 310 East Green Street, Pasadena, 626-578-0800
- **Pickwick Ice Arena,** 1001 Riverside Drive, Burbank, 818-846-0032
- **Van Nuys Iceland,** 14318 Calvert Street, Van Nuys, 818-785-2171

IN–LINE/ROLLER SKATING

The parks and beaches of Los Angeles are bustling with in-line and roller skaters. Rentals can be found at several shacks along the coastal path, in **Marina del Rey, Venice,** and **Santa Monica.** Beware, bicyclists and skaters turn the bike path into a veritable Autobahn on weekends. The weather is so good here, year round, that there are few traditional indoor skating rinks in the city. The ones that remain are listed below:

- **World on Wheels,** 4645 1/2 Venice Boulevard, Los Angeles, 323-933-3333
- **Moonlight Rollerway,** 5110 San Fernando Road, Glendale, 818-241-3630
- **Northridge Skateland,** 18140 Parthenia Street, Northridge, 818-885-7655
- **Robinson Park,** 1081 North Fair Oaks Avenue, Pasadena, 626-798-0926

For a unique experience, join the **Friday Night Skate,** 310-57-SKATE, a loosely knit group of bladers who get together the first and third Friday of every month. This becomes a roving 10-mile, traffic-stopping, three-hour long, noisy party on wheels in Santa Monica.

PADDLE TENNIS

Those aren't kiddie-sized tennis courts you see dotting the beaches along the bike path, they're paddle tennis courts. Paddle tennis is similar to tennis, but it is played on a smaller court with deadened tennis balls and paddles, rather than rackets. You can try your talent for this popular game at one of the following spots:

- **415 PCH,** Santa Monica, 310-458-8555; there are five paddle tennis courts located just off the beach at this former private club.
- **Culver City,** 310-202-5689; there are three courts at the corner of Culver and Elenda.
- **Venice Recreational Center,** 310-399-2775; there are eight paddle tennis courts located right on the beach.

ROCK CLIMBING

Climbing enthusiasts head out of the city for the big rocks like **Stoney Point** in Chatsworth. A quick drive from LA, this location is particularly crowded on summer weekends. A bit more time on the road can get you to the likes of **Vasquez Rocks Natural Area Park,** in Agua Dulce, 805-268-0840, and **Joshua Tree Rock Climbing School** in Joshua Tree National Park, 800-890-4745. The California State University, Northridge (CSUN) Leisure Studies Department, 818 677-3202, can provide additional mountain climbing training information. For alternatives a little closer to home, check with your local health club to see if they offer rock climbing walls. There's also indoor rock climbing centers like these:

- **Rockreation Sport Climbing Center,** 11866 La Grange Avenue, Los Angeles, 310-207-7199
- **Rock Gym,** 600 Long Beach Boulevard, Long Beach, 562-983-5500
- **Los Angeles Rock Gym,** 4926 West Rosecrans Avenue, Hawthorne, 310-973-3388

RUNNING

The miles-long coastal path along the beach provides a beautiful setting for runners. Another popular Westside running spot is the median park strip on **San Vicente Boulevard,** starting in Brentwood and continuing through Santa Monica to the cliffs above the ocean. In the Hollywood area, the path around the **Hollywood Reservoir** (also known as Lake Hollywood) provides a nice place to jog.

Some Santa Monica runners like to include in their loop a strenuous staircase that runs from the end of 4th Street, north of San Vicente Boulevard, and leads into Santa Monica Canyon. In fact, many people bike or drive over to this spot, specifically to trod up and down these 200 steep steps, known as the **4th Street stairs.** Aside from a beautiful ocean vista and a good workout, the stairs also provide an active social scene, particularly on weekends when it gets downright crowded. But if you want to give the steps a try, watch your manners; climbers don't appreciate perfume or cologne wearing, which interferes with their huffing and puffing, and be sure not to mess with the stones and other markers at the top and bottom of the steps, which help exercisers keep track of how many flights they have completed. Also, neighbors in this tony area have complained that some climbers walk or sit on their front lawns, leave empty water bottles around, or even use their hoses to cool off, so be considerate.

The Los Angeles Marathon gathers more than 20,000 competitors each March at the Los Angeles Memorial Coliseum. The course runs through Chinatown, Hollywood, and Echo Park. For more information, call 310-444-5544. For novice runners who have never accomplished a marathon or active runners who want to train with a group, the **LA Leggers,** 310-577-8000, has a $35, 30-week training program in preparation for the LA Marathon. Culver City hosts the **Western Hemisphere Marathon,** 310-253-6650, in December. Another popular running club (for gays, lesbians and friends of) is the **Los Angeles Frontrunners,** 323-460-2554.

SCUBA DIVING

Many private scuba schools as well as local parks departments offer scuba instruction. While the diving in the **Santa Monica Bay** doesn't provide the greatest visibility, day trips to **Catalina Island** and the **Channel Islands** near Santa Barbara offer beautiful and exhilarating dives. For those particularly interested in diving with marine mammals like seals and sea lions, the California coast is *the* place. Here are a few of the many dive shops/schools in the area; check your telephone directory under "Diving Instruction" for others:

- **Blue Cheer Dive & Surf,** 1110 Wilshire Boulevard, Santa Monica, 310-828-1217
- **Malibu Divers,** 21231 Pacific Coast Highway, Malibu, 310-456-2396
- **Pacific School of Scuba,** 9763 West Pico Boulevard, West Los Angeles, 310-286-7377
- **Reef Seekers,** 8612 Wilshire Boulevard, Beverly Hills, 310-652-4990

SOCCER

LA's large and growing Latino population makes soccer a popular sport here. Balboa Park in North Hollywood is a busy site for weekly organized matches between multi-ethnic club teams. Check your phone directory under "Soccer Clubs" for more information. Or contact the **American Youth Soccer Organization** 800-USA-AYSO for a soccer league in your area.

SURFING

Hey dude! As you can imagine, surfing is a major part of the beach culture in Southern California—all along the LA coastline there are beaches and coves where surfing reigns supreme. For information on where to surf, contact the **Department of Beaches & Harbors** at 310-305-9503. To buy a surfboard, check the telephone directory under "Surf Boards." To learn how to surf, you can drive up to Malibu for an afternoon, watch the veterans, then grab a board and give it a try. Trial by fire may be the most popular teaching method. Keep in mind that the locals can be territorial, and newcomers aren't always welcomed. If you have a buddy who already surfs, you might be better off letting him/her show you the ropes.

Before you head out, here are the numbers to call for surfing conditions: **Central Section,** 310-451-8761; **Northern Section,** 310-457-9701; **San Pedro-Cabrillo Beach Section,** 310-832-1130; **Southern Section,** 310-379-8471. On the Internet, visit www.surfline.com for surf reports, live beach cams and more. Another good surf resource page is www.sdsc.edu/surf.

SWIMMING

Aside from that big outdoor pool called the Pacific Ocean, there are several places you can go to swim in Los Angeles. Contact the **LA Aquatics Offices**: Valley, 818-765-0284; Metro, 213-485-5559; Pacific, 213-765-5391, for a complete listing of county pools and references to clubs. Many **YMCAs** offer use of their pool for a fee, as do several city-run parks and recreation facilities, including those listed below. All are open year-round.

- **Echo Park Indoor Pool** (one indoor Olympic sized, one outdoor shallow), 1419 Colton Street, Echo Park, 323-481-2640
- **Fremont Pool** (indoor), 7630 Towne Avenue, Los Angeles, 323-847-3401
- **North Hollywood Pool,** 530 Tujuna Avenue, North Hollywood, 818-755-7651
- **The Plunge,** 219 West Mariposa Avenue, El Segundo, 310-322-1677
- **Rancho Cienega Pool** (indoor), 5001 Rodeo Road, Los Angeles, 213-847-3406
- **Eleanor G. Roberts Pool** (indoor), 4526 West Pico Boulevard, Los Angeles, 323-936-8483
- **Roosevelt Pool** (Olympic sized, outdoor), 456 South Matthews, Los Angeles, 323-485-7391
- **Westwood Recreation Complex,** 1350 Sepulveda Boulevard, Westwood, 310-478-7019
- **Van Nuys-Sherman Oaks Pool,** 14201 Huston Street, Van Nuys, 818-971-6975
- **Venice Pool** (indoor), 2401 Walgrove Avenue, Venice, 310-575-8260
- **Woodland Hills Pool,** 5858 Shoup Avenue, Woodland Hills, 818-756-9363

Unfortunately, as with many **beaches** across the nation, the **Santa Monica Bay** suffers from pollution. For the most up to date water conditions, call the **Department of Beaches & Harbors,** 310-305-9503 or **Heal the Bay** (a volunteer group), 310-581-4188. Clean up efforts are underway, and actually the bay is safer now than in years past, though there are often swimming advisories near the major storm drains. If you want to swim in the ocean, you might want to head up to **Malibu.** For local swim clubs, such as the **Ancient Mariners** based in the Culver City YMCA, 310-390-3604, or the **Southern California Aquatic Swim Club,** 310-451-6666, check out the postings at any of the pools listed above. See **Greenspace and Beaches** chapter for more information about these and other area beaches.

TENNIS/RACQUET SPORTS

Year-round outdoor tennis and racquetball are among the many benefits brought by the area's good weather. There are public tennis and racquet courts throughout the city—some require a small fee in exchange for the ability to make a court reservation. (These pay-to-play courts are often in better condition than other public courts.) Tennis players may be interested in contacting the **Southern California Tennis Association,** 310-208-3838 for more resources. The **Mid-Valley Racquetball Athletic Club,** 818-705-6500 can also assist racquet sports lovers. Many popular public tennis spots also have racquetball courts, call the facility near you for more information or contact your local parks and recreation department. Here's a sampling:

- **Riverside Tennis Facility,** Griffith Park, 323-661-5318
- **Echo Park,** Echo Park, six courts, 213-250-3578
- **La Cienega Park,** Beverly Hills, sixteen courts, 310-550-4765
- **Lincoln Park,** Santa Monica, six courts, 310-394-6011
- **North Hollywood Recreation Center,** North Hollywood, six courts, 818-763-7651
- **Plummer Park,** West Hollywood, six courts, 213-876-1725
- **Westwood Recreation Complex,** Westwood, twelve courts, 310-473-3610
- **Van Nuys-Sherman Oaks Park,** Sherman Oaks, ten courts, 818-769-4415

VOLLEYBALL

Several beaches offer beach volleyball courts, including **Zuma, Malibu Lagoon, Will Rogers, Santa Monica State, Venice,** and the grand-daddy of them all, **Manhattan,** which has more than 100 courts. Additionally, many parks have volleyball courts, including the **West Wilshire Recreation Center,** 323-939-8874, **Palisades Recreation Center,** 310-454-1412, **Barrington Recreation Center,** 310-476-3807, and **Westwood Recreation Complex,** 310-473-3610.

To join a group, contact the **Amateur Volleyball Association,** 310-451-4776, or **California Beach Volleyball Association,** 805-642-2282.

HEALTH CLUBS

Los Angeles is the fabled land of "the beautiful people," and you will notice that physiques are trimmer and fitter here than elsewhere in the US. The good weather means it's pleasant to exercise outdoors, but it also means it's harder to hide an out of shape body under layers of clothing. It's safe to say that more people work out here than anywhere else in the country.

There are **YMCAs** located throughout the city (check the telephone directory for one near you), and many offer good workout options at reasonable prices. On the other end of the spectrum, the most luxurious fitness complex in town is **The Sports Club LA,** 310-473-1447, which offers everything from personal trainers to a gourmet grill restaurant.

Here are some of the major health clubs that fall in-between:

- **24 Hour Fitness,** numerous locations, call 800-204-2400 for the nearest one.
- **Bally's Holiday Spa Health Clubs** are located throughout the city. For the one nearest you, call 800-695-8111.
- **Family Fitness Centers** have 11 sites in the Los Angeles area. Check the telephone directory under "Health Clubs" for the one nearest you.
- **Gold's Gym,** the original Gold's Gym started in Venice, California in 1965. It was the place for the serious no frills workout. As a result, bodybuilders flocked to Venice, creating a famous outdoor work-out area known as Muscle Beach; 310-392-3005, www.goldsgym.com.
- **LA Fitness Sports Clubs,** call 800-LA-FITNESS for locations near you.
- **The Sports Connection:** Santa Monica, 310-829-6836; West Hollywood, 310-652-7440; West Los Angeles, 310-450-4464
- **Spectrum Club,** numerous locales, check the Yellow Pages under "Health Clubs."

SPORTS AND RECREATION FOR CHILDREN

COMMUNITY RECREATION CLASSES

Many communities have recreation centers where a variety of classes and sports are offered to children. Call the center for detailed listings.

- **City of Beverly Hills Recreation & Parks Department,** 471 South Roxbury Drive, Beverly Hills 90212, 310-550-4761; recreational classes for toddlers to teens.
- **City of Calabasas, Department of Community Services,** 26135 Mureau Road, Calabasas 91302, 818-878-4225; recreational classes for toddlers to teens.
- **El Camino Adult Education Center,** 5440 Valley Circle Boulevard, Woodland Hills 91367, 818-888-1491; parent and child classes for ages birth to 5 years.
- **Glendale Parks and Recreation Department (Brand Studios),** 1601 West Mountain Street, Glendale 91201, 818-548-3782; recreational classes for toddlers to teens.
- **Granada Hills Recreation Center,** 16730 Chatsworth Street, Granada Hills 91344, 818-363-3556; recreational classes for toddlers to teens.
- **Northridge Recreation Center,** 18300 Lemarsh Street, Northridge 91325, 818-349-7341; recreational classes for toddlers to teens.
- **Pierce College Community Education,** 6201 Winnetka Avenue, Woodland Hills 91371, 818-719-6425; recreational classes for toddlers to teens.
- **Santa Monica College Community Services,** 1900 Pico Boulevard, Santa Monica 90405, 310-452-9214; recreational classes for 5 years to teens.
- **Valley College Community Services,** 5800 Fulton Avenue, Van Nuys 91401, 818-988-3911; recreational classes for toddlers to teens.
- **UCLA Recreation-Youth and Family Programs,** 2131 John Wooden Center, Box 951612, LA 90095, 310-825-3701; recreational classes for toddlers to teens.
- **Westwood Recreation Complex,** 1350 Sepulveda Boulevard, LA 90025, 310-473-3610; recreational classes for toddlers to teens.
- **Woodland Hills Recreation Center,** 5858 Shoup Avenue, Woodland Hills 91367, 818-883-9370; recreational classes for toddlers to teens.

BASEBALL CLUBS & LEAGUES

- **Balboa Sports Center,** Encino, 818-756-9642
- **Granada Hills American Little League,** Granada Hills, 818-368-8441
- **North Valley Youth Baseball,** North Hollywood, 818-368-7663
- **Sherman Oaks Little League,** Sherman Oaks, 818-501-8626
- **West Los Angeles Little League,** West LA, 310-471-3226
- **West Valley National Little League,** West LA, 818-342-0826
- **Youth Softball/T-Ball League,** Santa Monica, 310-458-8540

If the above clubs or leagues aren't close enough to where you live, check with the community recreation center near you.

SWIMMING

Whether you want your child to become an Olympic diver or to just splash around, check below for a swimming school near you. Or try your local YMCA.

- **Australian Swim School,** 22235 Sherman Way, Woodland Hills, 818-883-9100
- **Beverlywood Swim School,** 2612 South Robertson Boulevard, West LA, 310-838-4088
- **Cottonwood Swim School,** P.O. Box 49291, LA, 310-472-7474
- **Lucile Cowle Swim School,** 1619 Peyton Avenue, Burbank 818-848-8008
- **Dolphin Swim School,** 23400 Park Sorrento, Calabasas, 818-222-7946
- **Gerrish Swim and Tennis Club,** 2713 New York Drive, Pasadena, 626-798-9909
- **Grandview Swim School,** 2318 South Garfield Avenue, Monterey Park, 323-728-7575
- **Jed Heller's Swim School,** 21633 Farmington Lane, Saugus, 661-297-0275
- **UCLA Recreation-Youth and Family Programs,** 2131 John Wooden Center, LA, 310-825-3701

SOCCER

Contact the **American Youth Soccer Organization,** 800-USA-AYSO for the soccer league in your area. Or, you might want to call one of the local soccer fields:

- **Balboa Sports Center,** 17015 Burbank Boulevard, Encino, 818-343-4143
- **Barrington Recreation Center,** 333 South Barrington Avenue, Los Angeles, 310-476-4866
- **La Cienega Park,** 8400 Gregory Way, Beverly Hills, 310-550-4625
- **Mar Vista Recreation Center,** 11430 Woodbine Street, Mar Vista, 310-398-5982
- **Roxbury Park,** 471 South Roxbury Drive, Beverly Hills, 310-550-4761
- **Valley Plaza Recreation Center,** 12240 Archwood Street, North Hollywood, 818-765-5885
- **Van Nuys-Sherman Oaks Park,** 14201 Huston Street, Sherman Oaks, 818-783-5121
- **Westwood Recreation Complex,** 1350 South Sepulveda Boulevard, Westwood, 310-473-3610
- **Winnetka Recreation Center,** 8401 Winnetka Avenue, Winnetka, 818-341-1430

OS ANGELES GETS MUCH NOTORIETY FOR ITS URBAN SPRAWL. What may be less evident, until you live here, is that this area is rich with open spaces including parks, both urban and rural, and of course, beaches.

GREENSPACE

Like mini-oases, urban parks dot the City of Los Angeles, offering amenities such as tennis courts, baseball diamonds, basketball courts, and plenty of grass on which to stretch out and relax. For a listing of the parks in your neighborhood, check the front section of your telephone book, or call the recreation and parks department for your area (see **Sports and Recreation**). Two of the largest urban parks in Los Angeles are Griffith Park and Cheviot Hills.

Located in the Hollywood Hills, **Griffith Park** is said to be the largest publicly owned park in the United States. It occupies 4,400 acres in the hills, and features the Los Angeles Zoo, the Griffith Park Observatory Planetarium and Laserium, Travel Town Train Park, and the Autry Museum of Western Heritage. There are also pony rides, tennis courts, a soccer field, merry-go-round, picnic areas, and 50 miles of hiking and horseback riding trails.

Cheviot Hills Park, located in West Los Angeles near Cheviot Hills, offers 14 lit tennis courts, a pro shop, archery, swimming, basketball courts, soccer fields, baseball diamonds, a par course, a driving range, and what is reputed to be one of the busiest public golf courses in the country, Rancho Park.

If you're looking to be near some water but don't want to head for the beach, **Silverlake** and **Echo Park** are nice places to cool off and relax or take a jog or a walk around the lakes. At Echo Park you can rent canoes or paddle boats, or use the tennis courts, baseball diamonds, and two pools, one indoor, Olympic-sized, the other outdoor and shallow. Echo Park's lake is usually stocked with fish for any interested anglers. Silverlake is actually a reservoir, so no water access is allowed, but it still makes for a pretty, calming site, and the park does offer basketball courts, playing fields, and a gymnasium for children. And, nestled beneath the famed Hollywood sign is **Lake Hollywood**, which is not really a lake at all but an irrigated flood control area. Nonetheless, it features much open space, a jogging path around the lake that is strictly for pedestrian traffic, and a children's play area.

In the Valley, the largest recreational park is the **Sepulveda Basin Recreation Area**. It spans over 2,000 acres, including a lake for paddleboating and fishing. There are three golf courses, an archery range, 10 soccer fields and three cricket fields. Tennis, handball, and basketball courts also abound. In addition, paved jogging and biking trails make this a very popular spot on weekends. There is also a Japanese garden that's open for tours by reservation only, call 818-756-8166.

The **Van Nuys-Sherman Oaks Park** is another grassy and tree-shrouded neighborhood recreational area, featuring six baseball fields, eight tennis courts, and walking trails. Additional intimate neighborhood parks perfect for a quiet picnic include the **Johnny Carson Park** in Burbank and **Verdugo Park** in Glendale.

For those times when you can plan ahead, a visit to the **UCLA Hannah Carter Japanese Garden,** 310-825-4574 in the hills of Bel Air is a restful excursion. Open to the public only two afternoons per week, reservations are required and visits are supervised. But if you can tolerate all those provisos, you'll be treated to ancient pagodas, devil-casting stones, wild boar scarers, and a mix of indigenous Japanese trees and plants. Even though the **Getty Center** is known primarily as a museum, the wooded walkway leading to its spiral shaped "floating" garden there is designed to reflect the personality of each season. Guided tours of the garden are available if you can get reservations, 310-440-7300. If botanical gardens are your cup of tea, you should also consider the 207-acre **Huntington Library and Gardens,** 626-405-2141 in Pasadena, the **Virginia Robinson Gardens,** 310-276-5367 in Beverly Hills, and the **Los Angeles County Arboretum,** 626-821-3211 in Arcadia. Rose aficionados should not overlook the Sunken Rose Garden at **Exposition Park**, across the street from the University of Southern California.

The canyon parks offer a much different experience. With only a short drive you'll leave the city behind, and a few minutes along a hiking trail can find you in a spot where cars can't be heard, houses can't be seen, and you're about as likely to meet a lizard or jack rabbit as a human being. The largest area of canyon parkland is incorporated into the **Santa Monica Mountains National Recreation Area**. The Santa Monica Mountains stretch almost 50 miles across Los Angeles, and most of the trails here are part of, or hook up to, the Backbone Trail. For more information about parks throughout these mountains, call 818-597-1036.

Located on the northeastern edge of the San Fernando Valley is **Angeles National Forest,** one of seventeen national forests in California. Though accessible at many different points, the nearest part of the forest to most Los Angeles residents is adjacent to Pasadena, in the **San Gabriel Mountains**. Here you'll find campgrounds, picnic sites, lakes, streams, and miles of hiking trails. For more information call 818-574-5200.

Nestled in the Santa Monica Mountains near Pacific Palisades is **Will Rogers State Historic Park**. The former ranch of actor, humorist, and columnist Will Rogers, the park features tours through the 31-room ranch home, a large grassy hill for picnics, and miles of trails behind the house. On weekend mornings you can sit alongside the polo field and enjoy the matches.

Other beautiful canyon parks are **Malibu Creek State Park,** with more than 15 miles of hiking trails, **Temescal Gateway Park,** a 20-acre site that includes a trail that travels more than 12 miles north to the Backbone Trail, **Topanga State Park,** with 10,000-acres and 32 miles of hiking trails, **Brookside Park** in Pasadena, home to the Rose Bowl, a great gorge called the Arroyo Seco, and a golf course, and Santa Clarita's 350 acre **Placerita Canyon Park and Nature Center**, with 10 miles of hiking trails, a nature center, and picnic and campsites. In the spring these parks are filled with wildflowers that make hiking a colorful experience.

For a thorough introduction to LA parks, visit www.cal-parks.ca.gov.

BEACHES

Of course, Los Angeles is famous for its beaches, and they too provide an alluring place to get away from it all. There's nothing quite like standing at the edge of the continent, comforted by the knowledge that although there may be millions of people and a bustling civilization behind you, there are no such distractions in front of you as far as your eyes can see.

A few words of safety advice about going to the beach: first, if you plan on swimming, stay in front of the nearest open lifeguard tower on the beach. Second, take care to protect your eyes and skin; cover up with

UV-safe glasses, hats, or clothing if necessary, and use sunscreen. Third, being alone or even in a small group on the beach after dark unfortunately is not a safe idea. Stick to beach combing as a daytime activity.

At Malibu's most northwestern end is **Leo Carillo State Beach,** named for an LA-born actor. The 1,600-acre beach features nature trails leading to tide pools, and three campgrounds. The water is good for surfing and swimming, and you can explore Sequit Point which has sea caves and a natural tunnel.

Further southeast is **Zuma Beach,** known for its scenic views and rough surf. Zuma features volleyball, swimming, surfing, fishing, diving, and a kid's playground. At nearby **Point Dume** you can explore tide pools, and perhaps catch a glimpse of the migrating California gray whales, which travel through the area from November through May. Malibu's **Surfrider Beach** is known for its surfing as the name implies, but also has volleyball courts and a marine preserve with tide pools and a nature center.

At the foot of Topanga Canyon are the small **Las Tunas State Beach** and **Topanga State Beach**. Although Topanga State Beach covers almost 22 acres, it is most populated at a mile-long sandy stretch near Topanga Creek. Further south is **Will Rogers State Beach,** a popular spot for surfing, bodysurfing, and swimming. It too has volleyball courts, as well as a diving area and a playground.

Santa Monica State Beach is one of the largest and most popular beaches in California, due to its close proximity to much of the city, and its amusement amenities, including the Santa Monica Pier, playgrounds, and basketball and volleyball courts. Though you will see many people swimming here, reports on the water quality at local beaches often rate this one poorly. If you do choose to swim, stay away from storm drains and the areas closest to the pier.

Venice Beach features 238-acres of sand, but it's the adjacent boardwalk that has made it famous and brings most visitors. (See **Venice** in the **Neighborhoods** chapter.) Bicycles can be rented at several vendors along the beach front, and there's a nice children's playground. This is not the beach to visit to escape humanity, but for people-watching, it can't be beat.

Marina del Rey's **Dockweiler Beach** is quieter, though popular with families and young, single professionals. Features here include three-miles of shoreline, swimming, surfing, a picnic area and a campground. Busy **Manhattan Beach** boasts more than 100 volleyball courts. One of the main attractions here is The Strand, a concrete promenade for jogging, skating, and walking.

THE LOS ANGELES AREA OFFERS PLACES OF WORSHIP FOR A WIDE variety of religious preferences. While LA is not known as a town of one particular religion, there is a large Protestant community, a large Roman Catholic community (due in part to the fact that LA has the largest Latino population in the United States), and the second largest Jewish population in the United States, behind the New York metropolitan area.

What follows is a sampling of available spiritual centers. A quick look at the telephone directory should provide you with all of the religious centers in your neighborhood.

CHURCHES

AFRICAN METHODIST EPISCOPAL (AME)

- **First AME Church,** Los Angeles, 323-730-9180
- **First AME Church,** 1700 North Raymond Avenue, Pasadena, 818-798-0503

ASSEMBLY OF GOD

- **Assembly of God First,** 1320 Arizona Avenue, Santa Monica, 310-393-5763
- **Faith Tabernacle,** Purdue and Olympic Boulevard, West Los Angeles, 310-473-3135
- **New Life Assembly of God,** 330 North Hill Avenue, Pasadena, 626-795-8592

BAPTIST

- **Community Baptist Church,** 1234 Artesia Boulevard, Manhattan Beach, 310-372-3516
- **First Baptist Church of Pasadena,** 75 North Marengo Avenue, Pasadena, 626-793-7164
- **First Baptist Church of West LA,** 1609 South Barrington Avenue, West Los Angeles, 310-826-8374
- **New Mount Calvary Missionary Baptist Church,** 402 East El Segundo Boulevard, El Segundo, 310-324-0644

CHARISMATIC

- **Oasis Christian Church,** 4929 Wilshire Boulevard, Los Angeles, 323-937-5433

CHRISTIAN SCIENCE

- **Christian Science Churches and Organizations,** 1133 South Bundy Drive, West Los Angeles, 310-820-2014
- **First Church of Christ Scientist,** 1401 North Crescent Heights Boulevard, West Hollywood, 323-656-2888
- **First Church,** 550 East Green Street, Pasadena, 626-793-5151
- **Third Church,** 2803 East Colorado Boulevard, Pasadena, 626-793-7345

CHURCH OF CHRIST

- **Church of Christ,** 3020 West Burbank Boulevard, Burbank, 818-848-0545
- **Church of Christ Culver-Palms,** 310-202-7667
- **Van Nuys Church of Christ,** 14665 Sherman Way, Van Nuys, 818-785-2623

CONGREGATIONAL

- **First Congregational Church of Los Angeles,** 540 South Commonwealth Avenue, Los Angeles, 323-385-1341
- **Mount Hollywood Congregational Church,** 4607 South Normandie Avenue, Hollywood, 323-663-6577

EASTERN ORTHODOX

- **Saint Mark Coptic Orthodox Church,** 1600 South Robertson Boulevard, LA, 310-275-3050

EPISCOPAL

- **All Saints Episcopal Church,** 132 North Euclid Avenue, Pasadena, 626-796-1172
- **Saint Mary's Episcopal Church,** 3647 Watseka Avenue, Los Angeles, 310-558-3834
- **Saint Michael's Episcopal Church,** 361 Richmond Avenue, El Segundo, 310-322-2589

EVANGELICAL

- **Christ Community Church,** 7911 Winnetka Avenue, Canoga Park, 818-341-5750
- **Comunidad Evangelica De Los Angeles,** 15234 Saticoy, Van Nuys, 818-786-1050
- **West Los Angeles Holiness Church,** 1710 Butler Avenue, West LA, 310-473-2130

FRIENDS

- **Bell Friends Church,** 4100 East Gage Avenue, Bell, 323-560-1429

INDEPENDENT/INTERDENOMINATIONAL

- **The Church On the Way,** 818-779-8000
- **Sunlight Mission Church,** 1754 14th Street, Santa Monica, 310-450-8802
- **Victory Celebration Center,** 3901 West Victory Boulevard, Burbank, 818-848-7022

JEHOVAH'S WITNESS

- **Jehovah's Witness,** 608 East Grand Avenue, El Segundo, 310-322-0788
- **Jehovah's Witness,** 2119 Virginia Avenue, Santa Monica, 310-452-3825

- **Jehovah's Witness East,** 3493 East Del Mar Boulevard, Pasadena, 818-449-4890

LATTER-DAY SAINTS/MORMON

- **The Church of Jesus Christ of Latter-Day Saints,** 10777 Santa Monica Boulevard, Westwood, 310-474-1549
- **Jesus Christ of Latter-Day Saints,** 1215 East Mariposa, El Segundo, 310-322-5370
- **Jesus Christ of Latter-Day Saints,** 13042 Burbank Boulevard, Van Nuys, 818-787-2321

LUTHERAN

- **Emmanuel Lutheran Church,** 6020 Radford Avenue, North Hollywood, 818-761-6124
- **Grace Lutheran Church,** 4427 Overland Avenue, Culver City, 310-559-1027
- **First Lutheran Church,** 808 North Los Robles Avenue, Pasadena, 626-793-1139
- **First Lutheran Church,** 1100 Poinsettia Avenue, Manhattan Beach, 310-545-5653
- **Sherman Oaks Lutheran Church,** 14847 Dickens, Sherman Oaks, 818-789-0215
- **St. John's Lutheran Church,** 1611 East Sycamore Avenue, El Segundo, 310-615-1072

MENNONITE

- **Cristo Es La Respuesta,** 9292 Beachy Avenue, Pacoima, 818-899-0093

METHODIST, UNITED

- **Crescent Heights United Methodist Church of West Hollywood,** 1296 North Fairfax Avenue, West Hollywood, 323-656-5336
- **Culver-Palms United Methodist Church,** 4464 Sepulveda Boulevard, Culver City, 310-390-7717
- **Holliston United Methodist Church,** 1305 East Colorado Boulevard, Pasadena, 626-793-0685

- **United Methodist Church,** 540 Main Street, El Segundo, 310-322-0051
- **Westwood United Methodist Church,** 10497 Wilshire Boulevard, Westwood, 310-474-4511

NAZARENE

- **Church of the Nazarene,** 12120 Strathern, North Hollywood, 818-764-5077
- **Church of the Nazarene,** 1001 18th Street, Santa Monica, 310-453-4445

NON–DENOMINATIONAL

- **All Nations Living Fountains Church,** 1435 South La Cienega Boulevard, LA, 310-289-9163
- **Encino Community Church,** 5535 Balboa Boulevard, Encino, 818-345-8085
- **Lighthouse Christian Church,** 7943 Canoga Avenue, Canoga Park, 818-992-4935
- **World Harvest Church,** 14539 Sylvan, Van Nuys, 818-781-0777

PENTECOSTAL

- **Santa Monica Pentecostal Church,** 836 Cedar Street, Santa Monica, 310-452-3876
- **Iglesia De Dios Pentecostal,** 11216 1/2 Vanowen Avenue, North Hollywood, 818-508-9749
- **United Pentecostal Church of Van Nuys,** 6150 Tyrone Avenue, Van Nuys, 818-780-8334

PRESBYTERIAN (USA)

- **Bel Air Presbyterian Church,** 16221 Mulholland Drive, Bel Air, 818-788-4200
- **Beverly Hills Presbyterian Church,** 505 North Rodeo Drive, Beverly Hills, 310-271-5194
- **Brentwood Presbyterian Church,** 12000 San Vicente Boulevard, Brentwood, 310-826-5656
- **Culver City Presbyterian Church,** 11269 Washington Boulevard, Culver City, 310-398-3071

- **First Presbyterian Church of Hollywood,** 1760 North Gower, Hollywood, 323-463-7161
- **Pasadena Presbyterian Church,** 54 North Oakland, Pasadena, 626-793-2191
- **West Hollywood Presbyterian Church,** 7350 Sunset Boulevard, West Hollywood, 323-874-6646
- **Westwood Presbyterian Church,** 10822 Wilshire Boulevard, Westwood, 310-474-4535
- **Woodland Hills Presbyterian Church,** 5751 Platt Avenue, Woodland Hills, 818-346-7894

ROMAN CATHOLIC

- **American Martyrs Catholic Church,** 624 15th Street, Manhattan Beach, 310-545-5651
- **Good Shepherd,** 505 North Bedford Drive, Beverly Hills, 310-276-3139
- **Saint Andrews,** 311 North Raymond Avenue, Pasadena, 626-792-4183
- **Saint Cyril's,** 15520 Ventura Boulevard, Encino, 818-986-8234
- **Saint Bernardine Catholic Church,** 24410 Calvert, Woodland Hills, 818-888-8200
- **Saint Monica's,** 725 California Street, Santa Monica, 310-393-9287
- **Saint Philip,** 151 South Hill Avenue, Pasadena, 626-793-0693
- **Saint Victor Church,** 8634 Holloway Drive, West Hollywood, 310-652-6477

SEVENTH-DAY ADVENTIST

- **Seventh-Day Adventist,** 1527 Purdue Avenue, West LA, 310-479-1605
- **Seventh-Day Adventist Church of Santa Monica,** 1254 19th Street, 310-829-1945
- **Seventh-Day Adventist,** 4824 Tujunga Avenue, North Hollywood, 818-763-7174

UNITARIAN UNIVERSALIST

- **Emerson Unitarian Universalist Church,** 7304 Jordan Avenue, Canoga Park, 818-887-6101

- **Unitarian Universalist of Studio City,** 12355 Moorpark Avenue, Studio City, 818-769-5911
- **Unitarian Universalist Community Church,** 1260 18th Street, Santa Monica, 310-829-5436

UNITED CHURCH OF CHIRST

- **Congregational Church of Northridge-UCC,** 9659 Balboa Boulevard, 818-349-2400
- **Westwood Hills Congregational Church,** 1989 Westwood Boulevard, 310-474-7327
- **Woodland Hills Community Church,** 21338 Dumetz Road, Woodland Hills, 818-346-0820

UNITY

- **Unity West Church,** Santa Monica, 310-459-7437
- **West Valley Unity Church,** 18300 Strathern, Reseda, 818-345-6011

WESLEYAN

- **In His Steps Ministry,** 5730 West Adams Boulevard, Los Angeles, 323-939-3987
- **Korean Central Wesleyan Church,** 7921 De Garmo Avenue, Sun Valley, 818-768-3773

MOSQUES

- **Islamic Studies and Recruitment Center,** 14534 Arminta, Van Nuys, 818-787-0911
- **Masjid Bilal,** 4016 South Central Avenue, Los Angeles, 323-233-7274

SYNAGOGUES

CONSERVATIVE

- **Beth Am,** 1039 South La Cienega Boulevard, Los Angeles, 323-655-6401
- **Kehillat Ma'arav,** 1715 21st Street, Santa Monica, 310-829-0566
- **Mishkon Tephilo,** 206 Main Street, Venice, 310-392-3029

- **Sephardic Temple Tifereth Israel,** 10500 Wilshire Boulevard, West Los Angeles, 310-475-7311
- **Sinai Temple,** 10400 Wilshire Boulevard, West Los Angeles, 310-474-1518

ORTHODOX

- **Beth Jacob,** 9030 West Olympic Boulevard, Beverly Hills, 310-278-1911
- **Chabad,** 1111 Montana Avenue, Santa Monica, 310-394-5699
- **Pacific Jewish Center,** 505 Ocean Front Walk, Venice, 310-392-8749

RECONSTRUCTIONIST

- **Kehillath Israel,** 16019 Sunset Boulevard, Pacific Palisades, 310-459-2328

REFORM

- **Beth Shir Shalom,** 1827 California Street, Santa Monica, 310-453-3361
- **Leo Baeck Temple,** 1300 Sepulveda Boulevard, Bel Air, 310-476-2861
- **Stephen S. Wise Temple,** 15500 Stephen South Wise Drive, Bel Air, 310-476-8561
- **Temple Isaiah,** 10345 West Pico Boulevard, West Los Angeles, 310-277-2772
- **University Synagogue,** 11960 Sunset Boulevard, West Los Angeles, 310-472-1255
- **Wilshire Boulevard Temple,** 3663 Wilshire Boulevard, Los Angeles, 323-388-2401

EASTERN SPIRITUAL CENTERS

BAHA'I

- **Baha'i Faith Los Angeles Center,** 5755 Rodeo Road, Los Angeles, 323-933-8291

BUDDHIST

- **Soka Gakkai International,** 1212 7th Street, Santa Monica, 310-451-4422
- **Wat Thai of Los Angeles,** 8225 Coldwater Canyon Avenue, North Hollywood, 818-785-9552
- **West Los Angeles Buddhist Church,** 2003 Corinth, West Los Angeles, 310-477-7274

GAY/LESBIAN SPIRITUAL CENTERS

- **Metropolitan Community Church,** 8714 Santa Monica Boulevard, West Hollywood, 310-854-9110

GIVING BACK TO THE COMMUNITY IS ONE OF THE MOST rewarding experiences one can have. Whether you are skilled at building houses, caring for the elderly, tutoring underprivileged children, or canvassing neighborhoods, you can find a volunteer project that suits your talents and beliefs. Helping out in your new community is also a great way to meet people and can make the transition to an unfamiliar place less stressful.

VOLUNTEER PLACEMENT SERVICES

The following organizations coordinate much of LA's volunteer activity, from feeding the hungry to counseling fire victims to mediation for the City Attorney's Office. Give them a call and they'll direct you to where help is needed the most. Or go online, www.volunteermatch.org (a national service) or www.la-volunteer.org for local listings.

- **LA Works,** 888-LA-WORKS
- **Retired and Senior Volunteer Program (RSVP),** 818-908-5070
- **Volunteer Bureau of Los Angeles,** 888-CARE-4-LA
- **Volunteer Center Assistance League of Southern California,** 818-908-5066
- **Volunteer Center of Los Angeles,** 213-387-7201

AREA CAUSES

Once you've settled in, you may want to become involved in some of the many charitable organizations in Los Angeles. The list below is just a small sampling of the many worthy organizations and causes that would appreciate your support. When calling, ask to speak to their volunteer coordinator.

AIDS

- **AIDS Project Los Angeles (APLA)**, 323-993-1600
- **LA Shanti Foundation**, 323-962-8197, 818-908-8849
- **LA Gay and Lesbian Center**, 323-993-7400
- **Minority AIDS Project**, 323-936-4949
- **Out of the Closet Thrift-Store**, 310-473-7787

ALCOHOL AND DRUG DEPENDENCY

- **Alcohol-Drug Council, West**, 310-451-5881
- **Alcoholics Anonymous**, 310-474-7339
- **Center for Chemical Dependency**, 310-855-3411
- **Cocaine Abuse Info**, 800-274-2042
- **Families Anonymous**, 800-736-9805
- **Narcotics Anonymous**, 310-390-0279
- **National Alcohol and Drug Abuse Hotline**, 800-252-6465

ANIMALS

- **Animal Regulations Department & Shelters, City of Los Angeles**, 888-452-7381
- **Last Chance for Animals**, 310-271-6096
- **Pets are Wonderful Support (PAWS)**, 323-876-7297
- **ResQPet**, 818-346-1410
- **Society for the Prevention of Cruelty to Animals (SPCA)**, 323-730-5300

CHILDREN

- **Big Brothers of Greater Los Angeles**, 323-258-3333
- **Big Sisters of Los Angeles**, 323-933-5749
- **Boy Scouts of America**, 213-413-4400
- **Catholic Big Brothers**, 800-453-KIDS
- **Children of the Night**, 310-276-9283
- **Girl Scouts of America**, 323-933-4700
- **Jewish Big Brothers**, 800-453-KIDS
- **Make-A-Wish Foundation**, 310-788-9474

- **School Volunteer Program of the Los Angeles Unified School District,** 800-933-8133
- **Starlight Foundation of California,** 310-286-0271

CRIME PREVENTION

- **LAPD Volunteer Programs,** 213-485-8890
- **Neighborhood Watch Programs,** 213-485-3134

CULTURE AND THE ARTS

- **Cathartic Art Center,** 909-517-4337
- **Hollywood Bowl,** 323-850-2000
- **Los Angeles County Museum of Art,** 323-857-6000
- **Los Angeles Philharmonic,** 323-850-2165

DISABLED ASSISTANCE

- **Association for Retarded Citizens,** 323-290-2000
- **Braille Institute,** 323-663-1111
- **Easter Seal Society of Los Angeles and Orange Counties,** 310-204-5533
- **Greater Los Angeles Council on Deafness,** 323-478-8000
- **Independent Living Center of Southern California,** 818-988-9525
- **Orton/Ryan Center for Dyslexics,** 323-748-9596
- **Los Angeles Caregiver Resource Center,** 800-540-4442
- **Westside Center for Independent Living,** 310-390-3611
- **Western Law Center for Disability Rights,** 213-736-1031

ENVIRONMENT

- **American Oceans Campaign,** 310-576-6162
- **Audubon Society,** 323-876-0202
- **California Conservation Corps,** 213-744-2254
- **Heal the Bay,** 310-475-2994
- **Sierra Club,** 213-387-4287
- **Tree People,** 818-623-4879

GAY AND LESBIAN

- **Gay and Lesbian Alliance Against Defamation,** 323-658-6775
- **Gay and Lesbian Counseling Center,** 323-936-7500
- **Gay and Lesbian Parents of Los Angeles,** 323-654-0307
- **Los Angeles Gay & Lesbian Center,** 323-993-7400
- **West Hollywood Cares,** 310-659-4840

HEALTH & MEDICAL CARE

- **American Cancer Society,** 310-670-2650
- **Juvenile Diabetes Foundation International,** 310-842-6742
- **Los Angeles Free Clinic,** 323-653-8622 or 1990
- **Lymphoma Research Foundation,** 310-470-4912
- **Project Support for Spinal Cord Injury,** 310-553-3411
- **South Bay Free Clinic,** 310-318-2521
- **Valley Community Clinic,** 818-763-8836
- **Venice Family Clinic,** 310-821-3484
- **Westside Hotline,** 310-226-7009

HOMELESS

- **Chrysalis,** 213-895-7777
- **People Assisting the Homeless (PATH),** 310-996-0034
- **Saint Joseph Center,** 310-399-6878
- **Step Up on Second,** 310-394-6889
- **Union Station Foundation,** 818-449-4596
- **VOALA Hollywood Shelter,** 213-467-4006
- **West Hollywood Homeless Organization,** 213-850-4040

HUMAN SERVICES

- **Catholic Charities,** 310-829-7944
- **Habitat for Humanity,** 818-765-2073
- **The Salvation Army,** 818-361-6462
- **American Red Cross,** 310-394-3733

HUNGER

- **The Salvation Army,** 818-361-6462
- **Meals on Wheels,** 818-761-6224
- **Project Angel Food,** 323-845-1800
- **SOVA Food Pantry,** 310-828-3433
- **Westside Food Bank,** 310-314-1150

INTERNATIONAL

- **EF Foundation for Foreign Study Cambridge,** 800-447-4273
- **Travelers Aid Society of Los Angeles,** 310-646-2270

LEGAL

- **American Civil Liberties Union (ACLU),** 213-977-9500
- **Bet Tzedek Legal Services,** 323-939-0506
- **Legal Aid Foundation of Los Angeles,** 213-650-3883
- **Westside Legal Services,** 310-396-5456

LITERACY

- **Southern California Literacy Hotline,** 800-372-6641
- **Los Angeles Central Library,** 213-228-7000

MEN'S SERVICES

- **The Parent Support Group,** 310-659-5289
- **YMCA,** 310-553-0731

POLITICS–ELECTORAL

- **League of Women Voters of Los Angeles,** 323-939-3535
- **Voter Registration,** 562-466-1373

POLITICS–SOCIAL

- **Amnesty International,** 310-815-0450

SENIOR SERVICES

- **American Association of Retired Persons,** 310-496-2277
- **Jewish Family Services of Los Angeles,** 323-937-5930
- **Retired Senior Volunteer Program,** 310-394-9871, 818-908-5070
- **Los Angeles County Community and Senior Citizens Services,** 213-738-2600
- **Senior Health and Peer Counseling,** 310-828-1243

WOMEN'S SERVICES

- **LA Commission on Assaults Against Women,** 323-462-1281
- **Planned Parenthood of Los Angeles,** 323-226-0800
- **Progressive Health Services & Wholistic Health for Women,** 323-650-1508
- **Safe Harbor Women's Clinic,** 213-622-4073
- **Santa Monica Hospital Rape Treatment Center,** 310-319-4000
- **Venice Women's Clinic,** 310-392-4147
- **Women's Commission for Los Angeles,** 213-974-1455
- **YWCA,** 213-365-2991

YOUTH SERVICES

- **Angel's Flight,** 800-833-2499
- **Exceptional Children's Foundation,** 323-290-2000
- **LA Works Youth Action Corps,** 323-936-1340
- **Los Angeles County Runaway Adolescent Project,** 323-466-5015
- **Los Angeles Youth Network,** 323-957-7757
- **McGruff House Program,** 801-486-8691
- **MidValley Youth Center,** 818-904-0707

WITH APPROXIMATELY ONE CAR FOR EVERY 1.8 PERSONS IN Los Angeles it is easy to understand why LA consistently ranks number one in the nation for traffic congestion. Los Angeles is famous for its "car culture," and with good reason. The city covers 467 square miles and while it is technically possible to get around by foot, bicycle, bus, and the new Metro light rail or subway, in most cases it is quicker and more convenient to drive. The South Coast Air Quality Management District (AQMD) is doing its best to encourage use of public transportation, carpooling, bicycling and walking, and many smog-conscious residents are trying to cut down on their driving, especially during peak commute hours. (There's even a hot-line that you can call, 800-CUT-SMOG, to report a vehicle that you see emitting visible exhaust for more than 10 seconds.) In addition, the AQMD has mandated that companies with one hundred or more employees must encourage smog-cutting transportation alternatives. In consideration of these mandates, some companies now operate on "flex time," which allows employees to work a compressed schedule of nine out of ten working days so that fewer cars are on the road. Nonetheless, the bottom line is that even though many are limiting their driving, cars are a way of life here.

CARS AND TRAFFIC

A quick glance at the map will tell you that Los Angeles is the land of freeways. Any way you look at it, morning (7:30 a.m. to 10:30 a.m.) and afternoon (3 p.m. to 6 p.m.) rush hours are a bear. If avoiding these hours is not possible, be sure to heed the "Sig-Alerts" (named after their inventor), these electronic freeway condition signs tell you where major delays can be expected. Caltrans, the city crews responsible for maintaining LA's massive freeway network, posts real-time road conditions on the Internet, www.traffic.maxell.com/caltrans, making it possible to check whether the 405 (or any freeway in LA) is at its usual crawl or moving faster.

In general, the freeways are still the best way to go long distances. **Interstate 5** runs north-south, and is the fastest, though not the prettiest route to the San Francisco Bay Area and other parts of Northern California. **US-101** is a more scenic route through the state, and cuts through the San Fernando Valley and Hollywood. **Highway 1**, known as the Pacific Coast Highway (PCH) in the Los Angeles area, runs up and down the entire California Coastline. Most agree that at one time or another, it's worth the extra hours on the road to take Highway 1 to or from Northern California, as it covers some of the most beautiful geography in the country.

Locally, **I-10** runs east-west, and is the most common way to get from West LA to downtown, and points in between. The **I-405** runs north-south between the Valley and West LA, and down through the South Bay, and can have punishing traffic so be forewarned. Going north-south in south-central LA is the **I-110** freeway, which features an elevated carpool lane that's an impressive sight in itself. The relatively new **I-105** (featured in the movie "Speed") provides quick access from south-central LA to the west and dead ends at LAX. The **I-101** runs north-south in LA (called the Hollywood Freeway), but turns southeast in the Valley (and becomes the Ventura Freeway). Highway **134** runs east-west and begins in Toluca Lake, then becomes the **I-210** in Pasadena.

Some of the stickiest interchanges in LA include the "four-level" in downtown, which is where on-ramps to the 110, 101, 10, and 5 freeways are clustered within a mile of each other. The interchange between the 405 and 101 is also tough, especially from the 405 to the 101. However, the city recently has approved plans to add an additional lane to ease congestion, but expect additional delays while construction takes place. The 405 near LAX is another trouble spot, especially on Friday and Sunday evenings. On the surface streets, the intersection of Wilshire and Westwood Boulevards (in Westwood) is the busiest in the city. The junction of Wilshire and Santa Monica Boulevards (in Beverly Hills) is also very heavy.

Most locals have their tried and true shortcuts around town (remember Steve Martin's cruise through alleys, parking lots, and front lawns in "LA Story"?), but they may be stingy about telling you what they are. After all, too much traffic on the shortcut defeats the purpose! It's worth experimenting yourself to see which byways move and which don't.

CARPOOLING

The majority of cars on local freeways typically hold one passenger—the driver. Carpooling lanes, located in the far left lane and marked by a white diamond and carpooling signs, are for the exclusive use of cars that have two or more people in them, including the driver (some diamond lanes require a minimum of three people). Carpooling can be a real time-saver and is certainly a pro-active approach to saving the environment.

Check with your human resources office at work for carpooling incentives. Many employers offer gas coupons and other freebies to those who carpool with co-workers. Car-poolers may use special parking lots set aside for carpool participants. These Park & Ride locations are dotted throughout the city.

For more information on commuter carpools and vanpools, call **Commuter Transportation Services** at 213-380-7433 or 800-286-7433. For door-to-door transportation referrals for seniors and mobility-impaired people, call the **Paratransit Information Referral Service** at 800-431-7882. For more information on transportation around the greater LA area, call the **Regional Transportation Information Network** at 800-2LA-RIDE. The **Smart Traveler Information Line** provides comprehensive information about every possible transportation option in LA, including ridesharing, 800-266-6883, www.smart-traveler.com.

PARK & RIDE LOCATIONS

Too many to list here (see your *Thomas Guide* index for a full list), but here are some:

- **Burbank Metrolink Park & Ride,** 201 North Front Street, Burbank
- **College of the Canyons Park & Ride,** 26355 North Rockwell Canyon Road, Santa Clarita
- **Glendale Metrolink Park & Ride,** 400 West Cerritos Avenue, Glendale
- **Hayvenhurst Park & Ride,** Hayvenhurst & Magnolia, Encino
- **Manchester Park & Ride,** Manchester Avenue & I-100, Los Angeles
- **Parsons Company Park & Ride,** Pasadena Avenue & Union Street, Pasadena

- **Pasadena Park & Ride,** Sierra Madre Boulevard & Corson Street, Pasadena
- **Riverton Park & Ride,** Riverton Avenue & Ventura Boulevard, Los Angeles
- **Sepulveda Pass Park & Ride,** 2350 Skirball Center Drive, Brentwood
- **South Pasadena Park & Ride,** 435 South Fairoaks Avenue, South Pasadena
- **Topanga Plaza Park & Ride,** 6600 Topanga Canyon Boulevard, Canoga Park
- **Van Nuys Boulevard Park & Ride,** 7724 Van Nuys Boulevard, Van Nuys
- **Veterans Administration Park & Ride,** Wilshire Boulevard & I-405, Los Angeles
- **Washington & Fairfax Park & Ride,** Washington Boulevard & South Fairfax Avenue, LA

CAR RENTAL

There are numerous car rental agencies near the airports, and throughout the city. Call the following phone numbers for information, reservations, and locations:

- **Alamo,** 800-327-9633
- **Avis,** 800-831-2847
- **Budget,** 800-527-0700
- **Dollar,** 800-800-4000
- **Enterprise,** 800-325-8007
- **Hertz,** 800-654-3131
- **National,** 800-227-7368
- **Payless,** 800-729-5377
- **Rent-a-Wreck,** 800-535-1391
- **Thrifty,** 800-367-2277

TAXIS AND SHUTTLES

Unlike New York or Chicago, Los Angeles is not a major taxi town. You will not, for instance, be able to step out of any building and flag down a cab. Nonetheless, there are taxis outside the airports, hotels, and tourist attractions. If you need a cab at a specific time, your best bet is to call and order one in advance. Group shuttles are almost always cheaper than cabs for one passenger, and may still be cheaper for groups. The listing below includes both taxis and shuttles.

- **Airport Shuttle,** 310-215-9950
- **Checker Cab,** 310-201-0307
- **Super Shuttle,** 818-556-6600
- **Prime Time Shuttle,** 800-733-8267
- **United Taxi,** 800-290-5600
- **United Independent Taxi,** 800-411-0303
- **World Shuttle Services,** 888-992-8600
- **Valley Cab,** 818-787-1900
- **Yellow Cab,** 310-207-0245

LIMOUSINES

Check the telephone directory under "Limousine" for a listing of the many companies that provide limo service—just don't expect to get a limo on the day of the Academy Awards.

BY PUBLIC TRANSPORTATION

Los Angeles has an interesting history with public transportation. Until the 1940s, like most major American cities, LA had an extensive system of electric trolley cars, known as "Red Cars." The old tracks can still be seen in Santa Monica, Beverly Hills, and other parts of the city. Pressure from automobile companies and "others" led to the demise of the system, and the story is now one of the region's great scandals. More recently, civic leaders tried to rectify the situation with the **Metro**, LA's first subway. The project, delayed by shoddy workmanship and cost overruns, was unpopular with Angelenos ("A subway in earthquake country?" was the question commonly asked by those opposed to it). So unpopular, in fact, that in 1998 a proposition to outlaw the use of tax dollars to fund the Metro, once lines are finished in the Valley, passed by a 68% majority. Today, however, ridership on the Metro subway is way up and commuters are beginning to take advantage of this clean, predictable and well-patrolled mode of transport. It is safe to say from this point forward the subway can only gain in popularity and that Metropolitan Transit Authority (MTA) officials will continue to be in the forefront of unpopular decisions. Their next battle, to prevent duplication of city services officials have proposed cutting bus routes in

Hollywood and the San Fernando Valley. This too is being met with heavy opposition by current bus riders who like things the way they are. Despite the political bickering, the Metro now has three lines. The **Blue Line** runs from downtown to Long Beach. The **Red Line** originates from the Union Station in downtown and runs through Hollywood, finishing in North Hollywood. The **Green Line** takes commuters through south-central communities, between Redondo Beach and Norwalk. Fares are currently $1.35 for one segment. An unlimited local travel monthly pass may be purchased for $42. Maps, timetables, tickets and passes may be purchased in person at the MTA customer service center at Union Station, downtown, 800 North Alameda Street, or by calling 800-COM-MUTE (out of state, call 213-922-6059 to purchase passes; 213-922-6235 for customer service). On the Internet, visit www.mta.net for Metro and bus timetables, or www.scag.ca.gov/transit for online assistance with planning your travel itinerary via public transportation.

Due to the limited nature of the Metro and perhaps out of habit, most residents who use public transportation rely on MTA buses to get around. Newcomers might want to request a Transit Guide, published by the **Southern California Transit Advocates,** 3010 Wilshire Boulevard #362, Los Angeles, CA 90010. This $5 booklet lists over 50 fixed route public transit agencies operating in Southern California, with tips on using the systems. Here is the low-down on bus travel:

- The **Culver City Bus** can be reached by calling 310-559-8310 for recorded information. It provides local service in Culver City and to Los Angeles, Los Angeles International Airport (LAX), Marina del Rey, UCLA, Venice and the Westside. Adult fare is 60 cents.
- LA Department of Transportation (**LADOT**) operates **Commuter Express** and **DASH**. The Commuter Express links the San Fernando Valley with other parts of LA, including downtown, Burbank, Glendale, Pasadena, and LAX. The DASH is a shuttle bus that runs in the Valley and Greater LA. Call 818/213/310-808-2273 for more information.
- The LA County **Metropolitan Transit Authority (MTA/Metro)** serves the Greater LA area with more than 180 bus, rail and light-rail routes. The base fare is $1.35, the unlimited local travel monthly pass is $42. For maps, fares, passes and other information, call 800-COM-MUTE; TTY, 800-252-9040, 6 a.m. to 8:30 p.m., Monday-Friday, 8 a.m. to 6 p.m., Saturday and Sunday; out-of-towners should call 213-922-6235, 8 a.m. to 4:15 p.m., Monday-Friday, or write to: Metro Customer Relations, 1 Gateway Plaza, Los Angeles, CA 90012-2952.

- The **Metrolink** is a long-distance commuter train service connecting Los Angeles to surrounding counties, including Orange, Ventura, and San Diego. There is also a Ventura County Line that takes riders from Union Station to Northridge, Van Nuys, Burbank, and Glendale. Fares are determined by distance traveled. Call 800-371-5465 for more information.
- **Santa Clarita Transit (SCT)** offers local bus service in the Santa Clarita Valley, as well as express buses to downtown LA, Westwood, and the Valley. Call 805-294-1287 for more information.
- The **Santa Monica Municipal Bus Lines** (Big Blue Bus) can be reached at 310-451-5444. The Big Blue Bus services Santa Monica and the Westside, and some routes extend to UCLA, LAX, and downtown.
- The **Smart Traveler Information Line** provides comprehensive information about every possible transportation option in LA, including ridesharing, 800-266-6883, www.smart-traveler.com.
- The **West Hollywood City Line** services the city of West Hollywood, fares are 50 cents or free with an MTA pass. Call 800-447-2189 for route and schedule information.

NATIONAL TRAIN AND BUS SERVICE

- **Amtrak** can be reached at 800-872-7245, www.amtrak.com. The Los Angeles station is **Union Station** and is located downtown, 8090 North Alameda Street. Amtrak offers a variety of departure times for long-distance commuters into nearby San Diego. Discount fares can only be found on their web site at rail sales, www.reservations.amtrak.com, offering savings of up to 60% on long-distance coach train tickets.
- **Greyhound** can be reached at 800-231-2222, www.greyhound.com. The Los Angeles terminal is downtown at 1716 East 7th Street, 213-629-8402.

BY AIRLINE

- **Los Angeles International Airport (LAX)** is the largest and busiest airport on the West Coast. It is located on the coast, just south of Playa del Rey. For information call 310-646-5252 or visit their web site: www.airwise.com/airports/us/LAX
  Terminal 1: America West, Southwest and US Airways
  Terminal 2: Northwest, Air Canada, Air New Zealand, Hawaiian, Virgin Atlantic and others

Terminal 3: Alaska, Frontier, Midwest Express, Reno Air and TWA

Terminal 4: American Airlines, Canadian Airlines

Terminal 5: Delta Air Lines plus partner airlines

Terminal 6: Continental Airlines, Lufthansa, SkyWest and United international flights

Terminal 7: United Airlines and Air Jamaica arrivals

Terminal B is The Tom Bradley International Terminal and serves most non-US airlines, including Air France, British Airways, Cathay Pacific, Japan, and Mexicana.

- **Burbank/Glendale/Pasadena Airport** is located at 2627 North Hollywood Way, 818-840-8840, www.bur.com. Alaska, American, America West, SkyWest, Southwest, and United offer domestic service directly in and out of Burbank.
- **Long Beach Airport** is located at 4100 East Donald Douglas Drive, 562-421-8295, www.lgb.org. For information on parking, call 562-425-9665. Two commercial airlines service this airport: West Airlines and American Airlines.
- **Ontario International Airport** is located about an hour southeast of Los Angeles, at Airport Drive and Vineyard Avenue in Ontario. For general information, call 909-988-2700, for parking information, call 909-988-2737. Most of the airlines servicing LAX also service Ontario.
- **Orange County's John Wayne Airport** is located at 18741 Airport Way in Santa Ana, 714-252-5006, www.ocair.com; parking, 714-252-6262. Airlines servicing the airport: America West, Northwest, Southwest, TWA, United, US Air, Alaska, American, Continental, Delta, Reno.
- **Santa Monica Airport** is at 3223 Donald Douglas Loop South, 310-458-8591. No commercial flight service is offered here, it is for the exclusive use of private planes and helicopters.
- **Van Nuys Airport** is at 16461 Sherman Way and is for corporate and private planes and helicopters, no commercial flights. Their phone number is 818-785-8838.

MAJOR AIRLINES

- **Alaska,** 800-252-7522, www.alaskaair.com
- **American,** 800-433-7300, www.aa.com
- **British Airways,** 800-247-9297, www.britishairways.com

- **Canada 3000,** 877-973-8000
- **Cathay Pacific.** 800-233-2742
- **Delta,** 800-221-1212, www.delta-air.com
- **Continental,** 800-523-3273, www.flycontinental.com
- **Japan Airlines,** 800-525-3663
- **Mexicana,** 800-531-7921
- **Northwest-KLM,** 800-225-2525, www.nwa.com
- **Southwest,** 800-435-9792, www.southwest.com
- **TWA,** 800-241-6522, www.twa.com
- **US Airways,** 800-428-4322, www.usairways.com
- **United,** 800-241-6522, www.ual.com

ONLINE AIR TRAVEL RESOURCES

Bargain airfares can be had by the savvy web-head. Many airlines offer Internet specials via their web sites. The best bargains, however, have to be hunted down. Try www.expedia.com or www.travelocity.com for flight, hotel and car rental reservations. Discounts on airline reservations are also available at Intellitrip, www.intellitrip.com. It scans other travel related web-sites to find the least expensive fare to your destination. Best of all, it's free, you'll just need to download the software. Or, visit www.cheaptickets.com to locate your cheapest fare based on your itinerary. TravelBids, www.travelbids.com has travel agencies bid on your trip, with the lowest bided fare winning. The cost is $5 to register and $5 for each listing. Another bidding option is through Priceline, www.priceline.com. Their motto, "Name Your Price and Save" says it all. Good luck!

A S A CITY WITH A HUGE TOURISM INDUSTRY, LOS ANGELES AND the surrounding areas have numerous hotels and motels. Accommodations run the gamut from utilitarian to ultra-luxurious. When reserving a room, be sure to ask about discounts or weekend packages. Some hotels offer senior citizen and/or automobile club rates. Many lodgings have un-advertised special rates that they offer only if customers inquire. Keep in mind that summer rates can be higher than the rest of the year, and that big conventions or other area events will cause hotels to fill up fast and rates to rise. Remember, the cost of living is high in Los Angeles, and hotel room rates reflect that fact.

Quickbook, 800-789-9887, www.quikbook.com, is a national discount room reservation service that offers reduced room rates for many hotels. Other similar services: **Express Reservations,** 800-356-1123, **California Reservations,** 800-576-0003, **Room Exchange,** 800-846-7000, and **Hotel Reservations Network,** 800-964-6835, www.hoteldiscount.com. These services are free, however, unlike booking a room directly with the hotel, many do not give a grace period before a charge is applied in the event you cancel your reservation.

The following list of hotels and motels is by no means complete. For more listings, check the telephone directory under "Hotels and Motels." If you know the area in which you wish to book a room, you might call the local Chamber of Commerce or visit the city's web site for a list of what's available. The LA Visitor's Bureau, 800-228-2452, www.lacvb.com, may also be able to make some recommendations based on your budget.

LUXURY LODGINGS

There is no shortage of luxury hotels in Los Angeles and the sky is the limit in terms of room rates ($5,000 a night for a suite at the Century

Plaza Hotel, where visiting presidents and dignitaries stay). Here are just a few of the many:

- **The Argyle,** 8353 Sunset Boulevard, West Hollywood, 323-654-7100; rooms begin at $225.
- **Beverly Hills Hotel,** 9641 Sunset Boulevard, Beverly Hills, 310-276-2251; rooms start at $300.
- **Century Plaza Hotel & Tower,** 2025 Avenue of the Stars, Century City, 310-277-2000; rooms begin at $375.
- **Hotel Bel Air,** 701 Stone Canyon Road, Bel Air, 310-472-1211; $315 and up.
- **Loews Santa Monica Beach Hotel,** 1700 Ocean Avenue, Santa Monica, 310-458-6700; rooms begin at $205.
- **The Peninsula,** 9882 Santa Monica Boulevard, Beverly Hills, 310-551-2888; rates begin at $350.
- **Regent Beverly Wilshire,** 9500 Wilshire Boulevard, Beverly Hills, 310-275-5200; one night costs $320 and up.
- **Ritz Carlton Huntington,** 1401 South Oak Knoll Avenue, Pasadena, 626-568-3900; rooms begin at $225.
- **Ritz Carlton Marina del Rey,** 4375 Admiralty Way, Marina del Rey, 310-823-1700; rooms go for $240 and up.

MIDDLE RANGE LODGINGS

For hotels with multiple locations, call and inquire on their rates and reservations, prices will vary according to location.

- **Marriott Hotels/Inns,** 800-228-9290; Marriotts are located in Century City, Long Beach, LAX, Marina del Rey, Torrance, and Woodland Hills.
- **Hilton Hotels,** 16 in the LA area, call 800-445-8667
- **Hyatt Hotels,** 800-233-1234, locations in Century City, LA, West Hollywood and Long Beach.
- **Radisson Huntley Hotel,** 1111 Hotel Santa Monica, 1111 2nd Street, Santa Monica, 310-394-5454, 800-333-3333; rooms start at $199.
- **Radisson Valley Center Hotel,** 15433 Ventura Boulevard, Sherman Oaks, 818-981-5400; rooms start at $110.
- **Shangri-La Hotel,** 1301 Ocean Avenue, Santa Monica, 800-345-7829; rooms start at $145.
- **Wyndham Checkers Hotel,** 535 South Grand Avenue, downtown, 213-624-0000; rooms start at $179.

BED & BREAKFAST INNS

The majority of B&Bs in Los Angeles are hosted, usually by the proprietors, and are reminiscent of a stay at a mini-hotel with a dash of an overnighter at grandma's house. Nearly all require a minimum two-night stay. It is possible to book reservations through a B&B directly, though some only list with an agency. In comparison to the number of hotels in LA, the selection of B&Bs is limited. The following agencies can assist you with locating a B&B that suits your needs and budget. Commissions, if any, are included in the price of the reservation.

- **B&B International,** 127111 McCartysville Place, Saratoga, CA 95070, 800-872-4500, www.bbintl.com; approximately 10 local B&B's are listed with brief descriptions, pictures, and reservation information on their web site, each location has been inspected by a B&B International representative for quality assurance.
- **Inn & Travel Network,** 2095 Exeter Road, Suite 80, Memphis, TN 38138, 901-755-9613, www.innandtravel.com; offers a database of 20,000 B&B's worldwide, including Los Angeles. There is no fee to obtain an inn's name and phone number; an annual fee is required to view more detailed descriptions.
- **LA Convention & Visitors Bureau,** 633, West Fifth Street, Suite 600, Los Angeles, CA 90071, 213-624-7300, www.lacvb.com; search their web site or call for free referrals to local B&B's.

SHORT TERM LEASES

- **Days Inn Extended Stay,** 800-DAYS-INN
  Glendale, 600 North Pacific Avenue, 818-956-0202
- **Execustay Inc.,** 800-388-0004
  Newport Beach, 3 Corporate Plaza Drive
- **Extended Stay America,** 800-398-7829 (call for more locations)
  Gardena, 18602 South Vermont Avenue, 310-515-5139
  Torrence, 19200 Harbor Gateway, 310-328-6000
  LAX, 6531 South Sepulveda Boulevard, 310-468-9337
  Long Beach, 4105 East Willow Street, 562-989-4601
- **Oakwood Apartments**
  Marina del Rey, 4111 Via Marina, 310-823-5443
  Los Angeles, 209 South Westmoreland, 323-380-4421
  West Los Angeles, 3636 South Sepulveda Boulevard, 310-398-2794
  Universal City, 3600 Barham Boulevard, 818-567-7368

- **Residence Inn by Marriott,** 800-321-2211
  Arcadia, 321 East Huntington Drive, 626-446-6500
  Beverly Hills, 1177 South Beverly Drive, 310-277-4427
  Long Beach, 4111 East Willow Street, 562-595-0909
  Manhattan Beach, 1700 North Sepulveda Boulevard, 310-546-7627
  Redondo Beach, 3701 Torrance Boulevard, Torrance, 310-543-4566
  Santa Clarita, 25320 The Old Road, Valencia, 661-290-2800

INEXPENSIVE LODGINGS

For hotels with multiple locations, call and inquire on their rates and reservations, prices will vary according to location, but generally range between $40 to $125.

- **Banana Bungalow Hollywood,** 2775 Cahuenga Boulevard, Hollywood, 800-446-7835; rooms are hostel-style singles with baths; no individual telephone lines.
- **Best Western,** 310-478-1400; there are various locations in LA, including Santa Monica, Pasadena, and Westwood.
- **The Beverly Laurel Motel,** 8018 Beverly Boulevard, Los Angeles, 800-962-3824
- **Beverly Terrace,** 496 North Doheny Drive, Los Angeles, 310-274-8141; offers pleasant if small rooms in a great location.
- **Comfort Inn,** 800-228-5150; there are 100+ locations throughout LA, including downtown, Burbank, Hollywood.
- **Econo Lodge,** 800-553-2666; a handful of Econo Lodges dot the LA area, including downtown, Hollywood, Glendale, and Inglewood. The accommodations are basic, but inexpensive.
- **Holiday Inn,** 800-465-4329; there are approximately 25 Holiday Inns in the Los Angeles area. Call for reservations and information.
- **Hotel Figueroa,** 939 South Figueroa Street, downtown, 213-627-8971
- **Howard Johnson's,** 800-654-2000; there are five Howard Johnson's in the Los Angeles area.
- **The Magic Hotel,** 7025 Franklin Avenue, Hollywood, 323-851-0800; cheery two-story lodge type building located near Hollywood tourist attractions.
- **Motel 6,** 800-466-8356; various locations, including Hollywood.
- **Ramada Inn,** 800-228-2828; multiple locations, including West Hollywood.

HOSTELS

There are three **American Youth Hostels** in the Los Angeles area:

- **Santa Monica,** 1434 2nd Street, 310-393-3413
- **Fullerton,** 1700 North Harbor Boulevard (nearest to Disneyland), 714-738-3721
- **San Pedro,** 3601 South Gaffey Street, #613, 310-831-8109

YMCAS

While there are multiple YMCA's in Los Angeles, the Glendale location (140 North Louise, 818-240-4130) is the only one that offers lodging. Dormitory rooms are for men only and are $26 per night. Vacancies are rare, so call ahead.

H AVE CAR, WILL TRAVEL. YOU CAN TELL A LONG WEEKEND JUST by the considerable increase in freeway traffic on Friday after-noon. Many Angelenos use the weekend as an opportunity for a quick escape from the city. San Francisco, Las Vegas, San Diego, Santa Barbara, and Mexico are popular weekend destinations, as are Catalina and Palm Springs. But with LA as big as it is, just driving into a different community across town, like Long Beach, can be a quick getaway in itself. Don't forget to review the **Greenspace and Beaches** chapter of this book for other relaxing ways to fill up a weekend. Also, call the **California Division of Tourism**, 800-862-2543 and request their fact-filled brochure on popular California getaway destinations.

Catalina Island is approximately 22 miles west of Long Beach. Accessible only by a two hour boat ride (or, for the financially blessed, a helicopter ride) across the Pacific Ocean. Getting to this resort town requires a little bit of planning but is worth the effort. Once you land in Avalon, the island's port, look into the bay to receive greetings from the bright orange fish that are native to the waters here. Since the island is so small, 28 miles long and 8 miles wide, rented golf carts are the only means of transportation for visitors. Take your cart on a loop around the island for a self-guided tour. Over 80% of the land has been set aside for preservation of native flora and fauna. Most hotels require a two night minimum stay on the weekends. Contact the Catalina Island Visitors Center, 310-510-1520 for trip-planning assistance.

Palm Springs is a popular (particularly with the gay crowd) golf and spa resort destination located in the upper Colorado Desert. And, national golf tournaments are frequently held here, making it a favorite destination for golf lovers. Upscale shopping is another prime activity. Don't miss the Palm Springs Tram, which whisks you from desert coun-try to an Alpine forest within 15 minutes and provides a beautiful birdseye view of the city. Contact Palm Springs Tourism Center, 800-347-7746, www.palm-springs.org, for more information. Or, request a Palm Springs Desert Resorts Vacation Planner, 800-417-3529.

San Francisco, charming and fresh, despite being a bit crowded. Popular sightseeing destinations: Fishermans' Wharf, the Golden Gate Bridge and Park, the Presidio, Alcatraz Island, Coit Tower, Chinatown, Union Square, and of course, their old-fashioned cable cars. A word to the wise, much of your sightseeing time can be spent seeking out street parking, especially critical on weekends. You're better off shelling out the bucks for garage parking. Contact San Francisco's Visitor Information Center, 415-391-2000 for planning assistance. With frequent cheap flights out of LAX and Burbank Airport to San Francisco, San Jose, or Oakland, you may opt to skip the 7- to 8-hour drive north and fly instead.

Laguna Beach, about an hour south of Los Angeles, is a picturesque artists' colony and resort town. Art collectors can, and do, spend entire weekends just checking out the local artists at the town's popular summer Sawdust Festival (from July to August). The frequently sold-out Pageant of the Masters, a live-stage recreation of famous works of art by community actors set to live music, is a unique must-see as well. Many area hotels offer overnight packages that include tickets to the show, be sure to ask. The Laguna Beach Visitor Information Center, 800-877-1115, can provide more detailed information.

Drive another hour and a half further south and you'll be in **San Diego**. Though it's now the second largest city in California, San Diego has still managed to maintain a laid-back beach town feel. Perhaps it's because the largest naval air station on the West Coast is based here. Home to the world-renowned San Diego Zoo, Sea World Marine Park, La Jolla, Old Town, and Coronado Island, San Diego is a popular destination for families. After a day of shopping and sight seeing, head over to downtown's Fifth Avenue, a popular street for nighttime dining, dancing and people-watching.

On the southern edge of San Diego are two international border crossings into **Mexico**. Young people jam the borders on long weekends (creating one-hour plus waits) and head into Tijuana's main drag, Avenida de Revolution, for serious bar hopping and partying. The San Diego Convention & Visitors Bureau, 800-892-VALU, www.sandiego.org, can provide additional information on San Diego and trips into Mexico.

Santa Barbara is another coastal community two hours north of Los Angeles. Highlights of this historically rich town include the El Presidio State Historic Park, Mission Santa Barbara, the Zoological Dens, and Sea Center. Antique collectors and flea market hunters should keep an eye out for **Summerland**, a tiny little town just five miles south of Santa Barbara. Many of the buildings along the town's main strip, Lillie Avenue, feature antique shops, cafes and houses constructed in the late 1800's. The Santa Barbara Visitor Information Center, 800-927-4688, can assist you with your vacation plans in both towns. Just off the coast of Santa Barbara are **San Miguel** and **Santa Cruz Islands**, which offer scenic hiking, kayaking, caverns, and a petrified forest. Both islands are accessible only by chartered boat. Contact the Channel Islands National Park, 805-658-5730, for additional information.

Big Bear, an easy two-hour drive east of Los Angeles, is a popular ski destination in the winter, and is one of the largest year-round recreational areas in the state. There are seven ski resorts here, offering a good selection of slopes with varying degrees of difficulty. Come summer, you can rent a boat, go horseback riding, hiking, camping or picnicking. Quaint bed and breakfasts abound, perfect for romantic getaways. Contact the Chamber of Commerce, 909-866-4608, for more vacation ideas.

From May through September flower lovers should take a lovely day trip to the flower beds of **Lompoc**. Many of the nation's flower seeds are harvested here, and the colorful flower fields are the primary attraction in this picturesque town. Its normal population of 37,000 multiplies by three during the Lompoc Valley Flower Festival, held over a weekend in late June. Formal bus tours are arranged for the many tourists. Contact the Lompoc Valley Chamber of Commerce, 805-736-4567, for detailed information.

Nature lovers should consider the five-hour drive out to **Sequoia & Kings Canyon National Parks**. Among the park's lush old growth pines, firs, and cedars are some of the world's oldest sequoia trees. In addition to camping in log cabins, there's hiking, fishing, climbing, and horseback riding in the spring and summer. During the winter, cross-country skiers delight in trekking through the snow-frosted sugar pine forest. Contact the Sequoia-Kings Canyon Park Services Company, 209-335-5500, for camping reservations and trip planning information.

And, on a completely different note, if you're in the mood for glamour and gambling, **Las Vegas**, Nevada is a mere four hour drive away. With popular themed mega-hotels in constant construction on the Strip, this city likely has more hotel rooms clustered in one town than anywhere else in the world. Best room bargains are to be found on the weekdays, and many hotels require a two-night minimum on weekends. The buffets aren't as good a bargain as they once were, but food is still relatively cheap considering it's all you can eat. This glittering, restless city offers one of the most economical vacations around—unless you lose it all at the tables. Non-gaming options include the Bellagio's art museum, the MGM theme park, the spectacular Red Rock Canyon, and Hoover Dam. Call the Las Vegas Convention and Visitors Authority, 702-892-7575, for more information.

NATIONAL PARKS & FORESTS

- The **National Park Service** takes phone reservations, call 800-365-2267, or go online to http://reservations.nps.gov for details about its camping facilities. For reservations at Yosemite call 800-436-7275, Carlsbad Caverns, 800-967-2283.
- The **National Forest Service's** toll free reservation line is 877-444-6777, TDD, 877-833-6777. They will take your reservation up to 240 days in advance. Their web site is www.reserveusa.com.

OTHER RESOURCES

For more ideas on quick getaways and packages, go online to www.latimes.com/travel, or check the **Online Air Travel Resources** section in the **Transportation** chapter.

FOR YEARS, WHEN YOU TURNED ON THE NATIONAL NEWS THERE always seemed to be some drama occurring in LA. Riots, earthquakes, fires, landslides, floods, or captivating trials–there was Southern California in the starring role. Well the riots are long over (though not the social issues that spawned them), the trials will probably keep coming (the Menendez brothers, Heidi Fleiss, O.J. Simpson, who's next?), but the one thing you can bet on as a part of life here is natural disasters.

Fortunately, most natural disasters like earthquakes, fires, landslides, and floods happen infrequently and seriously effect relatively few people. While you may be inconvenienced by increased traffic due to flooding or a temporary loss of power due to a temblor, the vast majority of LA residents have suffered no loss of property or bodily injury due to these disasters. On the other hand, for those few people who are victims, the results can be devastating. While most locals do not go through life in fear of these disasters, it is wise to have a healthy respect for Mother Nature's power, and, when possible take precautions to guard against it.

In addition to what follows, the **LA County Office of Emergency Management** has a number to call, 323-980-2260, for disaster preparedness information.

EARTHQUAKES

One of the biggest fears people relate about living in California is earthquakes. While most natives aren't too frightened by the swaying or bumps of small temblors, no one relishes the thought of the proverbial "Big One."

The 6.6 Northridge earthquake that rocked LA on January 17, 1994 killed 57 people, with 1,500 more suffering serious injuries. It is believed that casualties would have been much greater had it struck in the middle of the day, when the collapsed stores would have been filled with shoppers and the failed freeways crowded with cars. (However, most earthquakes occur at night.) Twenty-two thousand people were forced to leave their homes (either permanently or while repairs were made) due to quake damage, and more than 3,000 buildings were declared unsafe for reentry. Yet, when you consider the millions of people who felt the quake that early morning, the number of people affected in more than a casual way was relatively small.

While only chance dictates who will be in the wrong place at the wrong time during a quake, there are precautions you can take to aid your survival in an earthquake. Here are some for your to consider.

In your home:
- Place your bed away from windows and bookshelves, and don't hang heavy objects nearby.
- Heavy ceiling fans and lights should be supported with a cable bolted to the ceiling joist. The cable should have enough slack to allow it to sway.
- Store flashlights and batteries and a crowbar (in case your door gets jammed shut) in your bedroom.
- In an accessible closet, store a disaster kit. Local home improvement and specialty stores sell earthquake preparedness kits.
- Store heavy objects in lower shelves.
- Use brackets to bolt bookshelves, file cabinets, and other heavy pieces of furniture to the walls. Be sure to connect brackets to wall studs.
- Brace chimneys. (Usually a professional will need to do this for you.)
- Fasten down lamps and valuable objects, and use putty to hold breakables in place.
- Be sure your home is bolted to its foundation. This is especially a concern with older homes, many of which were not fastened to the foundation at the time of construction.
- Strap your water heater to the wall.
- Put latches on cabinet doors.
- Know where your water and gas valves are located, and how to shut them off.

In your car:
- Store the following: flashlight, batteries, portable battery-powered radio, first aid kit, maps, food such as trail mix or non-melting energy bars, water, tools, and cash.

In your office:
- Store the following: a portable battery-powered radio, flashlight with spare batteries, and a first aid kit. Most companies have emergency procedures in place to follow in the event of an emergency.

When an earthquake strikes:
- At the risk of stating the obvious or the seemingly impossible, remain calm. You can cause more needless disruption by irrational behavior than the earthquake itself may produce for you.
- Move away from windows and heavy objects that may tumble.
- If the shaking is severe, stand in a door jam, or crawl beneath a sturdy piece of furniture like a desk.
- Falling or sparking power lines present a real danger. Be alert for them if you run outside.
- If you smell gas after a quake, turn off your gas valves and notify authorities that you may have a leak.
- Your electrical power may be disrupted.
- Cordless telephones that run on electricity will not work if the power is down, so it's a good idea to have at least one phone that doesn't require electricity to work. Phone service may be disrupted, but often it is the high volume of calls within the quake area that causes overloads of the telephone lines. If you do have service, make only necessary calls. True emergency telephone calls may have a difficult time connecting because local people are calling around town to check on friends. Instead, designate a friend or family member outside the area (preferably out of state) who can serve as the point person to your circle of friends. Since calls to and from outside the area are often easier to make, your point person can keep track of who is okay and report to concerned family members and friends, thus saving vital phone lines.
- Remember, most earthquakes are over in a matter of seconds. However, aftershocks, sometimes strong ones, can continue for weeks or months after a quake.

DISASTER KITS

You may elect to purchase a prepared kit (see list of stores below) or do like most Angelenos do, make your own disaster kit. Any waterproof plastic container that's big enough to store all the items will do. The items in your list should be customized according to your specific needs, but generally, here are what experts recommend:

Portable radio and batteries
Flashlights and batteries
Candles and matches
Medical supplies
Canned and/or dehydrated food
Sleeping bags or blankets and sturdy shoes
Three gallons of drinking water per person in your household
Barbecue or camp stove
Toiletries, including diapers for those with little ones

Store your kit in a place that's easily accessible to the entire family. Don't forget to rotate your water and food every six months. And check that your batteries and first aid supplies are still fresh every other year.

Here are some mail order and walk-in stores that specialize in earthquake supplies:

- **Grabbit Emergency Pack,** 310-471-8608
- **Quake Kare Inc.,** 805-241-9898, www.quakekare.com
- **Recon-1,** 818-342-2666, 19423 Ventura Boulevard, Tarzana
- **Safe-T-Proof Disaster Preparedness Co.,** 888-677-2338
- **SOS Survival Products,** 800-479-7998, 15705 Strathern Street #11, Van Nuys

FIRES, LANDSLIDES, & FLOODS

Summer brush fires are a normal occurrence in California, especially in hilly canyon areas with a good deal of vegetation. If you live in such an area (for instance Malibu, Topanga Canyon, or other canyons), be sure to clear the brush around your home before the summer dry season.

Following are recommendations from wildfire specialists on how to shield your home, especially in areas of high fire danger:

- Get rid of a wood shake or shingle roof, and replace it with a steel or composition roof rated Class A (will not burn) or Class B (slightly less protective).
- Reduce or eliminate shrubbery that would act as fuel in your yard

and along your driveway. Remove "torch trees" close to your home, trim flammable, dead branches from older trees, and maintain thirty feet or more of "defensive space" in the form of protective landscaping around your home and one hundred feet or more downhill. The US Forest Service or National Park Service can provide you with information on protective landscaping.

• Be certain that your community has roads that are clear of vegetation within at least twenty feet on either side, to act as a firebreak and allow for safe evacuation and access by fire fighting equipment.

Burn areas are especially vulnerable to landslides in the rainy season, as the vegetation that normally holds the hills in place has been burnt away. But fire sites are not the only places that landslides occur. The sharp cliffs above the Pacific Coast Highway regularly slide during the rains, and slides are also common in all hilly neighborhoods. Residents often use sandbags to shore up iffy areas, and tarps to cover precarious hillsides.

These same neighborhoods are particularly susceptible to flooding. Remote canyon roads may be inaccessible during heavy rains, though not for longer than a few days.

Note that massive fires, landslides, and floods are seldom issues for people living in the most populated areas of Los Angeles.

WITH YEAR-ROUND GOOD WEATHER, IT'S NO WONDER THERE are so many things going on in Los Angeles. Hundreds of yearly events, including the popular Auto Show and Home & Garden Expo, take place at the LA Convention Center alone. Museums and individual communities host their own events year around, keep an eye out for flyers and ads in the local publications for more happenings. The following is just a sample listing of annual festivities:

JANUARY

- **Auto Show,** 213-624-7300
  Check out every major car manufacturer's latest models and concept cars too, at the LA Convention Center. Most of the new cars are open for viewing, touching, photographing, and dreaming.
- **Tournament of Roses Parade,** 626-449-7673
  The January 1st parade travels along Orange Grove Boulevard in Pasadena. Folks typically camp out on the sidewalks the night before for the best views. You can also pay a nominal fee to see the floats up close after the parade—wear comfortable shoes, even though all the floats are parked nose to nose, you will walk the equivalent of two miles to view them all.
- **The Rose Bowl,** 626-449-7673
  Watch the superbowl of college football as the champs of the Pac 10 duels with the champs of the Big 10.
- **Martin Luther King Jr. Awareness Day,** 818-899-4357, 323-290-4100
  A citywide celebration, featuring poetry, art, films, a gospel fest and lectures, culminating in the Kingdom Day Parade, 323-298-8777.

FEBRUARY

- **African-American History Month Celebrations,** 323-295-0521
  A citywide event featuring lectures, films, performances, etc.
- **Chinese New Year Celebration,** 213-617-0396
  Punctuated by noisy firecrackers and lion dancing, a parade, street fair and carnival are some of the celebrations to take place in Chinatown.
- **Mardi Gras Celebration,** 213-625-5045
  On Fat Tuesday, head downtown to the El Pueblo de Los Angeles Historical Monument for a parade, costume contest, and general revelry.

MARCH

- **Environmental Education Fair,** 626-821-3222
  A festival to increase environmental awareness held at the Arboretum of LA county.
- **LA Marathon,** 310-444-5544
  Nearly every community the marathon runs through, from Chinatown to Hollywood, throws a block party along the race route to cheer on the runners. A festival and fair are held in Exposition Park, the starting and finishing point of the race.

APRIL

- **Blessing of the Animals,** 213-625-5045
  A Catholic priest will bless your feathered or fury friend at this centuries-old ceremony at the El Pueblo de Los Angeles Historical Monument, downtown.
- **Brentwood Art Show,** 626-797-6803
  Art lovers flock to the VA Medical Center park grounds to admire the works of local artisans.
- **Feria de los Ninos,** 323-261-0113
  A Latin American festival featuring food, workshops, dances, and mariachi bands in Hollenbeck Park, Boyle Heights.
- **Fiesta Broadway,** 310-914-0015
  A popular block party in downtown celebrating Latin American culture.
- *Los Angeles Times* **Festival of Books,** 213-237-6503, www.latimes.com
  Held the last weekend in April in Dickson Plaza on UCLA campus, this free festival attracts over 100,000 book lovers of all ages. Over

300 booths are set up by booksellers, publishers, and cultural organizations. Events include readings and signings by well known and not so well known authors and poets.

- **Santa Monica Arts Festival,** 818-709-2907
Third Street Promenade hosts an impressive selection of handmade arts and crafts booths.
- **Thai New Year Festival,** 818-780-4200
The Wat Thai Temple in North Hollywood is host to food booths, performances, ceremonies and a beauty pageant. This popular festival is attended by Thais from all over California.

MAY

- **Affaire in the Gardens Fine Arts and Crafts Show,** 310-550-4796
None of the typical costume jewelry or clothing is hawked during this weekend at the Beverly Gardens. Over 200 artists from around the country display fine art from sculpture to paintings for the discriminating art collector. The show takes place again in October.
- **Children's Day,** 213-628-2725
Little Tokyo's Japanese-American Cultural and Community Center hosts games, food and crafts booths, and other fun activities for children.
- **Cinco de Mayo Celebration,** 213-625-5045
Celebrate May 5 with hundreds at the El Pueblo de Los Angeles Historical Monument in downtown.
- **Greek Festival,** 818-886-4040
Greeks celebrate their heritage at Saint Nicholas Greek Orthodox Church in Northridge with food, dance, and crafts booths.
- **Kids' Nature Festival,** 310-364-3591
Popular among families with young children, this annual event features face painting, storytelling, crafts, food, and animals. Held at Temescal Gateway Park in the Pacific Palisades.
- **Mother's Day Crafts Festival,** 818-880-8728
Over 100 artisans display their art and crafts for sale in Moorpark Park in Studio City.
- **SPCA 5K Dog Walk,** 323-730-5300, ext. 251
Pet lovers take a walk through Griffith Park with their four-legged friends to benefit the SPCA.
- **Renaissance Pleasure Faire,** 800-52-FAIRE, www.renfair.com
Starting in late May and running through June, this elaborate recreation of a medieval village takes place in the Glen Helen Regional

Park in San Bernardino County. Many people attend in period costume to watch jousting matches, wander the crafts booths, and enjoy a stein of ale with fellow wenches, knights, and royalty.
- **UCLA Pow-wow,** 310-206-7513
Native Americans and friends gather on the college campus to celebrate their heritage with song, dance, food, and displays.

JUNE

- **Boat Show,** 310-645-5151
Boating and water sport enthusiasts head down to Burton Chace Park in Marina del Rey to check out the latest in aquatic equipment.
- **Irish Fair and Music Festival,** 626-503-2511
A medieval Irish Village is recreated at the Santa Anita Park in Arcadia and features bagpipes, Gaelic sports, and food.
- **Gay and Lesbian Pride Parade and Celebration,** 323-860-0701
The West Hollywood portion of Santa Monica Boulevard is lined with bleachers for spectators of the gay and lesbian pride parade.
- **NoHo Theatre Performing Arts Festival,** 818-508-5155
North Hollywood's arts district, along Lankershim Boulevard in North Hollywood, celebrates with a weekend of music, food and crafts booths, and theatrical performances throughout the area's playhouses.
- **Playboy Jazz Festival,** 310-449-4070
Jazz aficionados flock to the Hollywood Bowl for performances by some of the top names in jazz.
- **Summer Solstice Folk Music, Dance and Storytelling Festival,** 818-342-7664
This is the country's largest folk festival, featuring workshops, concerts and exhibits and is held at Soka University in the city of Calabasas.
- **Valley Fair and Rodeo,** 818-557-1600, www.home.earthlink.net/ ~sfvalleyfair
Held over a weekend at the LA Equestrian Center, the rodeo is its main event, but the fair also features carnival rides, game booths, and gardening exhibits.

JULY

- **Best of LA Festival,** 888-BESTOFLA, www.efestival.com
Lectures, concerts, and demos supplement this grazing event where Angelenos wander among booths set up by LA's top restaurants to

purchase and taste samples of their signature dishes. This popular weekend event is sponsored by *Los Angeles Magazine*. Held in different locations year to year.

- **Fourth of July Celebrations,** 800-900-3473
  City-wide celebrations with fireworks displays from the Hollywood Bowl to Santa Monica. Contact the above number to locate the nearest fireworks show.
- **Hollywood Bowl Summer Festival,** 323-850-2000
  The Hollywood Bowl begins its summer season (through mid-September), featuring varying orchestras and all genres of music from classic to pop. For many Angelenos, packing a picnic dinner and taking in an evening concert is an annual tradition.
- **Lotus Festival,** 213-485-8744
  The largest lotus bed outside of China is located in Echo Park, a fitting host to a day filled with dragon-boat races, flower shows, and Pan-Asian food booths.
- **Malibu Arts Festival,** 310-456-9025
  Over 100 artists display their wares at the city's civic center.
- **Shakespeare Festival,** 213-489-1121
  Venues around the county pay homage to William Shakespeare by putting on professional productions of the bard's plays.

AUGUST

- **African Marketplace and Cultural Fair,** 323-734-1164
  A festival filled with food and entertainment to celebrate African heritage in Rancho Cienega Park in Crenshaw.
- **Children's Festival of the Arts,** 213-485-4474
  A wholesome event, held at Barnsdall Art Park in Los Feliz, filled with performances, food and crafts for the entire family.
- **Nisei Week,** 213-687-7193
  Little Tokyo celebrates its culture with weeklong festivities including a parade, street fair, taiko drums and ondo street dancing.
- **Westwood Summer Art Show,** 626-797-6803
  Yet another art show, held at Wilshire Boulevard and Veteran Avenue in Westwood.

SEPTEMBER

- **Los Angeles County Fair,** 909-623-3111
  This is billed as the world's largest country fair and is held on the Pomona Fairplex grounds.
- **Watts Towers Jazz and Arts Festivals,** 213-847-4646
  The Watts Towers Art Center plays hosts to a three-day event that includes a jazz festival, art exhibit and fair booths.

OCTOBER

- **AFI LA International Film Festival,** 323-856-7707
  Screenings for one of the largest film festivals in the country, hosted by the American Film Institute, are held in theaters around Hollywood and Santa Monica.
- **International Fall Fest Street Fair,** 818-884-4222
  Canoga Park celebrates ethnic diversity with family-oriented activities and booths.
- **Los Angeles County Arts Open House,** 213-972-3099, www.lacountyarts.org
  In honor of the National Arts and Humanities month, the first Saturday of October features free admission to participating museums within LA County. This event is well attended, especially along Museum Row. Wilshire Boulevard, between Fairfax and Curson is closed to cars, allowing the crowds to view outdoor performances.
- **Scandinavian Festival,** 323-661-4273
  MGM Plaza in Santa Monica hosts a Nordic costume parade, folk dancing, food, and entertainment.
  West Hollywood's Halloween, 323-650-2688
  Many might think of Halloween as a child's holiday, but in West Hollywood, adults claim All Hallow's Eve. An estimated one million people, usually in elaborate costumes, jam Santa Monica Boulevard (west of La Cienega Boulevard) to strut their stuff.

NOVEMBER

- **Arts of Pacific Asia Show,** 310-455-2886
  The Santa Monica Civic Auditorium hosts an impressive collection of Asian art and antique exhibits.

- **Dia de los Muertos,** 213-625-5045
  The Day of the Dead, a traditional Mexican festival to honor the departed, is observed at El Pueblo de Los Angeles Historical Monument, downtown.
- **Festival of Jewish Artisans,** 310-277-2772
  Artists, local and from Israel, exhibit their wares. A concert and other activities are held for families.
- **Harvest Festival,** 213-624-7300
  Angelenos head to the LA Convention Center to get a jump on holiday festivities and Christmas shopping among the hundreds of booths and vendors.
- **Hollywood Christmas Parade,** 310-537-4240
  The popular parade, held Thanksgiving weekend, is broadcast nationwide, but many Angelenos flock to Hollywood sidewalks with a thermos of hot chocolate to see it live.
- **Doo Dah Parade,** 626-449-3689
  Fans of the irreverent or bizarre will want to check out this popular spoof of the Tournament of Roses Parade in downtown Pasadena.

DECEMBER

- **Burbank Mayor's Tree Lighting,** 818-238-5320
  Many residents of Burbank attend the mayor's tree lighting ceremony at City Hall.
- **Holiday Boat Parade,** 310-305-9546
  Go to Burton Chace Park in Marina del Rey for the best viewing of decorated boats.
- **Kwanzaa Celebration,** 323-965-0935 or 323-291-5712
  This Afro-centric holiday is celebrated with entertainment, crafts booths, and more in Leimert Park Village.
- **LA County Holiday Celebration,** 213-974-1396
  The Dorothy Chandler Pavilion is the site of annual holiday music and festivities.
- **Toluca Lake Open House,** 818-761-6594
  Shops and restaurants along Riverside Drive in Toluca Lake stay open late the first Friday night of the month to offer free candy canes, cookies, and food samples. The neighborhood caroling truck also makes it rounds, adding to the charm of this holiday evening.
- **Santa Monica Open House,** 310-393-9825
  Same idea as the Toluca Lake open house, but held on the first Saturday night of the month along Montana Avenue in Santa Monica.

Above Los Angeles by Robert W. Cameron
   Incredible aerial views of the city.

An Actor's Guide: Your First Year in Hollywood by Michael Saint Nicholas
   Solid advice and tips for newcomers who seek a career on the big screen.

The Best of Only In LA: A Chronicle of the Amazing, Amusing and Absurd by Steve Harvey
   A humorous collection of trivia and oddities that can only be found in Los Angeles.

Buzzwords: LA Fresh Speak by Anna Scotti
   All the local slang and lingo demystified to have you talking like an LA hipster in no time.

The California Cauldron by William A.V. Clark
   An in-depth study of immigration and how it's affecting the state.

Hollywood Dish! Recipes, Tips, & Tales of a Hollywood Caterer by Nick Grippo
   A unique combination of celebrity gossip and food from a local caterer to the stars.

How to Communicate with Your Spanish Speaking Help and Friends by Liora Cohen
   English-Spanish guidebook for frequently used phrases in cooking, cleaning, child care, and gardening.

LA Unconventional by Cecilia Rasmussen
   A collection of anecdotes about the offbeat characters found in LA.

The Reluctant Metropolis: The Politics of Urban Growth in Los Angeles by William Fulton
   An examination of the urban planning and politics that shaped LA into what it is today.

Call 911 for all police, fire and ambulance emergencies. For 24-hour general information on public assistance from shelters to food programs, call the INFO Line of Los Angeles: 800-339-6993.

Note, not all listings below have web sites.

An asterisk (*) indicates a toll call.

ALCOHOL AND DRUG DEPENDENCY

- Alcoholics Anonymous, 310-474-7339
- Alcohol Abuse 24 Hour Hotline, 800-888-9383
- Cocaine Abuse 24 Hour Info & Treatment, 800-274-2042
- Narcotics Anonymous, 310-390-0279
- National Alcohol and Drug Abuse Hotline, 800-252-6465

ANIMALS

- Society for the Prevention of Cruelty to Animals, 323-730-5300, www.laspca.com
- Animal Regulations Department & Shelters, City of Los Angeles, 888-452-7381, www.ci.la.ca.us
- Dead Animal Pick-up, 800-773-2489
- Santa Monica Animal Shelter, 310-458-8594

AUTOMOBILES

- Automotive Repair Bureau, Department of Consumer Affairs, 800-952-5210

CALIFORNIA DEPARTMENT OF MOTOR VEHICLES
- LA, 213-744-2000, www.dmv.ca.gov
- Valley, 818-901-5500

PARKING CITATIONS
- LA, 213-623-6533

PARKING PERMITS

Beverly Hills, 310-285-2551
Los Angeles, 213-485-9543
Santa Monica, 310-458-8291
West Hollywood, 323-848-6392

BIRTH AND DEATH CERTIFICATES

- Los Angeles County Clerk, 800-815-2666, www.co.la.ca.us/regrec/main.htm

CHILD ABUSE AND FAMILY VIOLENCE

- Abducted, Abused and Exploited Children, 800-248-8020
- Child Abuse Hotline, 800-540-4000
- Childhelp USA, 800-422-4453
- Domestic Violence Hotline, 800-978-3600
- Elder Abuse Hotline, 800-992-1660
- Sojourn Services for Battered Women, 310-399-9239
- Victims of Crime Resource Center, 800-842-8467
- YWCA Battered Women's Help Line, 626-967-0658

CONSUMER COMPLAINTS AND SERVICES

- Better Business Bureau, 213-251-9696, 818-386-5510, www.bbb.org
- City Ethics Commission Complaint Hotline, 800-439-4666
- Los Angeles Consumer Affairs Department, 213-974-1452
- State Bar of California Attorney Complaint Hotline, 800-843-9053
- State of California Consumer Affairs Department, 800-952-5210
- US Consumer Product Safety Commission, 800-638-2772, www.cpsc.gov

COUNTY OFFICES

- Beverly Hills, 310-285-1000, www.ci.beverly-hills.ca.us
- Burbank, 818-238-5850, www.ci.burbank.ca.us
- Culver City, 310-253-5851, www.ci.culver-city.ca.us
- Glendale, 818-458-4000, www.ci.glendale.ca.us
- INFO Line of Los Angeles, 800-339-6993
- Long Beach, 562-570-4000, www.ci.long-beach.ca.us

- Los Angeles, 213-485-2121, www.ci.la.ca.us
- Los Angeles County Information & Services, 213-974-1311, www.co.la.ca.us
- Malibu, 310-456-2489, www.ci.malibu.ca.us
- Pasadena, 626-744-6000, www.ci.pasadena.ca.us
- Santa Clarita, 661-255-4391, www.ci.santa-clarita.ca.us
- Santa Monica, 310-393-9975, www.ci.santa-monica.ca.us
- South Pasadena, 626-403-7200, www.ci.south-pasadena.ca.us
- West Hollywood, 310-323-848-6400, www.ci.west-hollywood.ca.us

CRIME

- Crime in Progress, 911
- Crime Prevention, Santa Monica, 310-458-8473
- Central Fraud Reporting Line, 213-749-4266

CRISIS HOTLINES

- Boys Town National Hotline, 800-448-3000
- Pacific-Asian Family Crisis Hotline, 800-339-3940
- Suicide Prevention, 310-391-1253
- Suicide Prevention Hotline, 800-255-6111
- Battered Women Hotline, 310-392-8381
- Youth Crisis Hotline, 800-448-4663

DISCRIMINATION

- California Fair Employment and Housing Department, 800-233-3212
- Disabilities Commission on Los Angeles County, 213-974-1053
- Gay and Lesbian Alliance Against Defamation, 323-658-6775
- US Department of Fair Housing and Discrimination Hotline, 800-424-8590
- Women's Commission for Los Angeles County, 213-974-1455

ELECTED OFFICIALS AND GOVERNMENT

- Los Angeles County Board of Supervisors, 213-974-1411, www.co.la.ca.us
- Los Angeles Mayor's Office 213-847-2489, www.ci.la.ca.us
- Federal Government Information Center, 800-688-9889

EMERGENCY

- Police, Fire, Medical, 911
- American Red Cross Emergency Services, 800-540-2000
- Earthquake Recovery-Debris Pick Up, 800-498-2489
- FEMA Disaster Assistance Information, 800-525-0321
- Los Angeles County Office of Emergency Management, 323-980-2260
- Storm Water Hotline, 800-974-9794

ENTERTAINMENT

- Audience Associates, 323-653-4105
- Audiences Unlimited, 818-506-0067
- Los Angeles Cultural Affairs Department, 213-485-4581, www.lacountyarts.com
- Ticketmaster 213-365-3500, www.ticketmaster.com
- Tickets Los Angeles, 323-655-8587

HEALTH & MEDICAL CARE

- AIDS Healthcare Foundation, 800-343-2101
- California Smokers Helpline, 800-766-2888
- Healthy Families Information Line, 888-747-1222
- Los Angeles County Health Services Department, 800-427-8700, www.co.la.ca.us
- Los Angeles County Mental Health Services, 800-854-7771, www.co.la.ca.us
- Los Angeles County Sexually Transmitted Disease Hotline, 800-227-8922
- Los Angeles Urban Search & Rescue-Fire Department, 818-756-9677
- Minority AIDS Project, 323-936-4949
- Medi-Cal Information, 818-718-3500
- Nursing Home Info & Referral, 800-427-8700
- Poison Control Center, 800-876-4766
- Smog Conditions, 800-242-4022
- US Department of Health and Human Services, 800-336-4797

HOUSING

- California Fair Employment and Housing Department, 800-233-3212
- Culver City Housing Division, 310-253-5780
- Homeowners and Renters Assistance, Franchise Tax Board, 800-852-5711, www.ftb.ca.gov
- Fair Housing Information Clearinghouse, 800-343-3442
- Fair Housing, Santa Monica, 310-458-8336
- Fair Housing, Santa Clarita, 661-255-4330
- Fair Housing Congress of Southern California, 323-468-7464
- Fair Housing Council of San Fernando Valley, 818-373-1185
- Fair Housing Council, Westside, 310-474-1667
- Los Angeles City Housing Department, 800-994-4444, www.ci.la.ca.us
- San Fernando Valley Neighborhood Legal Services, 800-433-6251
- US Department of Housing and Urban Development, 800-669-9777
- US Department of Fair Housing and Discrimination, 800-477-5977, www.fairhousing.com/fhsc

LEGAL REFERRAL

- American Civil Liberties Union of Southern California, 213-977-9500
- Asian Pacific American Legal Center of Southern California, 213-748-2022
- Bet Tzedek Legal Services, 323-939-0506
- Los Angeles Gay and Lesbian Center Legal Services Department, 323-993-7670
- Legal Aid Foundation of Los Angeles, 213-640-3883
- Los Angeles County Bar Association Referrals, 213-243-1525
- Police Misconduct Lawyer Referral Service, 213-387-3325
- Public Defender Information Line, 213-974-2811

LIBRARIES

- Los Angeles Central Library, 213-228-7000, www.lapl.org
  See also **Libraries** in **Getting Settled**, and end-listings in the **Neighborhood** profiles.

MARRIAGE LICENSES

- Los Angeles County Marriage License & Ceremony Information, 800-201-8999, www.co.la.ca.us/regrec/main.htm

PARKS & RECREATION DEPARTMENTS

For parks and recreation department web sites, visit the city sites listed at the end of the **Neighborhood** profiles.

- Beverly Hills Recreation and Parks Department, 310-285-2537
- Burbank Parks and Recreation Department, 818-238-5300
- Culver City Recreation Department, 310-202-5689
- El Segundo Parks and Recreation Department, 310-322-3842
- Glendale Parks Recreation Department, 818-548-2000
- Los Angeles Recreation and Parks Department, 818-756-8891 or 310-837-8116 or 213-738-2961
- Malibu Parks and Recreation Department, 310-456-2489, ext. 235
- Manhattan Beach Recreation Department, 310-545-5621, ext. 325
- Pasadena Parks and Recreation Department, 626-405-4306
- Santa Monica Recreation Division, 310-458-8311
- Santa Clarita Parks and Recreation Department, 661-255-4910
- West Hollywood Recreation Department, 310-854-7471

POLICE

- Los Angeles County Sheriff, 213-974-4811, www.www.la-sheriff.org
- Los Angeles Police Department Divisions, www.lapdonline.org
- Valley Bureau Operations, 818-756-8121
- West Bureau Operations, 213-237-0080
- Central Bureau Operations, 213-485-6586
- Southern Bureau Operations, 213-485-2582

POST OFFICE

- US Postal Service, 800-275-8777, www.usps.com

RAPE AND SEXUAL ASSAULT

- Los Angeles County District Attorney Victim-Witness Assistance Program, 310-260-3678
- Los Angeles Commission Rape & Battering Hotline, 213-626-3393, 310-392-8381
- Rape Treatment Center, Santa Monica-UCLA Medical Center, 310-319-4000
- Sojourn Services for Battered Women, 310-399-9239

SANITATION AND GARBAGE

- Sanitation District of Los Angeles County, 323-685-5217, www.co.la.ca.us
- Los Angeles County Recycling & Hazardous Waste, 800-552-5218

SCHOOLS

- Los Angeles County Office of Education, 562-922-6111, www.lacoe.edu
- Los Angeles School District Boundaries, 213-625-5437
- Los Angeles Unified Parent Resource Network Hotline, 800-933-8133, www.lausd.k12.ca.us

SENIORS

- Alternative Living for the Aging, 323-650-7988
- California Medical Review, 800-841-1602
- Elder Abuse Hotline, 800-992-1660
- Elder Care Locator, 800-677-1116
- Jewish Family Service of Los Angeles, 323-937-5910
- Los Angeles County Area Agency on Aging, 800-510-2020
- Long-Term Care Ombudsman, 800-334-9473
- Los Angeles County Community and Senior Citizens Services, 818-897-2909
- National Council on the Aging, 213-365-0700
- Senior Services Referral, 310-551-2929
- Social Security and Medicare Eligibility Information, 800-772-1213

SHIPPING

- Airborne Express, 800-247-2676
- DHL, 800-225-5545
- Federal Express, 800-463-3339, www.fedex.com
- United Parcel Service (UPS), 800-742-5877, www.ups.com
- US Postal Service, 800-275-8777, www.usps.com

SPORTS

- California Angels, 888-796-4256, www.angelsbaseball.com
- Los Angeles Clippers, 877-522-8669; season seats, 213-745-0500, www.nba.com/clippers
- Los Angeles Dodgers, 323-224-1491
- Los Angeles Kings, 877-522-8669; season seats, 888-KINGS-LA, www.lakings.com
- Los Angeles Lakers, 877-522-8669; season seats, 310-419-3131, www.nba.com/lakers
- UCLA Bruins, 310-825-2101
- USC Trojans, 213-740-4072

STATE GOVERNMENT

- California State Senate, 916-445-1353
- California State Assembly, 916-319-2042
- Governor's Office, 213-897-0322
- Senator's Office, 310-441-9084
- US House of Representatives, 202-225-3976

STREET MAINTENANCE

- Caltrans Highway Information Network, 800-427-7623
- Los Angeles County Road Maintenance, 323-776-7552
- Pot holes, sidewalk repair, etc., 800-996-2489, www.co.la.ca.us
- Streetlight repair, 800-303-5267
- Traffic signals, sign repair, etc., 800-675-4357

TAXES

- Internal Revenue Service, 800-829-4477, www.irs.gov
- Los Angeles County Treasurer-Property Tax, 213-974-2111, www.co.la.ca.us
- State Franchise Tax Board, 800- 852-5711, www.ftb.ca.gov

TELEPHONE

- GTE, 800-483-4000, www.gte.net
- Pacific Bell, 800-310-2355, www.pacbell.com

TIME

- From any area code *853-1212

TOURISM AND TRAVEL

- Los Angeles Convention and Visitors Bureau, 213-624-7300, www.lacvb.com
- California State Parks & Recreation, 818-880-0350, www.cal-parks.ca.gov
- INFO Line of Los Angeles, 800-339-6993
- State Info-Line, 213-897-9900

TRANSPORTATION

- Commuter Transportation Services (carpools), 800-286-7433
- Commuter Transportation Information, 800-266-6883
- Cal Trans Highway Conditions, 800-427-7623, www.traffic.maxell.com/caltrans
- Los Angeles County Metropolitan Transit Authority (MTA/Metro), 800-COMMUTE, 213-922-6235, www.mta.net
- Highway Conditions, 800-427-7623, www.dot.ca.gov, www.traffic.maxell.com/caltrans
- Los Angeles Department of Transportation (LADOT), 818/213/310-808-2273
- Smart Traveler Information Line, 800-266-6883, www.smart-traveler.com

AIRPORTS

- Burbank/Glendale/Pasadena Airport, 818-840-8840, www.bur.com
- Los Angeles International Airport (LAX), 310-646-5252, www.airwise.com
- Long Beach Airport, 562-425-9665, www.lgb.org
- Ontario International Airport, 909-988-2700
- Orange County's John Wayne Airport, 714-252-5006, www.ocair.com

NATIONAL TRAIN & BUS SERVICE

- Amtrak, 800-872-7245, www.amtrak.com
- Greyhound, 800-231-2222, www.greyhound.com

UTILITY EMERGENCIES

- Los Angeles County Waterworks & Sewer, 626-458-4357
- Los Angeles Department of Water and Power, 800-342-5397, www.ladwp.com; Electric Trouble, 800-821-5279; Water Trouble, 800-499-4611
- Southern California Gas Company, 800-427-1420, www.socalgas.com
- Southern California Water Company, 310-838-2143
- Las Virgenes Municipal Water Company, 818-880-4110
- Los Angeles County Water District #29, 310-456-6621
- Pasadena Water and Power, 626-744-4409
- South Pasadena Water, 626-403-7200
- Santa Monica Water Department, 310-458-8224
- Santa Clarita Water Company, 661-259-2737
- Valencia Water Company, 661-294-0828
- Newhall County Water District, 661-259-3610
- Castiac Lake Water Agency, 661-257-6024
- Storm Water Hotline, 800-974-9794
- Underground Service Alert, 800-227-2600

VOTING

- California Voter Registration Hotline, 800-345-8683
- Voter Information, 562-466-1323

WEATHER

- Local weather conditions, 213-554-1212

ZIP CODE INFORMATION

- USPS zip codes request, 800-275-8777, www.usps.com

INDEX

JOAN WAI, a Southern California native, has resided in the Los Angeles area since 1987. A graduate from the University of Southern California's School of Cinema-Television, Wai pounds away at her computer as a professional screenwriter and freelance writer. Her most recent work is *Savvy Women Entrepreneurs,* a collection of true entrepreneurial success stories. Her favorite Los Angeles pastime, when not foraging for unusual restaurants, is people watching along the Santa Monica Promenade.

STACEY RAVEL ABARBANEL is a native of the San Francisco Bay Area, and has lived in the Los Angeles area from 1986-1987, and from 1990 to the present. Formerly the Promotion Manager for *Architectural Digest,* Abarbanel is a freelance writer. Her articles have appeared in *Meetings California,* a newspaper for the tourism industry, and *Ad LA,* a magazine for the Los Angeles advertising community. She is also the author of S*mart Business Travel.* Abarbanel and her husband reside in Santa Monica.

We would appreciate your comments regarding this third edition of the *Newcomer's Handbook® for Los Angeles.* If you've found any mistakes or omissions or if you would just like to express your opinion about the guide, please let us know. We will consider any suggestions for possible inclusion in our next edition, and if we use your comments, we'll send you a *free* copy of our next edition. Please send this response form to:

Reader Response Department
First Books, Inc.
3000 Market Street N.E., Suite 527,
Salem, OR 97301

Comments:

_____

_____

_____

_____

_____

_____

_____

_____

_____

Name: _____

Address _____

_____

_____

Telephone (   ) _____

3000 Market Street N.E., Suite 527
Salem, OR 97301
503-588-2224
www.firstbooks.com

FIRST BOOKS

THE ORIGINAL, ALWAYS UPDATED, ABSOLUTELY INVALUABLE GUIDES FOR PEOPLE MOVING TO A CITY!

Find out about neigborhoods, apartment and house hunting, money matters, deposits/leases, getting settled, helpful services, shopping for the home, places of worship, cultural life, sports/recreation, vounteering, green space, schools and education, transportation, temporary lodgings and useful telephone numbers!

	# COPIES	TOTAL
Newcomer's Handbook® for Atlanta	_____ x $14.95	$_____
Newcomer's Handbook® for Boston	_____ x $14.95	$_____
Newcomer's Handbook® for Chicago	_____ x $14.95	$_____
Newcomer's Handbook® for London	_____ x $17.95	$_____
Newcomer's Handbook® for Los Angeles	_____ x $17.95	$_____
Newcomer's Handbook® for Minneapolis-St. Paul	_____ x $14.95	$_____
Newcomer's Handbook® for New York City	_____ x $18.95	$_____
Newcomer's Handbook® for Philadelphia	_____ x $16.95	$_____
Newcomer's Handbook® for San Francisco	_____ x $14.95	$_____
Newcomer's Handbook® for Seattle	_____ x $14.95	$_____
Newcomer's Handbook® for Washington D.C.	_____ x $13.95	$_____
	SUBTOTAL	$_____
POSTAGE & HANDLING (*$6.00 first book, $1.00 each add'l.*)		$_____
	TOTAL	$_____

SHIP TO:

Name _____

Title _____

Company _____

Address _____

City _____ State _____ Zip _____

Phone Number (_____) _____

Send this order form and a check or money order payable to:
First Books, Inc.

First Books, Inc., Mail Order Department
3000 Market Street N.E., Suite 527, Salem, OR 97301

Allow 1-2 weeks for delivery

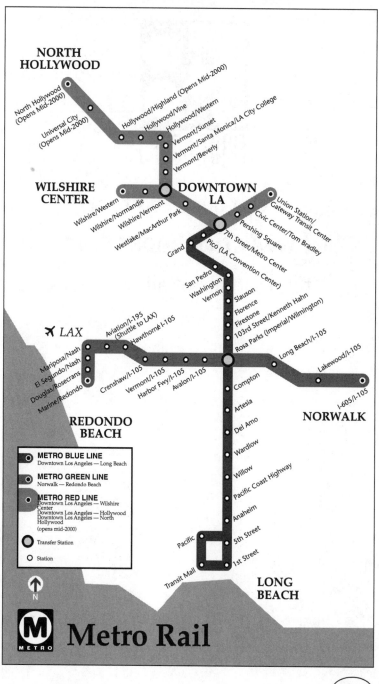

NORTH
HOLLYWOOD

North Hollywood
(Opens Mid-2000)

Universal City
(Opens Mid-2000)

Hollywood/Highland (Opens Mid-2000)

Hollywood/Vine

Hollywood/Western

Vermont/Sunset

Vermont/Santa Monica/LA City College

Vermont/Beverly

WILSHIRE
CENTER

DOWNTOWN
LA

Wilshire/Western

Wilshire/Normandie

Wilshire/Vermont

Westlake/MacArthur Park

Grand

Union Station/
Gateway Transit Center

Civic Center/Tom Bradley

Pershing Square

7th Street/Metro Center

Pico (LA Convention Center)

San Pedro

Washington

Vernon

Slauson

Florence

Firestone

103rd Street/Kenneth Hahn

Rosa Parks (Imperial/Wilmington)

Long Beach/I-105

Lakewood/I-105

✈ LAX

Aviation/I-195
(Shuttle to LAX)

Hawthorne I-105

Mariposa/Nash

El Segundo/Nash

Douglas/Rosecrans

Marine/Redondo

Crenshaw/I-105

Vermont/I-105

Harbor Fwy/I-105

Avalon/I-105

Compton

I-605/I-105

REDONDO
BEACH

NORWALK

Artesia

Del Amo

Wardlow

Willow

Pacific Coast Highway

Anaheim

Pacific

5th Street

1st Street

Transit Mall

LONG
BEACH

METRO BLUE LINE
Downtown Los Angeles — Long Beach

METRO GREEN LINE
Norwalk — Redondo Beach

METRO RED LINE
Downtown Los Angeles — Wilshire
Center
Downtown Los Angeles — Hollywood
Downtown Los Angeles — North
Hollywood
(opens mid-2000)

○ Transfer Station

○ Station

↑
N

M Metro Rail